# Peak Performance

# Peak Performance

*Business Lessons from the*
*World's Top Sports Organizations*

CLIVE GILSON
MIKE PRATT
KEVIN ROBERTS
ED WEYMES

HarperCollinsBusiness
*An Imprint of* HarperCollins*Publishers*

HarperCollins*Publishers*
77–85 Fulham Palace Road,
Hammersmith, London W6 8JB

www.harpercollinsbusiness.com

Published by HarperCollins*Publishers* 2000
1 3 5 7 9 8 6 4 2

The Authors assert the moral right to
be identified as the authors of this work

A catalogue record for this book is
available from the British Library

ISBN 0 00 257136 6

Set in Sabon by
Rowland Phototypesetting Ltd,
Bury St Edmunds, Suffolk

Printed and bound in Great Britain by
Caledonian International Book Manufacturing Ltd, Glasgow

# Contents

# Foreword

At some stage in our lives many of us are filled with an overwhelming desire or inspirational dream to achieve something that we know will stretch our abilities to the utmost. But all too often, sadly, the dream fades and we revert to being very normal human beings.

I have often been asked the question, 'When you have spent some years of your life devoted to achieving some great objective and you finally succeed – is there a sense of anticlimax and does life become rather empty for you?' I have known a few successful explorers who have confessed to me that when their greatest imaginable challenge has been achieved, they feel a little lost in the pressures of society. I have tried to re-ignite their enthusiasm and focus, to seek out other new challenges, for they are undoubtedly at their peak when they are attempting the seemingly impossible.

Although a person of modest abilities I have never experienced this problem – I have always had half a dozen other adventures churning around in my mind so when one is completed I can automatically carry on to the next. I can well remember standing on top of Mount Everest having reached the top of the world in every sense of the term and looking east towards the great unclimbed summit of Makalu. Instinctively my eyes followed up the mighty face of the mountain and I automatically picked out a route by which Makalu could be climbed – and was indeed climbed later by a strong French expedition. I had achieved an ultimate success but I was still looking for new and exciting challenges. Real success is a continuing process – one's objectives may well change but one always has an eye for something new and exciting. The authors of the book you are about to read call this 'peak purpose.'

During the eighty years of my life, my attitudes and purpose modified as my physical ability and experience developed. In my teens I was a reader and a dreamer about adventure. Then mountaineering captured my imagination and I strove with all my effort to be an outstanding member of each expedition. I was highly competitive and determined to be one of the leading climbers and my fitness and motivation carried me through. In my forties the challenges remained but now they were different. In my organizational life, I was now the leader and planner, selecting the teams, raising the funds and making the major decisions. They were great days in many ways. In later years I became deeply involved in a new inspirational dream – the welfare of the people of the Himalayas, building schools and medical clinics, mountain airfields and fresh water pipelines. Fund raising around the world is a major effort and I quickly learned that the old story of my ascent of Mount Everest, many years before, still gave my name rather astonishing prestige.

To use a term presented in this book, I developed important 'peak practices'. I learned early to select my companions carefully. Mostly my decisions were based on the previous performance of team members. My own personal experience of them was important too but I sometimes listened to the views of friends whose knowledge I respected. But it was always vitally important to me to search out people with a good sense of humour and community. I have never warmed to those who have an exaggerated sense of their own importance. And the people I remember with respect and affection are those who can laugh when the going gets tough.

I once interviewed a young man who I had never met before but who had a reputation as a powerful and successful climber. He was a very self-effacing person who I automatically liked but he was most reluctant to talk about his achievements. I finally discovered that apart from his climbing successes he had also won a New Zealand canoeing medal. This was more like it! I asked him, 'What do you have to do to be invited to participate in a canoeing championship?' He shrugged his shoulders. 'The main thing is to have a canoe,' he told me calmly. I chose him on the spot and he proved a great success.

There are some people who seem to be born leaders but most of us have to learn to be inspirational players in organizational life. You need to have a clear picture in your mind about what you plan to do and yet be prepared to make a rapid change if a better proposition is presented to you. You have to be ready to listen without losing executive control. It is advisable to have turned over in your mind all possible alternatives so if an emergency occurs you can act immediately and move effectively to overcome the problem. And it is enormously important that when total agreement has been reached you hand the task of implementation over to your colleagues, while ensuring that backup support is always available if something goes wrong. So I am a firm believer in both an individual and a team effort, but ultimately someone may have to make a final decision and that's the leader's responsibility. Naturally, it is important that it is a sound and sensible decision.

My programmes in the Himalayas are small yet complex, but over the years I have accumulated some expert assistants – both Sherpa and European. With their help we have worked together for 35 years responding to the expressed desires of the Himalayan mountain people. My life has been a busy one but I could have done little without the support of my family, friends and expert colleagues. We have worked together as a strong and motivated team – as indeed we did on Mount Everest – and it was reaching the summit of Mount Everest that made all the adventures and programmes possible.

Big or small projects carried out by the famous sports organizations featured here, or any business, demand a similar philosophy for success. I believe that the theory which is presented by the authors of this book also works rather well for our projects in the remote Himalayas. Peak performance is indeed the challenge.

Sir Edmund Hillary
Auckland
January 2000

# Acknowledgements

Our special thanks goes to all our case study organizations and in particular to those to whom we spoke and whose names are included within our narrative. Without them we would have had no book and no Peak Performing Organizations (PPO) Theory. We were honoured to be admitted as temporary honorary members of their PPO families, and the enduring friendships which have developed from the project are an ongoing privilege. Not all the organizations we interviewed made it through to the finals. We have not named those that were eliminated, but we nonetheless much appreciate the time and assistance they gave us.

The logistics behind this project were highly complex. Although every one of our informants enabled us to see and understand things better, we need to thank additionally those who spent considerable time and effort ensuring that our visits ran smoothly. We were always well aware that the daily demands placed on these organizations were huge, but our 'handlers' nevertheless generously gave up their valuable time for us. Our special thanks go to Jane Gorard (Williams), Bill Duffy (San Francisco 49ers), Bob Wolfe (Atlanta Braves), Steve Schanwald (Chicago Bulls), Pam Tye (Women's Hockey Australia), Carley Baker (Netball Australia), Gwen Lloyd (FC Bayern Munich), Ray Phillips (Australian Cricket Board), Kristen Sneyd (Team New Zealand), David Moffet (New Zealand Rugby Football Union) and Wolfgang Niersbach (German Football Association). Maryanne Schneider, from the University of Western Australia, hosted and helped to prepare our visits to Perth where we met Women's Hockey Australia officials and team members and Australia Cricket Board coaching staff.

Our project required thousands of pages of transcribing. Lorraine Brown-Simpson, who heads up the transcription services at the University of Waikato, and her staff, helped to bring the project to life by producing the raw data from our many interviews. Nicky Haisman also ably assisted by transcribing some of our final interviews.

We sincerely thank University of Waikato Vice-Chancellor Professor Bryan Gould for his support for our project and for his belief in its potential importance to the University. Our PPO project began as part of our search for a better way, beyond the MBA, and we continue to drive it to that end. We thank our colleagues at the University of Waikato Management School for stimulating conversations about excellence in organizations, and our students on MBA and PhD programmes for their critical and constructive feedback on early versions of PPO Theory.

Sarah Knox in particular, provided peak performing research assistance and critical commentary on our initial drafts. Many of our friends and colleagues, who spent considerable time reading early versions of chapters, provided vital feedback throughout the project. The unrelenting critical eyes and sharp reflections of Dorothy Gilson, Helga Pratt, Chester Spell, Delwyn Clark and Carolyn Boell of Saatchi & Saatchi undoubtedly improved the final product. Carolyn Boell also provided superb logistical support and field research assistance with women's teams. Bobbie Wisneski and Claire McIntosh manage the treasured memorabilia that we accumulated during our travels and expertly juggled logistics to facilitate our focus on writing.

We are indebted to Kate Pope of College Hill for patiently and engagingly introducing us to the world of global publishing. Our agent Mark Lucas of Lucas Alexander Whitley transformed the project by suggesting the idea of organizational story telling. Until Mark's intervention we had been proceeding down the path of a traditional business book, with chapters devoted to each element of the theory and examples drawn from all the research. Lucinda McNeile and Kate Morris of HarperCollins London enthusiastically encouraged us towards an ever more focused narrative and their attention to the last detail has been similarly transformational.

On a more personal level, we owe the most to our families and partners. They have encouraged us when things went wrong and excused our preoccupation when the project was in flow. They have shared our dream.

Clive Gilson
Michael Pratt
Kevin Roberts
Ed Weymes

# Introduction

Is it possible to achieve peak performance consistently, and to keep improving on that performance year after year?

Do organizations exist that have sustained continuous contention for the position of world-best in the long-term?

Given that people in organizations come and go, can we discover from such organizations the principles behind sustaining success over the long term?

To seek answers to these questions we chose to search in the most competitive domain of all human activities. Elite professional sport provides entertainment and involvement on a global scale. Fifty-five billion[1] television viewers are attracted to Formula 1 Grand Prix motor races during a season.[2] Nearly two billion people watched the 1998 World Cup Soccer final,[3] and the cumulative audience throughout the World Cup was thirty-seven billion.[4] Six billion people are expected to watch the America's Cup 2000. 133 million people in the USA and eight billion households worldwide watched the last American football Super Bowl contest . . .[5] Elite sport engenders passion, gruelling hard work, sacrifice and dedication to the greatest imaginable challenges in its participants. Riches beyond imagining are available for those capable of peak performance. But for the dedicated professional, sport is not just a job – it is a way of life. Millions of dedicated fans around the globe seek more than entertainment. They experience passion, elation and heartache, and they secure meaning and purpose from their commitment to their chosen team and sports code. For many, sport provides a vicarious dream of greatness in a world increasingly devoid of meaning.

We live in a world of organizations. Most people's lives are intimately intertwined with them. People are employed by them, manage them, participate in them voluntarily, or receive services from them. Some organizations are fun to work in, and are peak profit performers; others are losers. Some shine brightly, only to disappear quickly and without trace. A few organizations maintain their success for decades. It is these organizations in which we are interested.

Not every organization can shine on the world stage, but every organization has the chance of stardom in its own league. We believe there are general organizational practices which enable people to work together enjoyably and effectively towards common inspirational goals. Where better to search for these principles than in the teams and organizations of elite sports, the icons of the late twentieth century? One of the benefits of choosing sports industries to study highly effective organization relates to outcomes. Sport offers a simple yet effective measure of success – the win record.

Additionally, we chose sports organizations for our study because we found that ideas about peak performance, derived from sports psychology, constitute by far the most rigorously researched domain of elite human endeavour. We reasoned that, if we were ever to discover a coherent theory that explained peak performance, it would probably be found in the sports industry. In this sense, the choice of research domain was almost decided for us.[6] Elite team sports, by their nature, have significant organizations supporting them, and we hoped to observe peak performance within an organizational context. Given that all organizations, have experienced sustained success, and that players come and go, we assumed that organization would have a great deal to do with the winning formula. This proposition proved to be correct. We identify and explain generic organizational practices which will assist your organization to sustain the same levels of success and to work towards peak performance.

Our approach is profoundly different from that of conventional business books, which are rarely grounded in explicit data, and are usually marked by a rapid rush to assert how ideas might be implemented immediately. Even research-based business books often present only the authors' conclusions, which denies readers access to the deeper and richer insights available from directly comparing your own experiences with the research exemplars. In contrast, by telling stories of peak performance we will show you how we arrived at our theory and, hopefully, help you to discover your own path to greatness.

We would like to introduce ourselves. Clive Gilson is Professor of Human Resources Management, Mike Pratt is Dean and Ed Weymes is Associate Dean at the University of Waikato Management School (WMS). Kevin Roberts is a Senior Fellow of WMS and Chief Executive of Saatchi & Saatchi PLC. We have each lived on several continents. We all fly tens of thousands of miles a year in our roles as academics, consultants and executives. We have all chosen New Zealand as our home base. From this edge-dweller vantage-point, as practitioners and scholars of management, we have observed passing trends in organizational theory and attempted to apply them. And we have found them wanting.

We have experienced a parade of military models and metaphors for management over our working lives. We have devised strategies to destroy the competition, launched pre-emptive strikes; deployed sales forces to capture customers; and fired staff in re-engineering, rightsizing and restructuring exercises. We think managers and staff would prefer to go to work to have fun than to wage war. This book is about making work both fun and highly effective.

The search for effectiveness lies at the centre of organizational endeavour. Tools from traditional organization theory have proved to be less than useful – in effect they are tainted because they include data from all organizations, excellent or otherwise. In 1982 Tom Peters and Robert Waterman, in their book *In Search of Excellence*, narrowed down the data to those organizations that were deemed to be high performing, and spawned a new field of enquiry into high performing organizations (HPOs) that has been vigorously pursued by many authors. However, the concepts used to understand HPOs are still mired in the language and metaphors of organization theory, which distorts the picture. In contrast, our theory of peak performing organizations (PPO Theory) uses a single sharply focused lens and thereby transforms our understanding of organizational effectiveness.

We studied in depth ten of the world's consistently most successful sports organizations, across different sports codes, countries and cultures. They were FC Bayern Munich, WilliamsF1, Netball

Australia, The New Zealand Rugby Football Union, Womens Hockey Australia, The Chicago Bulls, The Atlanta Braves, The San Francisco 49ers and Team New Zealand. We talked to more than 300 people. We spent time in their organizations; we observed; we listened.

The sports we chose were team based and global, with a critical mass of competitors and high participation rates in the general population. The teams we selected were championship contenders at the time of the study, had exhibited continuous championship contention for at least a decade, and were recognized as leaders in the sport. We also ensured that we analyzed as diverse a range of sports organizations as possible.

Such is the passion engendered by sport that we know many readers will wish to challenge our selection, particularly if their team is not amongst our chosen elite! We wish to make it clear that these are not the only peak performing sports organizations that exist, and that in some cases we could have made a different choice. We believe that no one will dispute, however, the amazing records of success achieved by these organizations. Their inside organizational stories are fascinating and untold.

Our focus is on the role played by the organization, rather than on the teams themselves. In order to carry out this research, we gained unprecedented inside access to their stories. Our research question was, 'How do elite organizations sustain peak performance?' In our interviews this translated into a more colloquial, 'How do you keep on winning?'

The sporting organizations we spoke to were businesses, in many cases very large and successful businesses, with a razor-edged competitive spirit. By definition, the search for competitive advantage within each sports code is always relentless and unforgiving. All ten organizations exist within the fast-changing entertainment industry, where competition for disposable cash is fierce.

We spoke to a wide range of organizational participants, including, owners, players, coaches, managers, marketers, finance people, engineers, referees, board members, ticket sellers, fans and receptionists. In each case we watched games and went behind the scenes. For example, we spent time in the pit garage during the Grand Prix season with WilliamsF1, racing on the *Black Magic* boats with Team New Zealand, in the locker room with Michael Jordan and the Chicago Bulls, and at spring training with the

Atlanta Braves. We listened intently, and we observed. We were intrigued by the similarity of the answers across countries, cultures and codes, to our question, 'How does your organization keep on winning?'

We spoke to the teams to discover their perceptions of their organizations, and watched games and races to obtain what insight we could from elite performances. We found that many organizational practices emulated ways in which the teams themselves performed. We anticipated that it would be unlikely that a world-class sports team could be continuously in contention without world-class organization. You will see from the subsequent stories that this proved to be the case in practice.

We used multiple data-collection methods, including interviews, focus groups, participant observation and archival material. All interviews were tape recorded and subsequently transcribed. We amassed a staggering amount of data: 3,000 pages of transcripts as well as piles of archival material. Key to our research were our field notes of significant observations. These enabled us to focus on the important lessons from each case, as we agreed on these by consensus after each set of interviews or observations. Two or more researchers conducted almost all the interviews. The interviews were considered carefully after each round, and again after the transcriptions of the tapes had been completed. These conversations were pursued until there was a convergence of perceptions within the research team.

From our research we developed a set of principles, concepts and actions which, pursued in combination, can lead towards sustained peak performance. We describe this as our theory of peak performance organization, or PPO Theory.

## HOW TO READ THE PPO STORIES

A chapter is devoted to the organizational stories of each of the sports organizations that we studied. The stories are told in a way that captures the spirit of the organizations and their atmosphere of success. We share the insights and incidents recounted to us, together with our observations.

Each PPO has characteristics in common. They all have a long history of successful championship contention. They are part of the entertainment industry and the fitness industry – both good areas to be in so far as current social trends are concerned. Yet each PPO story is different. The teams are separated by geography, gender and game rules. The All Blacks (chapter 5) have a seventy-two per cent win record for the last 100 years. By contrast, some of our teams have only been top performers for about a decade. Some of the sports codes enable the players to earn millions of dollars; some are only just in the process of turning from amateur to professional. Through these differences, broader knowledge arises.

These contrasts mean that each story starts in a different place, and therefore reads quite differently. We determined our starting points after deciding the key distinguishing feature or lesson from each organization, and the chapters then proceed from this base. Wherever possible we tell the story in the words of those to whom we spoke. As you read you will see how similar their words are, despite their varying stories.

This book can be enjoyed on many levels, by managers, organizational participants and, of course, sports enthusiasts. The first ten chapters tell the stories of the individual sports organizations, while the final chapters offer a theoretical framework for peak performance organizing derived from the preceding narratives, which we hope will be transformational for the management practitioner or organizational scholar. In the final chapter we illustrate PPO Theory through a case study of Procter & Gamble, the consummate, corporate peak performer.

# CHAPTER 1

# FC Bayern Munich – More than 1–0

*'You cannot separate the Deutscher Fussball-Bund and Bayern Munich.'* – Franz Beckenbauer – 'The Kaiser'

Dedicated fans travel to FC Bayern Munich (FCB) games from Austria, Italy, Switzerland and all over Germany. On a cold, damp Bavarian winter's day, Borussia Dortmund, FCB's traditional great rivals in the German Bundesliga (premier professional league)[1] are in town, and once more the Munich Olympic Stadium will reverberate to the sound of 63,000 partisan voices. Although the facility was built for the 1972 Olympics, it now 'belongs' to Franz Beckenbauer – 'The Kaiser'. There, as a player, he led the German national side to a famous 1974 soccer World Cup victory. Beckenbauer rates this triumph as, 'the highlight of my life – the greatest of successes'. Yet the German people count winning the World Cup, as team manager in Italy in 1990, as an equally peak crowning moment of his career. In Germany, Beckenbauer is revered as a national hero. He continues to carry the torch as President of FC Bayern Munich, but his connection to the national side is ever present. He explains the origins of the link:

> In the last thirty years we all started as youngsters together. When we belonged to the German national side we were also winning European Championships – there were always five or six players from Bayern Munich. You cannot separate the Deutscher Fussball-Bund and Bayern Munich.

For Beckenbauer, a home game inevitably leads to media attention on a huge scale. Prior to the match an endless stream of dignitaries and hopeful Press, not to mention thousands of fans, lay siege to the part of the stadium which houses the FCB offices, and, in particular, the area that Beckenbauer inhabits before the game. To get within range is next to impossible. The cordon of officials and astutely deployed security is impenetrable except to those with special passes. By contrast, the right documentation dramatically clears the way. Doors open, as security guards, whose normal response to any potential invader is perfunctory dismissal, engage in an elaborate display of obsequiousness, helping to confer minor celebrity status upon those who have been granted access to the FCB president. Arms are waved dramatically, indicating to the next line of defence that a legitimate approach is underway.

Prior warning of this experience came during the taxi ride to the stadium. Upon hearing of our destination (VIP gate), and more importantly, the reason for the visit, the fare was promptly waived. Earlier, the hotel where we were staying got word of our agenda, courtesy of a carelessly left itinerary, and our rooms were automatically upgraded to presidential level. Requests for Beckenbauer's autograph followed thick and fast.

At the centre of it all, Beckenbauer is relaxed and looking forward to the upcoming game. As usual, at half-time and after the final whistle, he will provide nationwide television commentary and analysis of the game from a studio within the stadium. He reluctantly accepts the fame that has robbed him of privacy and solitude, although to secure a measure of seclusion he now lives in Austria, just a short drive across the border from Munich. His office in the stadium is unpretentious and functional. Dressed casually, with greying hair evident beneath an improbable baseball cap, Beckenbauer shows few signs of the youthful elegance and style that graced famous football stadiums around the world, but in explaining why FC Bayern Munich has been one of the global soccer giants for the last thirty-five years it becomes clear that he has lost none of his passion and enthusiasm for the game: 'Bayern Munich was founded in 1900, so we are coming up to our one-hundredth birthday! You really have to go back to tradition. I think it is tradition that explains our consistency, together with location.'

Beckenbauer, 'a player by the grace of God' according to Coach Sepp Herbeger, has been the figurehead of German football for twenty-five years, ever since the famous 1974 World Cup victory.

He collected 103 international caps, and sat on the coach's bench for sixty-six international matches. As president, Beckenbauer stands as the titular head of the FCB community, an extended family that definitely includes the thousands of fans in the Olympic stadium. The Kaiser is anxious to tell us how the national side and Bayern Munich both succeed by planning and tracking every last detail, but it is now getting seriously late. It's 3.30 p.m. – time for kick-off. A hurried knock on the door, and we are quickly ushered up the steps towards the VIP seating area. As our party, with Beckenbauer at the head, emerges into the sunlit majestic amphitheatre of the Olympic stadium, the crowd immediately recognizes the entrance of its finest inspirational player and roars its delight. The game can commence. Along with the Kaiser, we take our place at the very point where he received the World Cup in 1974. Over the next ninety minutes, we chat about the game, tactics and what it takes to build a great organization. At the final whistle Beckenbauer is immediately besieged by the media. Cameras, microphones and cassette tapes are dramatically thrust in his direction by journalists begging for commentary on the afternoon's victory. Time for us to leave.

Germany was the European Champion at the time of our visit, as it has been twice before, in 1972 and 1980. At the time of writing no other European nation has won more than once. The team has been crowned World Champions three times and placed second or third five times out of the sixteen contests since the inception of the World Championship in 1930, a record of achievement unequalled at the time of our visit. Unlike all other European nations since 1950 (the team was not allowed to play immediately after World War II) Germany has never failed to qualify for a World Cup. Deutscher Fussball-Bund Youth Teams secretary Bernd Barutta told us:

We are always criticized. If the German team is only one-up we will be criticized. We will be murdered if we fail to qualify. All other countries in Europe ... England, the Netherlands, France, Spain, Italy ... all of those countries have experienced a failure in World Cup qualifying matches. But we have never failed. If we don't qualify nowadays we are in big financial trouble with our sponsors and partners.

While other national teams wax and wane, Germany is always in contention, always expecting, and expected, to win.

## CONTINUOUS CONTENTION

At the heart of Germany's soccer success story is FC Bayern Munich. FCB has ruled the thirty-six-team German Bundesliga[2] through its thirty-five-year history, with fourteen Fussball-Meister titles, a further seven second-placings and three third-placings. They held the Fussball-Meister title at the time of our visit, and a few months later went on to win the Deutscher Fussball-Bund (DFB) Cup for the ninth time. In 1999 FCB were once again crowned Fussball-Meister, winning by a fifteen-point margin, the largest in the history of the league. No other German team comes close to this record of continuous contention in Europe's most consistently competitive soccer nation.

A million fans routinely attend home games during a season. There are 1,500 registered FCB fan clubs worldwide and 10.5 million fans. 'Kronen Wild Duck Haikon China' is not a new Chinese Restaurant – it is the new FCB official fan club in the People's Republic of China. FCB is a worldwide sports franchise of stunning proportions.

The Kaiser gave us his perspective on how this has all come about, but to explore the reasons for the relentless success of FCB more fully, we also needed to understand the national success of German soccer. A high-speed train ride took us to the headquarters of the Deutscher Fussball-Bund, nestled within woodland on the edge of Frankfurt-am-Main, where we carried out a series of interviews.

As we passed through the front entrance, a marbled foyer of football-field proportions appeared, decorated with the silver trophies associated with soccer supremacy over several decades. Purposeful Press and soccer officials were going about their business as a player disciplinary hearing was about to kick-off. Determined, efficient and elegant, the DFB headquarters stands proud in its history and tradition.

As our interviews progressed, the primary reason for the consistent success, both of the German national side and of the nation's crowning club, FC Bayern Munich, became clear – they are creating the future through investment in infrastructure, continuity and community. The DFB has six million members, 27,000 clubs, twenty-one 'Land', or district, associations and five regional associations. Each of the 'Land' associations has a *sportschule* fully equipped to provide world-class training facilities. The DFB is committed to offering the best possible organization for everyone, from the very young to seniors and players in fun-friendly leagues. Sophisticated scouting and development systems ensure that talent is identified and nurtured from a very young age. Club, district, regional and national leagues for all age groups hone talent through intense domestic competition. The role models provided by the elite club and national representative players create an ever-present incentive to achieve glory and financial fortune.

DFB General Secretary Horst R. Schmidt explained:

We believe that the consistency of our success is due to the strong structure of our clubs and our regional associations. That means that over the years we have been in a position to support talent. We can now look for talent at a very early age – under six. The kids in kindergarten are asked if they are interested in playing football. A lot of sports are competing for the children's attention, so it's understandable that clubs try to have them very young. By the age of nine or ten, coaches from the 'Land' associations are already looking for talented players. They are invited to training lessons and that continues over the years. Talented club players are noticed first by the talent scouts from the 'Land' association, then by the regional association, and the best players make it into the national squads for the various age groups. Clubs in the higher leagues look for talent in the smaller clubs. They used to have to pay smaller clubs a transfer fee before they would release them, but the European Court outlawed this system as a restraint on work. This created an unbelievable loss of money for small clubs all over Europe. We now have a completely free market, and players can change clubs with no charge at the end of their contracts. This makes the wealthy clubs very strong.

Creating the future through development is therefore a responsibility shared by the clubs and the DFB in a mutually dependent and symbiotic relationship. Both know that the success of the national team and the Bundesliga is dependent upon the continuous nurturing of new talent. The small clubs play a key role as the foundation of the pyramid, but are coming under increasing financial pressure as economic forces drive money towards the elite teams. Many of the Bundesliga clubs, such as FC Bayern Munich, have alliances with smaller clubs to extend the dream and build for the future. The very best young players move to the Bundesliga clubs at an early age, which suits the DFB, as Schmidt revealed:

> The talent scouts of the regional associations and the clubs work together because they have a mutual interest in ensuring the talent gets better and better for the club and national squads. The Bundesliga clubs try to attract talented players from the age of fourteen or fifteen from all over the country. That makes it easier for the DFB coaches to look for talent and to see how the players develop. Eighty per cent of talented players are members of the Bundesliga clubs and play in their teams by the age of sixteen or seventeen. The normal way is that these youngsters come to a Bundesliga club and then show up in the nationals.

The DFB coaching system is sharply focused on the development of talented players for the national squads for each age group from under-fourteen upwards. It is a systematic and relentless process, where the constant goal is to hone the skills of the very best inspirational players who will secure a place in the elite, senior national side. For the DFB all roads lead here. Schmidt described the process:

> The coaches think that the most important age for talent is between twelve and fourteen. We have an under-fourteen national side, then every age group through to the elite national squad. We have eight coaches. The coaches stay with their teams throughout the age groups and then start back with the under-fourteens. The best players become professional at eighteen, but often much younger players will have training contracts with Bundesliga clubs, and parents are very interested in this kind of contract. Our members number six million people, and we have to work to maintain the number of people in football.

Three or four million are really playing. A third of our members are parents, officials, referees or supporters. We have to ensure that these six million people become more, and we want to develop talent very early so that there is a good future for our national team.

Although elite sport is but one of three DFB goals, along with popular sport and social responsibility, it is clear that elite sport drives the dream. Without a successful national team, soccer would subside in popularity, meaning fewer funds and minimized magic with which to develop the broader goal of social responsibility.

After clearly setting out for us the relentless DFB development process, Schmidt, with much appreciated thoroughness, introduced us to Bernd Barutta, DFB Youth Team Leader, who provided us with further detail about the youth teams:

Through the fifties, sixties and seventies, youth football developed all over Europe, and finally all over the world, with different age groups, from under-fourteen up to under-eighteen, when players become seniors. The main work is done in our clubs and our regional associations. We pioneered a tournament for the twenty-one regional associations for the under-fourteen age group. Our coaches can take a close look at the players in the tournament, and we then take about fifty players and invite them to training sessions. We now do this for every age group. This way we can build up young players for the national representative squads. Nine out of eleven players in our World-Championship-winning team in 1990 had been youth national players first. Altogether, we have about sixty full-time paid coaches. We even have a football teacher's degree, run by the University of Cologne. The DFB educates their players and they gain experience. Without a successful national team the Bundesliga would decline, and the clubs realize this.

The DFB organization is unique in Europe in that it organizes everything to do with German soccer, including the professional leagues, the amateur leagues, the referees and relations with the Press. In most countries the amateur and professional leagues are divided. Schmidt:

We have been lucky enough to have both professional and amateur soccer managed by DFB – this is not the case in England, France, Italy or Spain. We are convinced that ours is the right way. The fact that we have a strong, concentrated organization has helped us to be very competitive over the years in our national squads, and this makes it attractive for youngsters and players from overseas to play soccer in the German leagues.

Over the years powerful DFB Presidents have ensured that the amateur and professional leagues have remained under one roof, despite the short-term financial considerations of some Bundesliga clubs which have led them to create pressure for greater ownership of the Bundesliga. Continuity in organization is a notable feature of the DFB. Since 1900 there have been just seven presidents, and while other nations sack their coaches at the slightest sign of a losing streak, in Germany just six coaches have developed the national representative squad in over seventy years. Schmidt sees this continuity as an important ingredient in creating the future:

Almost everybody in this association has played soccer, and this is what we prefer. We always have the same people from the DFB supporting each of the national teams, which means they know each other well, how they all think and what their needs are. The key players on the staff of the DFB have all been here for more than twenty years. The top national coach, Berti Vogts[3] started his career here in 1979 after the World Cup in Argentina. There is also another system, as in the Netherlands – they change their first coach very often. They are also successful, so you can't know which is the right way, but we think it's important to stay with the coaches. Knowledge of the young players as they develop is very important when selecting the national squads.

Just as continuity builds success over generations, so the tradition of winning is self-perpetuating. Schmidt:

The art of administration is directly related to what happens on the field. It is very important for the motivation of the people working in this association that we have successful teams. We are a powerful association which has always been very successful, and people are proud to be members of staff or members of committees. People want to belong to the DFB because of our traditions and our success. It does not matter if we are not always champions, but we have to be there, and to be a successful team playing football at the level that is expected. Winning is important, but the way you play for the public is very important. If you play with all your prowess, but you lose, people will accept this. If you win, but you don't play very exciting football, people will not accept this. We played one championship in Spain and got to the final, losing against Italy. Everybody in Germany was unhappy, not because we lost in the final but because of the way we played.

Wolfgang Niersbach, DFB Press, Publications and Public Relations Director, described the intensity of the media spotlight that is continually focused on German football:

We are sitting in a house of glass! In Germany we have a market with thirty TV channels and 170 radio stations, and now we have the Internet. Thirty million people buy newspapers in Germany every day. Let me give you an example. The national anthem is sung before international matches. Our coach Berti Vogts does not sing the national anthem because he needs that time for focus and concentration. So after every match I get about ten letters from fans asking why our national coach is not singing the national anthem!

Both the DFB and FCB embrace a symbiotic relationship with the Press, and systematically share the soccer dream through managed media relations, thereby extending the horizon of business possibilities. Niersbach:

We created a system whereby not all the players are available for the Press every day, but we offer something each day. We give them certain information and make available three or four players for special interviews, and the next day we offer other players. We work very closely with the clubs in this way.

According to Niersbach the DFB wants to share the dream globally.

We want to host the World Cup in 2006, based on our ideas of the relationship between professional sport, amateur sport and social action. This is not just about the German FA. It's about the whole country. We are a peaceful country, a new country, after reunification in 1990. This is not a development of Soccer only; it's about our country.'

No sport in our study has found its way into the soul of a nation to quite the same extent as soccer has in Germany. The passion of the DFB was palpable. Enthusiasm and energy infused our meetings, and were evident in the care with which the DFB ensured that we understood every detail of German football organization, and that all our questions had been answered to our satisfaction. Sharing the magic of the DFB community, even if only for a short while, was seductive. Niersbach summed up:

Everybody feels proud to work for the DFB. Nearly everybody will say, 'I have too much work, but I'm happy, I'm happy to work here, because it's not normal work, like for a bank.' It's a great feeling to be part of a success story. Next week we have our Christmas party for all the staff. Everybody, whether they are working in the front office, for the referees, for the cup competition or the Bundesliga or for the women's teams, is part of the success story. If I say to my friends I am working for the DFB, they say, 'Oh really, that's a good job.' Personally, I am convinced that the secret of success is to work in a quiet atmosphere, with discipline, in a strong organization. Look at the last European Championship in England. We didn't really have the best team, and we had so many injuries, but we won because of team spirit and the mentality and character of the team. We have the character to work for success, not to dance for success!

Our time with the DFB was concluded with exquisitely chosen gifts, all with discreet DFB logos, and a special extra item for one of us whose birthday it was.

On the Deutsche Bahn high-speed train back to FC Bayern Munich, we reflected that the formula of passion plus precision should put German soccer continuously in contention for a long time yet. By this time we had completed most of our global peak performing organization studies, so we believed that we could predict some of the reasons for sustained peak performance. But would they apply in Germany, where the language, culture and management traditions are very different to those of North American, English and Antipodean sporting organizations?

This was the question we had in mind as we prepared for our interviews with the staff of FC Bayern Munich. Our earlier research had revealed that the organization is studded with German soccer stars of the seventies and eighties. We were in awe when we found out that our first meeting was to be with the legendary stars Karl-Heinz Rummenigge and Uli Hoeness. In his playing days Rummenigge's name itself was enough to horrify opposing fans. He was the scourge of many a defence, breaking, on a regular basis, the hearts and hopes of spectactors not sporting the colours of either FC Bayern Munich or Germany. TV commentators had a grating habit of raising their voices and gutturally forcing his name out, as if his possession of the ball suddenly signalled imminent doom for the opposing team, which it often did. As an inspirational player, Rummenigge had it all: seemingly unlimited stamina, and strength; a vicious turn of speed; lightning reflexes; and a poacher's instinct for goals that was reminiscent of Gerd Muller, another FC Bayern Munich and German player still working with the organization after his retirement from the field. We wondered whether Rummenigge, one of the true icons of the world game, had made the transition to organizational life with the same ease with which he had sliced through opposing defences in his prime.

Robbed of a full playing career by injury, Hoeness was a dangerous inside forward who always maintained a flamboyant style of play, whether pulling on the shirt for FC Bayern Munich or Germany. A ubiquitous chaser of the ball, Hoeness was a celebrated member of the victorious 1974 German World Cup side, and is now FCB's manager.

We arrive early for our interviews at the FC Bayern Munich headquarters and training grounds in the sleepy Munich residential suburb of Harlaching. Celebrated in soccer circles, Säbener Strasse 51 is the FCB *Schaltzentrale* (nerve centre). Decorated in the distinctive Bayern Munich colours, the buildings symbolize the scale of activity carried out at FC Bayern Munich. With 64,000 members, FCB offers professional and amateur, women's, youth and school football as well as basketball, handball, squash, table tennis and more. It is both a social club and a superbly successful global business in one.

On the right, club rooms, restaurant and travel bureau are all commencing their day's activities. Professional changing rooms and apartments and offices for the FCB youth teams are in midfield. The gift shop and fan boutique are on the left. Behind the building the professional team practice is underway in preparation for the forthcoming season highlight match against arch rivals Borussia Dortmund. Spectators stand idly by, hoping for a glimpse of one of the FCB inspirational players. Directly ahead is the entrance to the ticket office, followed by the professional players' rooms and administration offices. Inside are the sophisticated weight rooms, training facilities, swimming pool, spa baths, and physiotherapy and medical facilities, which provide the ultimate in technical support for peak performance.

Punters, players and the Press, are moving in a disciplined manner towards the FCB offices, despite the earliness of the hour. We follow, keeping in the central area. This is clearly a place dedicated to fans. They are buying tickets, making enquiries, and soaking up the FCB magic. There is a family atmosphere, and people seem at home here. TV crews and the Press are all around, although quite who or what they are interested in never becomes apparent, since this appears to be an ordinary working day. A friendly receptionist responds to our enquiry in halting German for FCB Manager Herr Hoeness with clear directions in English. Throughout the building symbols of Bundesliga supremacy appear to be accepted as natural by the polite, yet persistent, fans who are purposefully going about their business. We are more easily distracted by the impressive array of trophies, pictures and soccer memorabilia, which dates back to the club's foundation in 1900. No corner could be found without magical representations of the tradition of winning.

We are expected, and shown into an interview room where coffee, soft drinks and nibbles are provided as a matter of course. The FCB logo is etched into the smoothly polished dark wood table, and more memorabilia adorn the walls. Hoeness appears moments later, relaxed, informal and immediately understanding and sympathetic towards our project. No longer the youthful athlete who contributed to English's international soccer misery during the seventies, Hoeness nonetheless exudes organizational energy and passion. It is clear that this inspirational player continues to lead his organization with all the flourish, drive, discipline and tenacity that he exhibited on the field. We suspect Hoeness has much to do with FCB's fame and fortune, and Rummenigge confirms this: 'For the last thirty years we have always had big players, thanks especially to Hoeness, who has been here for twenty years. He is always buying more.'

Hoeness is for ever famous for bringing down Johan Cruyff, thus conceding a penalty in the first minute of the 1974 World Cup to a rampant Dutch side which had already dispatched favourites Brazil 2–0 earlier in the tournament. When we asked him how he felt about securing his place in history this way, his demeanour still betrayed depths of guilt and disbelief. From this shaky start the German 1974 World Cup squad went on to a great victory in which Hoeness's flamboyant football played a major part. We asked what it was like to win the World Cup. Hoeness's evident pride in this achievement, even twenty-five years on, really needed no words: 'It was incredible. We hadn't won the World Cup since 1954, twenty years before and to win in Munich in our own country, you know . . .'

'He won it,' said Rummenigge, 'I lost it twice in the final. Let me tell you what that's like!':

> We lost to Argentina in 1986. I was very angry about that, because we had played very hard. The German Chancellor Helmut Kohl came into the locker room, and we were damaged and hurt. I was the captain, and he came to me and said, 'Oh, Mr Rummenigge, the team was fantastic today, and you are a really good ambassador for our country.' And I said '**** off Chancellor!' He said, 'No really, you were very good.' We were so devastated that I walked away. He just did not understand our passion to win. We didn't need to be told we were very good just then!

With inspirational players like Beckenbauer, Rummenigge and Hoeness engendering the passion to win it's not hard to understand the growth of the FCB franchise. Hoeness gave us his explanation:

The most important time for German football was in the seventies. FCB won three European Cups in succession from 1974 to 1976, a record never since equalled. Then, in 1974, Germany won the World Cup with five FCB players in the squad. These successes formed the foundation for our subsequent pre-eminence. When I was injured in 1979 I was twenty-seven. I hadn't played for six months and FCB President Neudecker asked me to become manager. I discussed with my doctor how long my knee would be stable and he convinced me to finish immediately. When I came here in May 1979 we had revenues of 12 million marks, eighty per cent of which came from entrance fees. This year we had revenues of 165 million marks and only sixteen per cent came from the gate. Next year we will have 200 million. Opel and adidas are big sponsors and we make a lot of money out of royalties on various merchandise. Back in 1979 we had twenty people in our organization – now we have hundreds. The team brand is a fantastic name, known throughout the world – even in Japan and China everyone knows our name. It was necessary to build our story around this town, and I think we were successful in that from early on. Many of the great names from the past help us today. The way we select inspirational players for the future, and combine them with the personalities of the past tells you everything you need to know.

Players who have been inspirational on the field in the past are positioned throughout the organization to pass on the dream of greatness. Franz Beckenbauer (396 FCB Bundesliga games and 103 games for Germany) has been president since 1994. Karl-Heinz Rummenigge (310 FCB Bundesliga games and 95 games for Germany) is vice-president. Uli Hoeness (239 FCB Bundesliga games and 35 games for Germany) is manager. Sepp Maier, who played a record 473 games for FCB, and 90 games for Germany, is assistant coach. Gerd Muller (427 FCB Bundesliga games and 62 games for Germany) is amateur trainer. Raimond Aumann (216 FCB Bundesliga games and 4 games for Germany) is fan club manager. Wolfgang Dremmler (172 FCB Bundesliga games and 27 games for Germany) is scout. And Hans Pflügler (276 FCB Bundesliga games and 11 games for Germany) is team leader in the merchandise and fan department. These living legends are the conduits from the past and the drivers of the dynasty, providing constant reminders of FCB's legacy of greatness. They have known success and continue to expect it. They encourage others to exceed their personal best.

Even though the players of Germany's famous seventies soccer squads were the catalysts for FCB supremacy, there are clearly other ingredients which lead to sustained peak performance. Echoing the infrastructure and commitment to long-term development that is also the hallmark of the Deutscher Fussball-Bund, Franz Beckenbauer emphasized continuity through the ranks of the organization, from the team to the administration:

> The financial situation in the seventies was very, very limited. We couldn't afford to buy Pele, but at this time the youth programme was very, very good at Bayern Munich. So all of us – Sepp Maier, Paul Breitner and Uli Hoeness – we all came from the youth levels. And many of the Bayern team of the seventies are now working in the organization itself.

Hoeness agreed, explaining that this strategy continues to the current day:

> When I was young everyone played football; I could play on every street corner. Today, the interests of the young kids are so different: some play computers, and they play ice hockey or basketball, so we have to look after them to keep young players coming to the club. We have fourteen flats for young players, and we have young players from all over the world. We have people who look after them, and teachers who help them with their classes in the afternoon. We always try to bring fresh blood into our main team of twenty-five players. We have a third-division team, and about five players from the main team play in the third-division side, with the rest made up from normal amateurs. We also have junior amateur teams. About half our team comes from our youth programme and the other half we buy in to fill certain positions, as they are needed. We choose people for their characters. We don't buy people who are just fantastic players. In this age when people get so much money, it is important that you buy character and vitality. We don't have too many people from outside Germany, because they

don't usually intend to stay here for the rest of their lives, and we don't get the same commitment. It's into the money machine for them and then they go back, so they cannot create a special identification with this club. Players from South America find it hard to learn the language and don't like the snow!

Andreas Jung, Manager, Sponsoring and Event Marketing, told us how FCB uses alliances to help create the future:

We have an agreement for technical co-operation with a second-division club called Unterhaching; it's a small city in the suburbs of Munich. Our younger players will go there so they get good experience, and if the club has any very good players we have got first option. We have eleven league teams, eleven youth teams, two women's teams and two women's youth teams. We have one chief coach, and all teams, from the eldest youth team to the youngest, play the same system as the FCB professional teams.

The continuity of inspirational players and staff, combined with the systematic way in which FCB creates the future through a carefully constructed game plan of development and judicious buying, harmonizes the community. Gwen Lloyd, Administrator in the Manager's Office who is English by origin but a fluent German speaker, explained the inside story of working for FCB:

It's really really, great. It's like a big family, you have complete trust and you feel that you could go to anybody at any time if you had a problem. It's such a different job. Most office jobs tend to be dull and boring, and here the work is not that much different from that in another office that I left to join FCB. But everything that happens around the work is interesting. We patent people I suppose . . . people who you know other people admire and go to the stadium every week to see. We all get involved with the football. Every worker gets two season tickets. Everyone works very well together, and it doesn't really matter what department they come from. Downstairs, whatever . . . they'll call us, we'll help them. If we need something then they help us. Everyone's prepared to help everybody else and I think that's the main thing that makes everything work and flow smoothly.

Jung offered some more examples of how the organization makes magic and builds community:

If at the end of the season the team is successful, the staff get a month's extra salary as a bonus, and they get a paper personally written and signed by the president, Mr Beckenbauer, congratulating them on their hard work and how it contributed to the success of the team. One year we were invited to go on a ski trip for three days. Next week we will have our end-of-year party where everyone is invited, including the players. All these things mean that now, at Christmas time, or when there is a big match, you don't say, 'I'm starting my work at 8.30 a.m. and I am going to finish at 5.00 p.m., if there is a crowd of people here waiting for tickets. People are not looking at the clock, and they do what needs to be done. The players and administrators are all part of the FCB family. The majority of staff will have personal contact with the players because they come here to practise. They are known by name and none of them are arrogant. They go through the building, say hello, and talk small talk to the staff. There is no hierarchy. Most of the staff have played football themselves, so we all talk the same language. We get thousands of applications, so we choose people who we think can do the job, have a passion about the game and fit into the FCB community.

Germany is known to scholars of management as the home of Max Weber, father of the theory of bureaucracy. We were interested to know the extent to which Weber's bureaucratic tradition would play itself out on the field of German soccer organizations. Since we had found very little of rules, regulations, policies and procedures in our peak performing organizations thus far in the study, we approached FCB with, we confess, an expectation that here we would find an outlier.[4] We asked Hoeness whether job descriptions and formal performance appraisals are used, and whether strategic plans, mission statements, goals, or objectives are in existence. He replied, 'Nothing really, no. We have no plans. I only know that we will make a profit every year!' This is not the 'death of bureaucracy', for it has never lived in FCB.

In response to our rather persistent questioning abut job descriptions Gwen Lloyd smiled: 'People don't have detailed job descriptions because the jobs change so quickly and everyone has too much work! I know how to do my job you know; otherwise I wouldn't be working for them!' We were a few kilometres from Max-Weber-Platz and no vestiges of bureaucracy were in sight. We persisted with our prejudices, causing Gwen increasing amusement. 'Perhaps your managers will sit down and discuss performance over the year with you? At FCB they don't even start . . . because we are working closely together, and we get told all the time that we are doing a good job. Come to think of it, my father does that sort of thing working for a big company, but we don't need it here . . .'

Focus substitutes for bureaucracy. Crystal clear understanding of, and deep belief in, the organization's purpose minimizes the need for policies and regulations. Franz Beckenbauer confirmed the importance of focus on the field:

> German football is not as creative as Brazilian football. It is simple, but with ambition, spirit and willpower. Some countries, for example the southern countries in Latin America, are more sensitive than the Germans. If they get to a certain point in a tournament they become afraid when they realize that they can win, and they get the shakes! But the Germans say, 'Come on, let's go.'

Jung emphasized the same focus in the off-field team:

> I think the most important difference is that our players do not have to do anything else; the team focuses on the match, on playing football. Our task is to do everything around the match: the allocation of ticketing; the event itself; the trip of the team; and all the technical questions for the team. We do these things perfectly down to the last detail. Everyone is focused on winning goals and the goal of winning.

The passion to win and the focus on winning is universal. Hoeness told this story:

The most important thing is that the team is successful. We once had a coach from Argentina. The Argentinians play creative football; he worked hard and the players liked him. Then I read an interview with him, and he said he cannot understand these people who are always willing to win, and he likes to play creatively to entertain people. Two or three weeks later he was off – chop. I told him, 'You play a very attractive ball game; very entertaining. Please do it wherever you want but not in Bayern Munich!'

Hoeness sums up the FCB focus in a simple phrase: 'We have to abolish losing!' Everyone knows this.

FCB has a continuity and tradition that come with its rich history and strong community, but at the same time flexibility, learning and the relentless pursuit of game-breaking ideas are ever present. Hoeness described to us his relaxed style of management, which we had already sensed: 'I never know when I come in here, what my plan is for the day, after lunch and so forth. The most important thing is that you are flexible. For me it is a laugh every minute. I cannot imagine working for another club. It is something special to work here.'

Rummenigge was proud of FCB's tradition of winning through game-breaking ideas on and off the field:

Our 1974 team were intelligent guys, clever guys, winners. This was the first generation to make big money out of soccer, but nothing like what we see today. Generation by generation, soccer is changing. It's different and harder than before, because you always have to come up with new ideas. But the organization knows how to have success and the economic side is very successful. So our job is to convince new people that these are the right things to do. We ask whether a new player is really confident. Is he willing to believe that the team must be perfect?

If we couldn't find stereotypical German bureaucracy, surely we would see much vaunted German precision. Indeed, it was everywhere, in the careful explanations that were given to us until our hosts were sure we understood every detail, and the extensive statistics and other material that appeared without our asking.

Franz Beckenbauer confirmed the perfectionist attention to the last detail:

> Yes! The organization is great – well, you know the Germans – the planning and the tracking of every last detail. I was team manager for six years and my assistant, who died two years ago, Horst Schmidt, planned everything, like a 'cake' for us to eat. I tried to overturn some of it, but he told me not to bother him – told me to shut up – to go and do something else, and at the end of the tournament I found out he was right!

This confident community keeps on winning through a magical mix of game-breaking ideas and precise attention to detail. It is never satisfied, and the passion to win is all-pervasive. Through winning, FCB sustains its dream to be 'The World's Greatest Soccer Club'. Hoeness explained that, 'It's really winning that provides the money, because winning gives you more TV time and media coverage, and that's what sponsors like.'

The Munich Olympic Stadium holds 63,000 people, and all of these seats could be sold as season tickets. However, unlike in North American sports franchises, where season-ticket sales are kept high as a protection against poor performance, FCB is sure of its success. Hoeness:

> We have 65,000 members of FCB, but that doesn't meant they are all season-ticket holders. We sold about 20,000 season tickets. We didn't want to sell more, because if you always have the same people in the stadium you don't make money on merchandising. We have six to eight million fans in Germany, and if you have so many fans and nobody is able to get a ticket, the dream fades.

FCB sells symbols of association through four FCB shops, four mobile vans and by mail order. The distinctive red, white and dark blue colours and logo extend the FCB brand into a range of clothing, memorabilia and merchandise as diverse as mountain bikes, watches, school equipment, kitchen equipment and toys. The FCB Meister Katalog offers a rich array of branded goods for the squads of enthusiastic fans worldwide. The range and extent of these dream catchers is the most impressive and comprehensive among all our project organizations. With a print run of one million copies, the Meister Katalog is big business, and the financial pay-off feeds the dream. There are about 120 people in distribution of tickets and merchandising. Service and image drive the dream, with 'everyone treated very friendly', according to Jung.' 'You do not know what they want to have; maybe they want a ticket, maybe a tie, magnet, shirt, you don't know but you treat everyone the same. And if you treat them friendly, the chance that they will buy is better.' Sponsors are partners in extending the dream:

> Opel and adidas are our two premium sponsors. Then we have other sponsors to whom we offer standard packages of benefits plus further special options. Cross promotion is very important between our sponsors. We often suggest that a sponsor goes together with another to get greater benefits. Also, we want successful sponsors, because then we have a transfer from sponsors to the club and from the club to the sponsors. We had 350 hours of TV coverage last season and 3,467 million people contacts. About twenty-five per cent of our income comes from sponsorship.

The revenue derived from sponsorship, merchandise and ticket sales enables FCB to fund the development of youth players and to play a role in the DFB's commitment to social responsibility. For example, inspirational players take decisive positions against drugs and smoking, in nationwide and local campaigns, aimed at the young. The FCB is at the forefront of an ongoing 'Say No To Drugs' campaign. Rummenigge was one of its initiators: 'Drug abuse caused a tragedy in the family of a close friend of mine. So, I immediately agreed to do whatever is necessary to warn our youngsters.'

The FCB dream is more than just winning. More than filling the stadium, year-in year-out. More than selling symbols of association. More than just a 1–0 win. Winning attractively is important, but beyond winning, FCB is committed to being a partner in society, and takes its social responsibilities for popular sports, and especially, youth, seriously. This commitment extends throughout the DFB. Niersbach:

A key moment happened at the World Cup in Mexico, when we saw homeless children a couple of metres away from the World Cup stadium. We were there as guests of the country, but we wanted to help. The Mexico Foundation in Queretaro has now existed for more than ten years. It was not just a momentary reaction to say we have brought you money for the homeless children. We established an orphanage, and now we have raised more than two million marks for Mexico, and we feel that our whole association understands the idea. So you have a referee meeting or a Christmas meeting and afterwards they bring money to the foundation: 20 marks, 200 marks, 1,000 marks. The German embassy in Mexico is involved and each mark goes directly to the children.

One million volunteer coaches throughout Germany teach young players skills and values that go well beyond the four corner flags of a football field. 'A young girl or boy in an amateur club should learn good social attitudes for life, for example, how to win and lose, and to accept a weaker partner,' says Niersbach, 'It's the task of sports, whether it's Munich or a very, very small club, to offer training and match competition, but also to offer a certain social attitude. Most clubs think this way.' The shared symbiotic dreams of winning attractively with social responsibility bring meaning to the German soccer logo 'More than 1–0.'

## CONCLUSION

The dream is the theme. As we boarded our southern-hemisphere bound Boeing we were left with a permanent impression of the passion that is German soccer. We continue to share the dream and follow their fortunes. The official song of the Deutscher Fussball-Bund, sung by Anna Maria Kaufmann and Joey Tempest, provides an apposite conclusion to our story.

> Running with a dream,
> Burning deep inside,
> Don't let them bring you down,
> Don't let the chance go by.

Running with a dream
Only we can show
How far this road will lead
And what it means
To be running with a dream.

Sometimes it seems like you've got it all
And everybody wants a share;
Sometimes your back is against the wall.
And nobody seems to care.
We've tried so hard and we've come so far,
We are the ones who don't give in;
The world will take us for what we are,
Whether we lose or win,
But we're
Running with a dream.

# CHAPTER 2

# WilliamsF1 – We are all Racers Here

*What really makes Williams tick is that it is one huge great family and every single member of that family has got one goal. That is to be a winner, whether that is by their technical contribution or in some other way. Every single one of us is completely focused on one thing. Winning.* – Jane Gorard, Media Manager

The numbers are simply staggering. On the sixteen race weekends that comprise a full Formula One season, over two and a half million spectators will visit the race circuits. Each Grand Prix is watched by an estimated worldwide TV audience of over 350 million, making an aggregate total of 56 billion loyal viewers. The 'need for speed' makes Formula One the world's most popular spectator, and breathtakingly spectacular, sport. For the last twenty years, WilliamsF1 has established the best record, out-pacing by a substantial margin the Ferrari constructors' team which is more obviously associated with the romance of motor racing.

Having won the coveted FIA Formula One World Constructors Championship nine times, and the better-known FIA Formula One World Drivers' Championship seven times, the trappings of victory are all around the Williams factory at Wantage, in Oxfordshire. As Managing Director, Frank Williams's opinion is that, 'Grand Prix racing attracts and creates more true passion than any other sport.' This can clearly be seen in the people who work for WilliamsF1. Yet in the mid-sixties, Williams was sleeping on a sofa in a shared flat in Pinner Road, Harrow, on the outskirts of London, trying to establish a spare parts business. Twenty years

later, that business had become Williams Grand Prix – the dominant force in the world of Formula One.

The present Williams factory, which was originally sited at
Didcot, some twenty-five kilometres from the new facility, has
been in operation since the beginning of 1996. Employing over
275 highly skilled employees, its output is at best modest, making
just seven cars each year. However, it takes 250,000 person hours
to build a single car, produced from over a thousand complex
technical drawings, and finally constructed with over 3,000
machined components worth over US $1.5 million. Additionally,
each car is completely stripped down between races, subjected to
over 200 diagnostic checks, and then rebuilt. Overall, the factory
machines over 200,000 components each year. The organization
also boasts one of the most advanced, fast and accurate half-scale
model wind tunnels in the world, allowing round-the-year aerody-
namic testing. The Williams car, like other Formula One vehicles,
can reach 200 k.p.h. from a standing start, and then stop within
seven seconds. Straight-line speed is well over 340 k.p.h. Just as
important as the Grand Prix cars are the test cars which complete
over 30,000 kilometres each year, a vital element in ensuring that
the work carried out by everyone in the organization is directed
towards making the car go faster.

The atmosphere in the factory is a heady mixture of engineering
and the romance of victory. The entrance way into the facility
opens out to a large atrium. In the middle of this space lies a
vivid reminder of the *raison d'être* of the organization – Jacques
Villeneuve's peerless 1997 World Championship winning car.
Even for those unmoved by the sport of motor racing, the sight
of this car, with its blue-and-white livery and wide wheels, makes
an impressive statement – no other car in the world does it better.
And it belongs to Williams. One corner of the atrium is reserved
for an assortment of trophies, shields, plaques and other mementoes that celebrate the winning years. Elsewhere, the walls offer
a rich array of framed photographs, memorabilia and nuggets of
information that provide tantalizing glimpses of Williams' history.

The shrine-like qualities of the atrium are amplified by the Formula One museum. Close to the reception booth a pair of sturdy
double doors opens to a priceless collection of Formula One cars
that represent twenty years of Williams' engineering. The cars, all

in pristine running condition, carry the names of the great drivers who helped take Williams to the peak of motor racing. The cars of World Champion Alan Jones, Keke Roseberg, Nelson Piquet, Alain Prost, Nigel Mansell and Damon Hill, along with those of many other Grand Prix winners, are all on display. If there is an inner sanctum to the world of Formula One, it is here. Adjacent to the museum is the plush, state-of-the-art Ayrton Senna Lecture Theatre, which hosts conferences, media presentations and launches of new products from Williams' sponsors.

The production areas that adjoin the atrium and museum bear little resemblance to a traditional engineering factory. It is an unparalleled, world-class facility where the highest skill level is employed. Every section or work station maintains a surgical cleanliness. Only the racks of titanium rods and alloys reveal the true nature and intent of the operation. Placed near to each other to ensure maximum co-ordination are Computer Aided Design systems, which play an integral part in the research, design, development engineering, production and testing. Three autoclaves which deal with new carbon fibre composites are housed in a clean room which would not be out of place in a NASA launch-vehicle assembly area. The bays where the cars are finally constructed and tested have the ambience of a large hospital operating theatre.

High technology, precision engineering and a strong sense of professional discipline are immediately apparent. The in-house factory capabilities include composites, fabrication, machining, electronics, pattern and model making for the half-scale model wind tunnel, hydraulics and various ancillary support functions. Approximately half the total workforce is directly involved in vehicle construction. Echoing the traditional working methods of skilled artisans, some forty design and research engineers collaborate closely with craftsmen to ensure that all tasks related to the making and assembly of each car are effectively conceived and executed. The race and test teams are each staffed with a mix of twenty engineers and mechanics. Another forty people working in administrative capacities round out the morphology of the organization. Within this latter group are sixteen marketing and media personnel who are responsible for sponsorship deals, public relations and generating US $70 million annual revenue.

During the year the facility holds several open days when friends and family of the workforce can see plant operations for themselves. In preparation for such occasions, some of the work spaces display small pieces of wreckage from spectacular accidents that are undeniably part of the thrill of motor racing at its fastest. Poignant reminders of the hazards, danger and expense of Formula One motor racing, they offer a surprisingly immediate connection for those peering in from the outside. 'This is a mangled piece of suspension wishbone from Jacques' [Villeneuve] shunt in the Belgian Grand Prix,' factory worker Bernie Jones explains. 'Course, we don't expect an apology,' he adds with a wry smile. As long as there is no proprietary engineering involved, and the driver suffered no more than a dent to his dignity, these trophies, once seen by 350 million television viewers, are carried off to many an Oxfordshire mantlepiece.

Even though the Grand Prix season winds up in late October, the factory is already in high gear, designing and preparing new components for next year's WilliamsF1 car. New FIA technical regulations governing the specifications for the coming season are made available to the constructors well before the last Grand Prix race has been run, giving them time to design components afresh to conform to the new rules. The 'off' season is also an important opportunity to begin experimenting with reconfigured components that offer the tantalizing hope of a faster car. One work station is honing a newly designed wheel nut that might reduce the time it takes to change a tyre during the all-important pit stop. 'This innovation might cut 0.2 of a second off our pit-stop times,' explains craftsman Steve Pieri. Although the component looks immaculate, Pieri is not impressed. Meetings will take place between the design engineers, the Technical Director, Patrick Head, and the factory specialists over this and an unspeakable number of other critical components. However, at the end of the day, it is craftsmen like Steve Pieri who have to machine the impeccable part, a responsibility he is proud to hold. During the race season this process may need to be concentrated into a much shorter period of time. David Williams, General Manager:

It is not unusual for the company to design a part today, manufacture and test it overnight and fit it to the car tomorrow. Naturally, this means that the emphasis is on each employee to take full responsibility for his or her work, with maximum freedom to act.

Work activity is seemingly relaxed and unhurried, yet Alan Challis, Race and Test Team Co-ordinator, a twenty-year veteran at Williams, observes in understated fashion that, 'At Williams, every day is a defining moment.'

Celebration is never far away. In the canteen facility hangs a large, evocative photograph of the Williams pit-lane crew at Suzuka, Japan, in 1996 cheering the final chequered flag victory that secured Damon Hill the Drivers' World Championship that year. The enlarged picture is personally signed, and dedicated by Hill to the Williams team. Similar artifacts, including scaled models of Formula One cars, can also be found in and around the offices. These objects embody a magic–making environment and a relentless ambition to be first. To win. This clear organizational focus comes directly from its two iconoclastic inspirational players, Frank Williams and Patrick Head, Frank's partner and technical director of the team. Head explains:

Frank and I have relatively straight aims which are clearly visible to our organization. We're just motor-racing nuts really. Everybody in the company is aware that we have very, very focused aims. I'm sure we have degrees of complexity, but, put simply, we worked out quite a long time ago that if you can be successful on the track, other things, particularly the commercial aspects of the company, tend to look after themselves. They tend to be a hell of a lot easier to run when the technical and the performance side is right. A company is more difficult to run if you turn that focus around.

We've always been very focused on the purpose of the company. I don't think that this is totally the case with all the other team principals. There are some teams in Formula One who give the impression that profitability comes first, and then they try to do the best job they can within the level of profitability. Whereas nobody here has any confusion about the Williams company. They know that the driving motivation is always to be successful and to win. Not just to be profitable, and if it become necessary to sell assets in order to be successful, that is what we would do.

# THE DRIVING FORCES

Kay Young, Head Receptionist, observes of Frank Williams, 'We still think of him being a mighty figure.' It is a sentiment that is easily understood, although Williams himself is more matter of fact in his personal assessments. 'Since the age of four or five I have always been interested in cars. In the late 1940s maybe only one family in twenty had a car. To ride in one was a major event. To race them with friends . . . it just happened.' Frank Williams is the consummate inspirational player. While fulfilling his own passion for speed he took a corner too fast and 'cocked it up'. The crash, which happened in France in 1986, left Williams tetraplegic and permanently wheelchair bound. Despite this setback, which almost cost him his life, he has continued to lead Williams successfully.

Apart from having amassed a lifetime of Formula One motor-racing knowledge, Williams is known for his great business acumen and, in particular, his skills at making critical deals with suppliers, sponsors and contractors. In the early days of Williams his ability to find sponsorship funds was about survival, whereas his current dealings are more likely to be about fine tuning the organization to enable it to maintain its success. In conversation Williams misses nothing. Urbane commentary combined with razor-sharp observations ensures the maximum attention of those within earshot. Whether in the office or in the pit garage his presence lifts those around him. His friendliness and kindly demeanour sit uneasily with the popular belief that Williams is the hard man of Formula One.

More importantly, his sheer grit and determination has provided the platform for others to establish their engineering and racing credentials, and make real their dreams of speed as well. Patrick Head, who, as a 'promising' racing-car engineer, joined Frank Williams in 1977, is a Formula One icon in his own right, famed for his unrivalled expertise. Dave Jones, Chief Inspector, notes that:

He is totally committed to racing. Patrick can walk into your department and if you have ten bits on the table, he can look at them, and if one has something slightly wrong with it, he'll pick it up. He knows every little bit of that car.

Head's legendary knowledge and passion for his work are truly inspirational. Although he has the appearance of a grizzled factory superintendent, he combines unparalleled engineering skill with an avuncular and infectious joviality. He is always willing to demonstrate his love for motor racing. While relaxing in the pit garage, only hours before the start of the Canadian Grand Prix, Head toys with a small, irregular-shaped defective engine component. Fixing his gaze purposefully on the offending object, resting on the tips of his fingers, he animatedly launches into a detailed technical explanation of why the engine part had recently failed. Quick to recognize that his audience is somewhat out of depth, he generously wraps up the one-sided discussion with the simple observation that, 'It's a design fault really, we'll fix it next week.' Still, he leaves the strong impression that he is personally insulted by the presence of the compromised object.

He talks effortlessly and very positively about the great drivers associated with Williams, although he has a more reflective and deliberate cadence when referring to the great Ayrton Senna, who tragically died in a Williams car three months after joining the team. 'You knew you were in the presence of someone special when working with Senna. After testing or qualifying he would never discuss the session until he had seen the telemetry on the tyres, which he considered to be the key variable in motor racing.' Contrary to uniformed opinion, Head also considered the Williams FIA Drivers' World Champion of 1996, Damon Hill, to be 'a very fast driver indeed'. Coming from Head this is little short of the ultimate accolade in the racing world, although such sentiments failed to secure Hill a drive in the 1997 Williams car. Great drivers come and go, and although the Williams team usually try to contract true racers who'll give it 'some welly', when the chips are down, the unmistakable reality is that the car is the star. In the past, the organization has eschewed other World Champion drivers for seemingly lesser talent, and when Hill's contract handlers tried to out-muscle Frank Williams in negotiations, the 1996 world champion was left to find another drive on the circuit.

Peter Yonge, Chief Buyer, describes Frank Williams and Patrick Head as 'the prime movers, the shareholder owners who from day one have been the common denominator'. For Lindsay Morle, Media Executive, their presence creates a special aura of association:

> It is very hard to describe actually, but there is something magical about Williams. It took me two years to get this job. There is such a history to it, especially with what Frank has gone through, and with himself and Patrick coming from the bottom to be a winning team. I think it inspires people to work as hard as they have done to get where they are. Everyone wants to be part of the Williams team.

With such a passionate desire to belong, the WilliamsF1 organization does not need to search for a mysterious formula that will unleash seemingly unlimited employee motivation. Jim Wright, Head of Marketing, offered an eloquent testimony as to how the organization sees its key inspirational players:

> The magic of Williams can be summarized in four words. 'Frank Williams' and 'Patrick Head'. They are the inspirational leaders. We all draw our motivation for our quest for supremacy from those two guys. Clearly, in a marketing role, I don't have too much contact with Patrick, so my inspiration comes mainly from Frank Williams. He motivates me in what I try to do, and that obviously penetrates down to my staff, who I try to motivate in the same way. But Frank is an extraordinary man. This is probably the only organization that I have ever come across where everyone reveres the boss. That is a very, very rare thing. Everyone loves Frank, because he has got time for everyone. He's tough, but he's fair, and he will always, always support his staff. I have never seen an occasion where he hasn't supported his staff. Even though they may have been in the wrong, he has given them support, and sorted it out later. I think that people have the utmost respect for both Frank and Patrick.

The daily impact of inspirational players cannot simply be captured by reference to 'the art of delegation' or overwhelming charisma. These attributes clearly apply to both Williams and Head, but another defining feature, observable in the organization at all levels, is that there are no 'followers'. Each and every person plays a key role in the life of the community. Not surprisingly then, Williams attracts those who strive constantly to better themselves.

Jane Gorard, Media Manager, until 1999, personified peak performance under pressure. She and another colleague were the conduit through which a stunned world learned of the tragedy of Senna's untimely death. In addition to dealing with the external demands of the media, who maintain a voracious appetite for any titbits of information, Gorard also handled the internal dispersion of information throughout the organization. Adroit and astute in her professional dealings during the Grand Prix season, Gorard brought a balance and perspective to her work which helped to define the contours of the Williams community. Equally at home on the factory floor or in the finely appointed visitors' room, her talk was of pushing for improvement in everything, everywhere. In this she was not alone. The Williams community thrives on personal accountability. Gorard believes that the maverick instincts of the two giants of Formula One act like a magnet for those who may be lured to experience other pastures:

> There is so much respect for Frank and Patrick, because of what they have done, and, in particular, how they haven't always toed the party line – they have bucked the trends. They have done it because of their desire and their passion for motor racing, and that filters through to all of the people who work here. Although people have left Williams and gone to other teams, the grass is greener on the other side of the fence only for a while. Many have returned, because they lose that feeling of being part of a big family. I don't believe you get that in other teams. Internally, we benefit from their attitude, which is wonderful. This is something very special, that you probably wouldn't ever get anywhere else. Frank and Patrick have enormous respect for all of the 270-odd people who work here.

# SUSTAINING PEAK PERFORMANCE: A MAGNIFICENT OBSESSION

Frank Williams knows that *constant* peak performance is not the same as *sustaining* long-term contention at the top of motor racing. For this reason, he sees that humility and winning go hand in hand:

There is no constant supremacy. I never believe that we are supreme in any way. We are always fearful of being given a good thrashing the next time we turn up to a race. It is not an exaggeration to say that we know that we are not that sharp. We think that there are better-organized teams out there in Grand Prix racing. It is very competitive, but no more competitive than any other world-class sport like American football or soccer. There are some very clever people working here, but the biggest advantage we have is magic.

Most people here are nuts about what they do. People here love cars, and the epitome of competition, currently, is Formula One Grand Prix Racing. Once you are involved, it is a whirlwind that sets up a non-stop challenge. Just participating, just being around the cars and entering a race is exciting. The drivers are very special human beings. All twenty drivers on the grid would give you the ride of your life in a touring car. Their control is prodigious, especially in the wet. They have 750 horsepower to control and the car weighs, with them on board, around 600 kg. In the wet they can't see anything and yet off they go. I once said to Nigel Mansell, 'How do you know when to brake in all that spray?' Nigel replied, 'I wait for the front wheels to lift off, pause and then I brake.' It wasn't exactly what I expected.

The magic and excitement of racing reaches everyone. No one gets left out at Williams, and a strong sense of ownership prevails. Kay Young sums up the community atmosphere: 'Everyone wants to be fast and successful. When we win, everyone's part of it. Not just the engineers and the aerodynamics people, it's not just them, everyone plays a part in it.' Bryan Lambert, Test Team Manager, offers additional confirmation that inclusion is a natural feature of the organization: 'It is the group of people as a whole. It is not just Frank Williams and Patrick Head. All of the employed people here work as a team.'

Each race during the season provides an opportunity for the organization to come together. Watching the race from afar, however, provides only a partial explanation for the extraordinary bonds between people who do very different jobs. Bringing back the trophies and displaying them is another powerful mechanism of inclusion, but there are also far more important activities which are critical to the maintenance of a tight-knit family environment. In this organization, everyone is kept informed. On average, thirty-five people out of the total 275 actually go to the Grand Prix. After each race there is a technical debrief between Head, Williams and the engineers who were actually at the race when they will discuss whether the race strategy was correct, or with new parts, whether they worked, and what amendments might be considered for the next race.

Equally important, if not more so, are the debriefs which Head conducts after several of the Grand Prix races. They are attended by all members of staff. Jane Gorard:

> Patrick, who is never lost for words, will talk about the build-up to the race weekend, he will talk about 'free practice', he will talk about qualifying, and if appropriate, something specific that happened to one of the other teams. He communicates the whole tone of the weekend. He will congratulate and if necessary chastise, if that is the right word. If there is a department which has to pull its socks up, because that is where we were let down at the weekend, then he will say so. Patrick discusses exactly why the team believes that, for example, the suspension broke. It could be a fault in manufacture, it could be a fault in materials or it could be a fault in the building of the car. Depending on which it is, then obviously that particular area has to be focused on.
>
> He will also talk about gossip, pointing out that one of the other teams obviously had a good weekend, because they had topless models all around their car, but that unfortunately it did not make their car go any faster. It always adds a bit of humour, but really the purpose of it is to bring the race back to the team, so that we all feel that we were there. Even if we have all sat and watched it on TV, it doesn't matter. There isn't

a single person in this place, or member of family, who is not going to be glued to the TV when a Grand Prix is on. For the Australian Grand Prix they will all be sitting there at 4.30 or 5.40 in the morning, having had parties the night before that just run through until the race starts.

The debrief is not taken lightly by anyone. Kay Young is absolute when describing who actually attends:

Everybody does. When we are down there, nobody takes any calls. We just tell everyone to call back. Patrick's got a booming voice, and when he talks everyone takes notice. Although we are obviously not technically inclined, we know what he's on about. It is nice to know. And he puts in a few funny little bits, and makes it very light-hearted in some respects. It's his voice, he's got presence. Everyone listens.

Held frequently throughout the racing season, these informal gatherings are special occasions which create strong ties and loyalty to the Williams community. At the same time, the external wisdom is that the organization is a cold and clinical engineering outfit. The most dramatic image that fuels this perception is the television view from each Grand Prix, which always shows Frank Williams in the pit-lane garage staring, expressionless, at a bank of monitors, absorbing an endless stream of data transmissions. Jim Wright drily reflects on a fundamental misunderstanding:

That is the difference between the workforce and the viewing public. The first comment I get when I tell people what my job is, 'Oh, Frank Williams, he's such a miserable git. You never ever see him smiling.' That is the TV image, but I carefully explain that you have to remember that he's looking at several monitors, and he's listening to two radio channels, and he's concentrating. He's working! The reality is that he is one of the most fun-loving people you would ever meet. Any one of the 275 employees can walk up to Frank's office and request to see him. There is never a problem with that. He knows all of them, and if any of them has got a problem they go to Frank. So I think that's pretty important.

Frank Williams himself ensures that the organization does not slip into the habit of adopting a deferential attitude to authority figures. Standing on ceremony for either himself or Patrick Head is positively discouraged. His arguments are simple yet persuasive:

> There is no room for formality in a building full of pressure. We are a Christian-name company, which is something I am very proud of. Nobody here is Mr. Everybody is a Christian name. I don't know all the surnames, but that is partly by design. When you are starting off on a Christian-name footing, as we do with new people, they tend to get on better and they are more productive.

The informal and friendly attitude that Frank Williams cherishes so much is embodied in people like Dave Jones, Chief Inspector, who has worked at Williams for twenty years. He draws a direct link between atmosphere and doing great work:

> Informal? Yeah. People outside think we are pretty serious. I have got a new guy in my department who has just come from Benetton and he was told, 'You don't want to go and work there, they are really serious and they do not know how to have fun.' But we are always larking about in our department. People enjoy themselves. Many people have been here a long time – the actual staff turnover of senior members is negligible. Most of the guys in the shop have been here for twenty years. It's continuity. Everybody knows what's going on. If you want something done quickly you know who to talk to and you can get it done. They came in last Friday to get a new flap to go out to Australia. The jig was drawn by the office, machined and finished by Saturday afternoon, and was in the composite department by Sunday morning and then winged out by Sunday night. You can get things done that quickly.

Knowing what to do, who to talk to and how to get things done is a competency that Williams has built up in the organization over many years. Guidance, however, does not come from formal job descriptions, and individual performance is not driven by detailed appraisal systems. In the factory annual, informal assessments are carried out between foremen and workers, but the structure of the organization is relaxed. Frank Williams:

> From time to time communication takes place by formal meeting. But really, informal corridor meetings are taking place morning, noon and night, seven days a week. You might say that that is a bit strange – a bit sloppy – but it works most of the time.

By contrast, in the mid-nineties, Williams began a fruitful relationship with Andersen Consulting, who developed an Enterprise Resource Planning (ERP) system which was designed to tighten up the working cycle for building a Formula One car. ERP linked design and production with purchasing, inventory and financial controls throughout the continuous cycle of design-build-test-implement. Alongside the ERP system, informal teams spring up and disband as needed. There are no formal cross-functional or self-managed teams that have 'official' status or can be identified as part of the formal governance process within the organization. Structure, such as can be recognized, ebbs and flows around functional expertise. For this to work, the stability of the workforce is a vital element in creating the future. The security of employment enjoyed by the workers is underscored by Frank Williams' observation that:

> I don't think we have ever made anyone redundant. I remind myself that most great companies make people redundant in their time. It has to be coming to us one day. I worry about it all the time. However, when we expand we try first to promote from within.

With the benefit of the trust and commitment that this attitude engenders, ongoing corridor meetings and focused, yet impermanent teams are able to create a firm basis for working in a state of flow. For Dave Jones, this way of working has hidden dividends:

> Someone might come up with an idea to improve the speed of the car, but because we have worked together for many years, we can say, 'No it didn't work. We tried that four years ago.' At some of the other teams, because they tend to change staff

quite quickly, they will say, 'Oh yeah, we should try that,' and that way they make costly mistakes.

What works in the factory goes for the office too. Lindsay Morle:

> We are not really that formal. There is a lot of banter. It's a lot like a community. If someone is snowed under we will all pitch in. It is not like, 'That is not in my job description. I'm not doing that.' You do it because you know it needs to be done. We are always working together, pulling as a team. We don't use performance appraisals to get things done. No. That kind of structure just doesn't exist.

The demands of Formula One ensure that the synergies of informal teamwork are used to their maximum potential. All aspects of organizational life are influenced by the quest for improvement and, in this respect, a Formula One car never finishes being built. The car that Williams rolls out of the box and tests for the first time at Silverstone at the start of the racing season has made leaps and bounds forward, from a technical point of view, by the time it performs at the opening Grand Prix in Melbourne, Australia. This process of development and design continues relentlessly throughout the season.

The informal and flexible, yet disciplined, processes that define the Williams organization are well suited to demands for constant iterative change and game-breaking ideas. Although much of the design and precision engineering is carried out by a cadre of highly skilled, qualified craftsmen, no stone is left unturned in the quest to find extra speed. Bryan Lambert:

> Ideas come from lots of people. Obviously, the main people are in the drawing office, in the design office, but they will listen to anybody that has an idea, whether it be from the design office, or the guy sweeping the floor to keep the place tidy – anybody – if they think that the idea is worth trying, then we will try it.

The ever-increasing technical sophistication needed to compete in Formula One inevitably pushes involvement in the direction of those who are scientifically qualified, yet Frank Williams has no intention of cutting off a powerful supply of innovative ideas – the shop floor.'

As engineers in a highly competitive environment we have to respond to the continuous staircase of change. People working with the suspension, carbon composite material etc., must all contribute ideas, especially if it is a critical change which involves safety. Certain directors or the chief designer approve the drawings, so there are procedures.

Patrick Head argues that innovation can only flourish when the fear of failure has been taken out of the organization:

We try to create an atmosphere where innovation gains credit, where it is recognized. However, innovation often goes through considerable periods of failure before it is seen as a visible success. If you have an environment where failure is not tolerated and is openly criticized, or where people are looking for failure in others, you can get an environment in which nobody will innovate for fear of failure. You have to run the organization in a manner which is not inward-looking, where each department tries to pick out faults in the other. We have values here so that the first response to failure is not to pick out the individual and crucify him. The focus is on how you're trying to put it right, not to blame someone for why it's not right.

The constant move forward with new ideas creates an ongoing sense of urgency. Expectations are extremely high, both in the factory and in the office. People who join the organization from outside are well positioned to reflect on the pressures to contribute from the moment they enter the organization. Jim Wright:

When I arrived, no one took me by the hand and led me in gradually. Here you were, joining an elite workforce, and you were coming into a position where people were already expecting you to deliver. In fact, I've seen that since I have been here. I had been here for a couple of years when we hired an in-house lawyer. We had never had one before. People just expected him to know all the FIA rules. You have to really get on to it. I think that these guys all around me are really good, and I have to perform at the same level. No one rolls out the red carpet for you. No one is hostile, but you are simply expected to perform because they perform.

Peter Yonge, another twenty–year veteran of the organization, has observed similar experiences when new people join the workforce:

There are people here who have come from other industries, the Air Force in lots of cases, who can't initially understand speed and the immediacy of things. They are used to a machining environment where they make something which might sit on a shelf somewhere in Malta or Kuwait and never see an aeroplane. Our guys can make a component on Thursday afternoon and watch it going round a track in Brazil on Sunday afternoon. This makes for very good morale. It is very immediate.

Although the drama of working in the world of Formula One has its share of pressure and tension, the high expectations create an invigorating atmosphere which is conducive to innovation and change. Jim Wright:

This is an enjoyable experience. It is an ever-changing experience. It is not something for which there is an established routine. It is a constantly evolving process. I have been here three years and four months, and it is ever-changing. You are always focusing on something new, a new programme or something else to go out and sell. So it is very motivational from that point of view – you don't feel as though you are doing a routine job week in and week out.

These sentiments are typical across all occupations at WilliamsF1. There exists a strong suspicion that all employees represent the very best in their personal field of expertise. Personal responsibility counts for a great deal here, and individual pride ensures that state-of-the-art knowledge is employed at every turn. This is most evident in the test teams, who pursue to the last detail improvements that can be measured in fractions of a second. As the Test Team Manager, Bryan Lambert has one of the most demanding jobs in the organization. He is responsible for overseeing the thousands of test miles that are the backbone of Formula One success. His role is to drive engineering capabilities to the very edge, a task which calls for precision and discipline:

> The people who work for me are people who are interested in development – they are not interested in just working on a car. We are there purely for development, and obviously if the development is successful the car will go quicker. We are not there to beat other teams' times, we are there to beat our own. For me personally, it's important to make sure that the test goes like clockwork from start to finish, because it is all down to me at the end of the day: the logistics of the trucks; the people; the organization during the day; every element; and, yes, every detail. This type of organization is very important.

In a similar vein, Chief Inspector Dave Jones bristles with confidence when describing how commitment to technological innovation and exceeding one's personal best, is a natural component of the work ethic: 'I think everyone has such commitment to new technology. Part of your job specification is that you keep up-to-date with the latest technology and you maintain all your equipment. It is the individual's responsibility.' Head himself admits to a perfectionism that motivates him to improve constantly: 'Frank and myself, we're always looking at ourselves to see what we can do to improve. Organizationally, anything that is running well tends to get pushed out of my head, because there are always plenty of bits that I'm not happy with.'

The focus on winning and the passion to exceed personal best are best revealed when the organization turns up to race. Senses are sharpened as the effort of many is concentrated into the frenetic activity of the few, which in turn is vested in the two drivers who carry the final burden of performance.

# IN THE PIT GARAGE

It is mid-afternoon, and the qualifying session for grid position in the 1998 Canadian Grand Prix is over, as are the never-ending impromptu pre-race Press conferences that the Formula One drivers have to endure. Apart from the sound of the occasional pneumatic drill, the pit garage has for once fallen silent. Standing alone in front of one of the monitors is Jacques Villeneuve, the 1997 FIA Formula One World Drivers' Champion. Like his father, Villeneuve is already a racing legend, respected and fêted by the Grand Prix community and, especially, by the Williams crew in the pit lane. He is watching one of the junior Formula Atlantic races that helps to fill the race weekend. As he focuses on studying the form of the drivers who aspire to claim his coveted title one day, the odd mechanic drifts by unnoticed. A casual reminder from one of the engineers about the upcoming drivers' race briefing is greeted with a knowing smile and a nod of the head.

Closer to race time, Villeneuve is apt to pad around the garage with his racing full-body jump-suit undone, and the top half sprawling around his hips. The idea is to ventilate body heat to stave off possible dehydration towards the end of the race. In the pit garage at least, glamour takes a back seat. Humour is not far away either. At one point during the race weekend, Villeneuve accidentally spills his hot drink all over one of the computers that processes the race car telemetry, and in the process wrecks the critical keyboard and mouse. The entire garage nearly collapses in stitches as one of the crew dryly observes that this is the cheapest accident Jacques has had all year. Prior to discovery of this minor calamity, the World Champion, aided and abetted by a willing accomplice, actually contemplated an elaborate cover-up of the deed, but in the pit garage nothing goes unnoticed for long.

Such a relaxed, informal atmosphere seems barely possible. By definition, the pit garage is the focus of all the raw power, high technology and surges of adrenalin that are associated with Grand Prix motor racing. Notably, the unexpected burst of noise as a Formula One engine kicks into life is startling, but in other respects the pit garage offers seemingly transparent activity conducted with a minimum of tension. The highly visible pit stop, conducted at breakneck speed against an unforgiving stopwatch, is usually cited by management gurus as a fine example of teamwork, yet this activity represents a mere fraction of race activity. More importantly, the pit stop consists of a pre-ordained set of manoeuvres that is barely related to the rest of the weekend's efforts. The pit garage calls for far more complex activities – many discretionary, invisibly co-ordinated decisions, are made in a split second. And no one is obviously in charge.

Throughout the Grand Prix weekend the pit crew are in a constant state of activity. Making the car go faster rests on supreme technical knowledge applied against an ever-changing backcloth of conditions. Air temperature, track temperature, track conditions, circuit layout and a whole host of new iterations brought in from testing between races have to be factored into the settings on the car. A mixture of free practice and qualifying sessions allows the team to adjust, recalibrate and try again. Small group debriefings on tyres, engines, gearboxes, suspension and, finally, race tactics take place in trailers at the back of the compound. This seemingly endless flow of interaction sees both race cars being built and rebuilt many times during the weekend. However, technical advantage, while precious, amounts to little without a feel for it all. Intuition and personal judgement rest not simply with the driver, but with every single person in the garage.

Unquestionably, the pit garage is a special place to be. Cramped and seemingly chaotic, it offers a surreal experience. Sitting unobtrusively in a corner of the garage is one of the disassembled engine blocks that generates over 750 horse power, the 'grunt' at the heart of the raw attraction of Formula One racing. There is a stack of wings here, a row of nose-cones there. A range of chocolate bars lies invitingly atop a vending machine that dispenses both hot and cold drinks. Traffic around this section of the garage is brisk, with the average length of each visit, at around eight seconds, matching the time, if not the drama, of the real pit stops that are undertaken in each Grand Prix race.

In amongst the computers, the boxes of spare parts and the tables at the back of the complex, where food is hastily consumed when time allows, are tyres, lots and lots of tyres. And then there is the crew, engaged in an endless flow of activity. The stacks of tyres are constantly rotated, as each set of 'boots' nears its turn to take to the track, while the ones already used are taken to the back of the garage. Parts of the car are being assembled, drilled, honed, attached, disassembled and reassembled.

Few words are spoken between the pit crew. A brief nod, a longer than usual meeting of the eyes followed by a raised eyebrow or a facial expression contain information as vital as telemetry from the state-of-the-art pit-garage computers. The ability to communicate this way was probably borne out of necessity, since the deafening roar of a single Formula One engine renders traditional conversation ineffective. The advent of the radio headset provided for more normal discourse, but this is usually restricted to formal confirmation of a known situation. Being in the pit garage feels as if you are walking through a basketball court while the Chicago Bulls are in a play-off game, and the ball is going around and over you while your presence remains largely unnoticed. Only after two days or more is there any recognition that 'someone else is in the garage'. The level of sustained concentration needed by the pit team is phenomenal. James Robinson, Senior Operations Engineer, believes that it takes at least two years, possibly three, before a member of his team is fully able to understand his role:

> I think it's fair to say the Williams way is that everybody is focused on their particular area, their particular expertise, and getting down to it and trying to do the best job they can. It needs very little paperwork, very little in the way of formal systems. You don't have to go over a problem twice, you don't have to ask if something has been done. You identify the problem and you can walk away, knowing that in a week's time the problem will be solved. You are looking at a period of two to three years before you think that person is in a position to be truly trusted.
>
> If we have a problem this weekend, we know somebody has got to look at the design side of it, somebody has got to look at the manufacturing side, and someone will be generating the right parts, either internally or from outside of our own processes. But those parts will be available in the factory before the next race. There is no follow-up system to say has it happened, has it been drawn, has it been stressed, has it been made, are the materials right, has it been painted, has it been tested in the labs, has it gone to the track to be tested, if so was it quicker, was it slower, did it break, did it not break, and, finally,

did it need looking at again? A lot of that is basically done with two lines on a piece of paper. Every two weeks we are racing and we are problem solving in that time period. As long as that is managed in such a way that it produces a safe and quicker car, then I think that is a very good way to operate.

For the pit-lane crew, especially, this calls for high levels of individual technical ability and accountability.

However, individual technical skills alone are insufficient – more important still is the network of relationships between crew members. Intense awareness is also a vital part of the working landscape, both in the factory, and, more decisively, in the pit garage, where the rubber literally hits the road. Task and process unite in a state of flow – a combination of head and heart. For James Robinson this is not accidental:

Williams has always been run on an engineering basis, creating a very strong group of focused, purposeful engineers. A lot of it is knowing your job. Our people have come through the ranks, whether they be mechanics or even Formula One drivers. You have to learn quickly what is required and what is needed. No one says, 'You should be doing this now,' or 'This should be happening.' It needs very little guidance or management. Rather, it needs pointing, not leading.

Heinz Harald Frentzen, who joined the team upon the departure of Damon Hill, has a unique perspective on Williams. Coming from the much smaller Sauber team, Frentzen was surprised that Williams was 'so well organized'. Reflecting on his two years with the team, Frentzen points out the difference between Williams and other constructors:

People here are workaholics. They live day and night with the problems. Patrick Head, the technical director, has so much experience. From his experience he already knows so much, and yet he still wants the chance to learn more and more things. As far as I know, as a technical director, there is really no comparison that can be made with him. He is the motor.

I also think that, apart from Patrick, the flexibility in the team is based on many good people who have lots of very good experience. They know the research and the direction they must go – the team knows itself perfectly. Here in the pit garage they have a very special 'procedure', it's a kind of special rhythm.

It is a rhythm which can incorporate disruption, distraction and the demands made upon it by the external world. Ffiona Welford, Motorsport Press Officer for Williams during the 1998 season, dealt directly with the journalists who constantly want access to the world-famous drivers and any pit-lane action that will land them the big story of the Grand Prix. Sponsors too, and a bevy of celebrity superstars have to be kept happy in a Grand Prix weekend. She has to maintain a delicate balance between the pressure-cooker atmosphere of racing and the need to satiate the media. It is a crucial interface that has to be managed to perfection. Ffiona Welford:

> I am the main point of contact with the media on circuit, so technically speaking I need to know what is happening throughout the race weekend. Frank, Patrick and the crew will give me anything I need to know, things that I should probably be telling the media, and then I can go out and keep them up to speed with what's going on. The trust has to be there between us. If I need to ask them a question for the media, the fantastic thing about them is that they can be absolutely 'rushed off their feet busy', but if I say, 'I need to ask you this,' they've always got the time to tell me, always got the time to give me an answer. From my first year here, nobody has ever brushed me off and said come back later. They answer straight away because they know I need to keep the media informed. Nothing is too much trouble for anyone.

Co-operation between the different roles in the pit garage takes place in a seemingly effortless, tranquil zone, which contradicts the popular image of Grand Prix racing as drama-filled, frenetic and frequently dangerous. Although drama and tension are always just below the surface, the pit-garage experience rests at the confluence of a well-oiled organization which knows how to win.

# CONCLUSION

Frank Williams feels that his organization is 'not important to the central thread of life', yet those who either work for, or who are associated with, WilliamsF1, will tell you a different story. Although Frank Williams and Patrick Head are most strongly associated with the history and current direction of the organization, the dream belongs to all. From Head's Grand Prix story telling, to Williams' insistence on informality, the traditional mental model of hierarchy and separated occupational classifications collapses in favour of personal discipline and identification with a collective vision – the goal of crossing the winning line before anyone else. The whole organization is geared up to ensure everyone's total contribution towards this end, and, without fuss or fanfare, the people at WilliamsF1 continually contribute by exceeding their own personal best performance at work. There is a relentless pursuit of development which includes coming forward with new, game-breaking ideas to make the car go faster, and ruthlessly dealing with each and every last detail. A positive attitude towards failure is encouraged as part of the critical development process. This keeps WilliamsF1, if not in, knocking on the door of the winner's circle. Finally, there is a seamless integration of all aspects of organizational activity without the traditional methods of managerial control.

The legacies which Frank Williams and Patrick Head are manufacturing at WilliamsF1 will remain long after they have retired. The powerful stories and mystique associated with these inspirational players has influenced the very fabric of organizational life, and sustained the dream of winning.

*

In recognition of his services to the motor sport industry, Frank Williams was knighted in the 1999 New Year's Honours list. On 23 February 1999, Sir Frank Williams proudly received his knighthood from Her Majesty the Queen on behalf of everyone who has worked for the Williams team, both past and present. The research for this chapter was conducted during February 1998.

# CHAPTER 3

# Netball Australia – Finding Flow

*We both said exactly the same answer at the same time. Like somehow there's this mental link; it's quite amazing. I think we all just learn; it's not taught to us. It's intuition.* – Carley Baker, National Marketing Manager, Netball Australia

In netball you must pass the ball or shoot within three seconds or incur a penalty. There are no time-outs, and few set plays. As a consequence netball is a fast, free-flowing sport, that requires supreme athleticism, agility and anticipation, consisting of four quarters of fifteen minutes each, with brief intervals between quarters. As a spectator spectacle, it has an attractive media profile because of its intense action. Netball has a higher number of active participants than any other sport in the Commonwealth.

Karen Miller, Australia 21 elite player explains the magic:

I saw the World Championships on TV and from then on I became very involved in netball. They were winners. When you are a kid growing up you always want to play for Australia, and once you start at the club and district level you can see the progression from there. We play because we love the sport. I have been playing since I was six years old. Netball was within our family I suppose, and that's really why I chose it. When you are ten you put a whistle in your mouth and you start umpiring; when you are thirteen or fourteen you start coaching. I think Australia is ahead of anywhere in the world in players, coaching, administration; everything all comes together and that's what makes us World Champions.

# WORLD CHAMPIONS

Netball Australia has globally dominated this 100-years-old-sport for more than three decades. The Australian Netball Team has won eight of the ten World Championships since their commencement in 1963,[1] and won the inaugural Commonwealth Games gold medal in 1998. They are the champions of one of the world's most popular women's sports, with more than seven million participants in forty-five countries around the globe. 'Why don't you have a brand name for your elite team, like the New Zealand Silver Ferns netball team, or the British Lions rugby union team?' we asked National Executive Director Pam Smith. She replied, 'We do, its World Champions!'[2] They have achieved this record, the best of the international teams in our research, because they have long understood how to organize for peak performance.

Australian netball provides participants with the opportunity to excel and achieve recognition in an exciting and entertaining sport that attracts huge public interest through a range of escalating competitive challenges in club, regional, state, national and international championships. It also encourages lifelong participation in a range of different activities within the local, regional, state, national and global netball communities, including administration, coaching and umpiring.

Netball Australia's focus is to develop the netball brand as Australia's number one participation sport, both nationally and internationally. Competition for the elite athlete, both in relation to other women's sports such as hockey and in relation to non-sporting activities, is intense – it is vital to ensure that new generations of players are both attracted to and remain involved with the game. The recruitment and development of potential elite players provides the foundation for achieving the enduring challenge of remaining World Champions.

Recruitment and development require infrastructure. With over 375,000 registered competition netball players in Australia, the demands placed on central co-ordination are acute, but because Australian netball is organized federally there is only a small central group of professional staff at the All Australian Netball Association Ltd (Netball Australia) national office. Each netball association in the states and territories of Australia is itself incorporated – they are completely separate legal entities with considerable autonomy from Netball Australia. States, territories, regions and local clubs maintain their own vigorous identities, as evidenced by separate web sites, brands and sponsors. All the states have their own professional staff who make their own sponsorship, events and marketing arrangements, independent of the national body.

Independence breeds fierce inter-club and inter-state competition, innovation and diversity of coaching and playing traditions. This intense domestic rivalry is the driving force behind Netball Australia's global dominance. Inter-dependence comes into play when external challenges need to be faced. The states and territories meet twice annually in the form of the National Council for administrative and governance purposes. The Council operates with sixteen members, two from each association, and has a significant measure of stability in the membership. A separate board of eight people, elected by the Council on the criteria of skills and passion for the sport, together with an appointed National Executive Director, has overall governance responsibility for Netball Australia. 'We have a proactive board,' explains National President Sue Taylor; 'It's a mostly female board. All debate is open, frank and to the point. We are all busy people with other lives and can't afford to 'pussyfoot' around.' Pam Smith, National Executive Director, attributes their enduring success to strong leadership:

> I honestly believe that the major reason for Australian netball success has been the fact that it has been run and led by women. Business is controlled by the old boys' network. Our female athletes are the most successful in the world, but they don't have the same social standing as their male counterparts. Because we have had to struggle in this difficult environment we have got to put in that much more effort and try that little bit harder to get our piece of the profile, but we know we can do it. We've got the perseverance.

Pam Smith is the only appointed director of the board. As well as being a full voting member she is also the driving force behind the national office that operates the business. The board's brief is to develop netball as a global sports entertainment brand, while remaining true to the dream of grass-roots netball as the foundation of elite player potential.

Pam Smith explains that the basis for working together rests on infrastructure:

> Netball is just like a central government structure, with the three tiers of federal, state and local government. We have a national approach to a range of things: overall branding, elite player development, sponsored national and international competitions, playing rules, coaching and umpiring accreditation, and curricula. Activities more specific to the states include coaching and development, scouting and regional competitions. And then the local associations and clubs are the final level of operation – they are the grass-roots of the netball community.

The central organization strives for close liaison between all facets of netball administration, from national down to club level, with a balance between being entrepreneurial and working for the common good. Despite the potential for conflicting interests to be reflected in the activities of the board and the national office, the organization has created a powerful community that is marked by inclusion. Netball Australia is the only organization that insisted on beginning its interview schedule with us as a team, before spinning off into individual meetings. During the group meeting, seven members of the board, national office and the state associations gave commentary on every aspect of the organization. According to Pam Smith, unity in the face of considerable diversity depends on a passion for the sport and a steely determination to employ a wide range of skills in the most effective manner possible. These elements, she argues, provide for automatic commitment.

Pam Smith herself is a key inspirational player who is responsible for effective co-ordination at the 'centre'. A no-nonsense person, she relies heavily on her ability to create leverage through an extensive network of relationships. People know very well that conflict and disagreements are not going to unhinge her:

> In the overall scheme of things, everybody works together. Our organization is about a team sport, and the philosophy of being in a team extends off the court as well. So, we're all committed

to a philosophy of collaboration. Nor are we backward in coming forward in telling one another what we think. I separate personal issues from professional issues – I have people that I can work with and have fun with, as well as have a large disagreement with them. I don't have time for getting back at people – I think that stuff is rubbish.

On the more personal level, she describes her style:

Most of the people who I work particularly well with on the board would say that my background in politics has been a bonus for the sport. Another strength is that I don't get overly concerned when people disagree. I certainly get frustrated at times, but I'm not the sort of person who goes home and tosses and turns, and worries about what's going to happen the next day. I believe that's just negative energy, and wasted time. If a decision's been made, I'm quite happy to live with it, even when it's the wrong decision, because once you've made up your mind, you've gone ahead and done something, there's no point worrying about it. It's too late!

As the link between the national office and the board, Pam Smith has to tread a fine line between operational activities and issues of a broader strategic nature. One of the most important relationships that she nurtured is between herself and the President of Netball Australia and Board Chairperson, Sue Taylor. Pam Smith:

As a friend, I don't think I will ever lose track of Sue, probably because we think in a similar way. She's bloody stubborn. I know where I stand with her. We can totally disagree on an issue, but I feel very comfortable in putting my point of view forward without fear of being ridiculed. She's blunt, she forthright, she's intelligent, and she's not motivated by a desire for personal glory. She's on the board because she believes she can contribute to a sport that she's been involved in all her life, and she's got a passion for it.

Peak performance is about enduring inspirational relationships. Netball Australia has benefited from a succession of presidents who have provided both stability and direction, and sustained and energized the dream, from the grass-roots up. Pam Smith says that Netball Australia has a 'legacy of inspirational administrators such as Eunice Gill, Lorna McConchie, Gwen Benzie, Marg Pewtress and Joyce Brown'. Sponsorship, gate receipts and related marketing activity provide funds for the elite, but like all sports netball is largely dependent on a volunteer workforce at the grass-roots. This combination of volunteers and inspirational administrators, many of whom have themselves been elite netballers, make up the administration of the Australian netball community.

The headquarters of Netball Australia is based in a nineteenth-century character-house, nestled within the concrete high rises of Paramatta NSW. The outward calm of the building belies an energized, colourful interior, where a sense of enjoyment and fanatical enthusiasm prevails. Fun sustains and is sustained by a peak performance work ethic, which is in turn sustained by the power of community belonging, and a potent sense of purpose. Carley Baker, National Marketing Manager, encapsulates the spirit of the place. She explains that when selecting staff, 'We are looking for work ethics; we know the type of people who will fit into our working environment.' Somewhat diminutive alongside the elite squad, she more than makes up for this with an effervescent and dynamic presence which enables her to sustain a schedule of activity that would exhaust most. Conversation is frequently disrupted by the mobile phone, which cannot be switched off. She is the glue. A missed call cannot be contemplated:

> Some days I think to myself, I would love to go home to bed after we have been on tour for two weeks. We have missed two weekends, a public holiday and we are all back in the office ready to go again. You know we have got to get this thing done and you know it doesn't matter how many people say, 'Take your holidays, don't come back from your holidays, switch your mobile phone off.' You know that at the end of the day you are accountable for that, and your work habits are so strong that you don't want your reputation to go down at all.

As one of a small number of professional staff in the national office, Baker occupies the hot seat. It is her responsibility to deliver a viable product for public and media consumption. Much of her work is based externally, in particular she has to work closely with the states and their different marketing campaigns. For Baker, this is all about 'accountability in terms of picking up our numbers – from sponsors to game attendance to the television audience'. To achieve this she holds 'sit-down marketing meetings' with the states, where common national themes for marketing and events are established. At the same time, she works hand-in-glove with both media and sponsors to ensure maximum coverage of the sport. In a competitive industry, Baker wins plaudits all around. Telstra Executive Adam Jeffreys, who is responsible for Telstra's sponsorship agreement with the Women's Hockey Association, recognizes that the netball marketing machine is one of the best in all of Australian sport. It is no surprise that Pam Smith characterizes her marketing guru as 'Ms million miles an hour!' Baker's work with the states, media and sponsors means that she also plays a key role with the national squad. She is the conduit through which much of the organization's activities are communicated to the team. Sponsors develop campaigns around key players: 'Our twelve elite players go out into schools and do information sessions; we have shopping centre appearances; we use their faces on our marketing and on our cardboard cut-outs. We send them to business lunches and other celebrity events.'

She works so closely with the elite players that the boundaries between different areas of responsibility begin to blur. She is no longer simply in charge of marketing. She is respected by the players. She knows when and when not to approach them for media work, or the circumstances under which it is possible to co-ordinate the autographing of uniforms, match-balls and the like. More importantly, she monitors closely the mood and general condition of the players:

> On a recent tour we didn't get the chance to sit down to ask the players if they were happy with everything. A few days after the test matches were over I gave them an open book with some pens and said, 'Spit out whatever you want to spit out.' They are over the moon with this consultation process, because we take on board their concerns and address them.

Baker describes her activity within the organization as providing a 'mental link'. Pam Smith is more effusive about her role: 'She's brilliant. Sponsors love her.' Nowadays, Baker invariably travels with the team on tours abroad. Smith's greatest fear is that her marketing manager will be 'pinched from me.'

Current captain of the Australian Netball Team Vicki Wilson has been a key factor in Australia's supremacy for over fifteen years. She is a brilliant, ruthless shooter and a fast, articulate speaker. As one of the greatest players of all time she is well placed to define the qualities an effective sports administrator needs:

> Good administrators can understand a player and think like a player, but can then step out of that environment and know exactly where they are heading as an administrator. I believe that a good administrator can come in and mix with the players so that there is good communication, and then return to do the job they are supposed to do.

Organizational excellence creates and sustains the winning tradition. Chris Burton, National Director of Umpiring, explains that countries outside the top three, including England where the game began 100 years ago, are far behind in terms of their administrative infrastructure: 'New Zealand and Australia are miles ahead; South Africa is not far behind.' Although the UK has the largest number of school-age netball players, it lacks centralized playing areas, cohesive networks and well-co-ordinated local, regional and national competitions. As a consequence, interest in the game falls off beyond school level. Pam Smith:

> Other countries don't appear to have the same access to sports sciences or realize the importance of rest, recovery and diet. Their coaching fraternities do not appear to have the same commitment to best practices. Our coaches look at a whole range of innovations in other sports. For example, we have people who run ball skills and eye-handling co-ordination skills for rugby football. Our coaches work with soccer players to assist their co-ordination. We actually cross-pollinate with other sports and take their best bits and pieces. Its more about organization and knowledge than it is about money, although I would love to have the massive money that England get from their lottery.

The Netball Australia infrastructure 'works for the grass-roots, which eventually comes through and feeds into the Australia team', explains Liz Ellis, Australia netball team Goal Keeper. The infrastructure creates the future through tremendous depth. Children aged five to seven are taught motor-based skills and activities through the nationwide 'Fun Net' programme, while 'Netta Netball', a modified version of the game with smaller goal posts and ball, provides friendly competition for ages eight to ten. Graded competition commences from age eleven. Club, regional and national competitions provide a staircase of graded challenges for junior athletes. This hones their skills, giving them ongoing opportunities to exceed their personal best. 'The 21 & Under development programme for our younger players ensures that they have had world-class international exposure prior to making it into the national team,' says Sue Taylor. The elite players are closely involved in development. Vicki Wilson:

One hundred per cent of A grade players have coached; all of them have coached a team or can go in and take coaching clinics on their own. Through coaching and umpiring you can analyse games better. You can see where the game is breaking down and you can whisper in someone's ear, 'Hey why don't you try this or that?' You can analyse the opposition and work out where their strengths lie. And when you umpire you get a better knowledge of the rules and you can think quickly and know what the call is going to be.

Coaching in all walks of life develops the coach as much as the coached.

The shift in elite netball from sport to entertainment flowed from the 1997 Netball Australia partnership with the Commonwealth Bank of Australia. The domestic inter-state competition was redeveloped into the National Netball League (NNL), which competes for the Commonwealth Bank Trophy (CBT). This institutional change of focus was designed to increase media coverage and sponsorship opportunities for Netball Australia. Pam Smith:

The NNL gives us a netball elite season with a televised profile which starts in April and continues through until September. As a consequence we get requests to be part of other television magazine and sports shows, and the newspapers ring us for comment on sporting and social issues beyond netball.

The new league brought new sponsors, eight new teams, each with bird brand names – Firebirds, Kestrels, Phoenix, Orioles, Sandpipers, Swifts, Thunderbirds, Ravens – eye-catching new uniforms, and a format designed to maximize entertainment and fan appeal. Logos and team colours enable fans to identify easily their team. Pam Smith:

> We have a centralized approach to our National Netball League for the Commonwealth Bank Trophy. We own all the logos and marks and we secure sponsors for the teams, pay their airfares and uniforms, and pay the teams to be in the competition.

This continuously competitive domestic environment for Australia's elite players provides them with probably the best domestic competition in the world,' says National President Sue Taylor. 'This makes sure our top players are exposed to tough on-court challenges on a regular basis. Carley Baker is now trying to build netball into our sponsors' advertising. Someone like Fisher and Paykel can buy so much space on television.' 'The administrators are doing a great job getting sponsorship then allowing the players to get out on court and show their wares internationally as well as at home,' confirms Lisa Beehag, Assistant National Coach.

The CBT is a high profile competition which gives young players the opportunity to worship and learn from their heroes, and it provides career pathways in coaching, playing, administration, umpiring, public relations and marketing. Women's team sports do not feature highly in the global market for sponsorship and media coverage; the NNL marks a significant breakthrough. Vicki Wilson dreams of seeing women's team sports offering top quality live entertainment on a par with men's sport, arguing that, 'It's even better in the flesh, like alive. Nothing better than coming out to a live game. It is fast, it is exciting, and we are skilful, and we are athletic, and we do sweat!'

Fisher and Paykel, the innovative domestic appliance manufacturers, have sponsored international competition with the other global top teams, New Zealand and South Africa. Carley Baker:

If you weren't aware that Fisher and Paykel has been involved with Netball Australia, then all of a sudden this massive truck delivers your washing machine, and its got three elite netball players throwing a ball on the side of the truck; its going to hit you really, really quickly. Women have purchasing and buying power. Sponsors see netball as a prime medium to get their messages out, alongside our message encouraging women to get involved with netball. We give the sponsors a vehicle to get their brand and product into the market place. They use the profile of our players, our logo and our branding to align themselves with us.

John Bongard, White ware Manager for domestic appliance manufacturers Fisher & Paykel:

Families are central to the Netball Australia brand. By associating with the highest levels of netball we install the Fisher & Paykel brand as standing for the families of Australia. Fisher & Paykel thereby gains connection to a huge following of netball fans and we are seen to be a company that supports women's sport. The relationship we have with Netball Australia is great. The officials are enthusiastic and co-operative and the players are great ambassadors for Australia, their sport and their sponsors.

The CBT and international competition together create a demanding annual schedule which builds to a crescendo in World Championship or Commonwealth Games years. In addition to the NNL there is a National Championship sponsored by Qantas in which the eight states and territories compete, which further intensifies domestic competition.

The Australian Institute of Sport (AIS) has done much to promote the success of Australian athletes. Netball has had a residential programme at the AIS since 1981, which is aimed at assisting junior elite athletes to achieve their peak potential, with training based on the skills and tactics used by the national squads. The large majority of Australia's championship team members are graduates of the AIS. Wilson explains the importance of the AIS in the development of the netball community:

I believe that the Institute programme played a big part in making elite netball like being part of the family. You left home and you had to get on with the other players. You lived with these people for two years and so you got to know them really well, and you became close.

The AIS has recently decentralized and now provides youth training throughout Australia. In collaboration with Netball Australia it gives younger players the opportunity to participate in international competition. Pam Smith: 'For example, the South Australian AIS may come to New Zealand and play some regional matches. Or we may send a group to England made up of the Australia 21 Team and AIS scholarship holders.

Netball Australia has nurtured its infrastructure to develop an enduring sense of community which sustains the netball dream of providing a lifetime of opportunities for achievement and recognition, and satisfies the players' social needs. Vicki Wilson has a unique perspective on the Netball Australia community:

You enjoy others' company, and there have been some wonderful friendships made over the years; there have been great times on tour, there have been funny times and sad times. We experienced the highs and the lows, and if you did that on your own I think you would be quite lonely. But when you can do it with a bunch of people who are out there and trying to achieve something, these memories stick with you for a long time. Going out to achieve something that is common to us all unites us even closer, even though we come from very different backgrounds.

The unity of the elite squad is reflected in the organization as a whole, and in the teams and clubs throughout Netball Australia.

Like all elite sports, netball is intensely competitive. Ensuring that individual competition does not destroy community is essential to maintaining the magic. Player selection provides a good example. 'They used to announce team selection at the end of a training weekend,' explains Carley Baker:

On a Sunday they might finish training at 2 p.m. and go home or go into the changing room for a shower. They would be back at 3 p.m. and the list would be read in alphabetical order. If they weren't in the team and had been dropped after being in the sport for say nine years they would be devastated. So in the last two years they have felt that players would prefer to ring someone such as myself. This gives them a few hours to think it through, and then they ring the coach later on for a discussion about their career.

According to Vicki Wilson, 'All the players are given the opportunity to be involved in advising on the selection process. They run it by us and we have a vote as to how we want to do it.' It is a matter of trust, respect and dignity.

Lisa Beehag, Assistant National Coach, describes how fun and practical jokes relieve tension and foster community:

> I played for New South Wales for ten years. We always had a lot of fun and practical jokes, but we also knew the time to get serious. You have got to have the skills, but there are plenty of athletes who have the skills. It is finding the extra that make the difference, and I think fun and enjoyment are two high priorities.

Community doesn't mean the players live in each other's pockets. Liz Ellis, National Team Goal Keeper:

> One comment made to us a few years ago was that we don't spend a lot of time together. We sometimes go out to different places and do different things, whereas you often saw the Kiwis doing a lot of things together. That was perceived to be the best way, but I think this team has got so many strong personalities that if we spent too much time together it could damage community.

Netball Australia shares the dream with participants and players, spectators and sponsors through community, combined with a passion to win and celebration of achievement. The 1995 World Championship earned the Australian Netball Team a ticker-tape parade through the centre of Sydney, the first time an Australian women's sport had received such an accolade. Carley Baker experienced the magic 'over in Birmingham in 1995; after the match I went into the changing rooms; the celebrations were just amazing; it's something that will stay with me for the rest of my life'. PPOs celebrate peak performance whenever and wherever it occurs. Celebration and tradition help to create the magic, and success flows from success. Vicki Wilson describes the importance of tradition:

Even when we have a change in the team experienced players remain who can teach a little bit of history of the game. I think it's important that we teach about the history, inject some traditions into the game, and value what's happened in the past. It's all about the magic and significance of wearing the green and gold uniform.

International competitions such as the Commonwealth Games, the World Championships and the Fisher and Paykel International Series create a global focus. Netball Australia co-operates with other countries to build the Netball industry. For example, Jill McIntosh, National Coach, regularly travels to Asian and the Pacific countries to share the netball dream, help identify talent and run coaching clinics. This expands both the reach of the game and the commercial opportunities. Netball Australia then competes intensely within the larger arena it helped to create.

The expanded context provides new challenges for the athletes. Lisa Beehag, confirms the importance of renewed challenges in maintaining the focus necessary for peak performance: 'For the older players in particular the Commonwealth Games have given them a new focus, a new lease of life. It's a new carrot dangled in front of their eyes.' Netball Australia went on to win the Gold medal in the 1998 Commonwealth Games. Embedded in human nature is a desire for renewed purpose, and renewed reason for the sustained effort and concentration which lead to peak performance. Pam Smith:

In 1999, when South Africa were soundly beaten in all three tests of their New Zealand tour, their coach came out with the statement that it was apparent that New Zealand are the team to beat. That comment was relayed back to our team, who said, 'Well, OK what was the biggest winning margin between New Zealand and South Africa?' Somebody says 45, and the next thing our team comes out with is a 62-goal win.

Peak performance requires focus.

Jill McIntosh notes that, 'The players leave problems off the court and focus on what they have to do.' It's vital to concentrate upon the actions necessary for peak performance, not upon the result required. Carley Baker describes the absolute respect for focus that exists on match days:

> Australian teams have a focus on a match day that is so intense; the coach is anti-publicity. There is lots of respect. Players don't autograph balls or uniforms – they go on the game court, train, go out for a team lunch, come home and sleep, go to a team meeting and get ready to go to the match. That's pretty much the secret for the day.

The same intensity exists throughout the organization.

Vicki Wilson describes how individual focus has to fuse into team focus:

> You have to focus on your own performance and you have to focus on the team as well; you have your own goals and you have team goals. You focus on the game at hand; or you can even break it up into each quarter of the game and then every five minutes. On the way to the game you are imagining what you want to do and how others will react when you first step onto the courts.

And so it is with all teams, on and off the court, both in sports and in business organizations. Individual performance lifts the team performance, and the team lifts the individual. Exceeding personal best and exceeding organizational best go hand in hand.

In netball a 'flow on' is one movement where you catch the ball, step and throw to make forward movement within the context of the 'less than three seconds' and 'no running with the ball' rules. It is a fundamental element of court craft and is the basis for a fast-paced, flowing game. The pass has to be almost intuitive, using peripheral vision. 'They work on peripheral vision a lot,' explains Team Manager Bronwyn Roberts. 'They will do a flow on and the coach will pull out a colour and the player has to throw to that colour coming down really fast.' 'We work on our skills, getting the flow pattern in the team,' says Jill McIntosh. The game is all about court craft, vision and intuition. The art is to create as many leads as possible. Vicki Wilson: 'Lots of things happen off the ball, because I created space for others. On the court the game is so fast I can't control what's going on.' Intuition does not just happen – it comes through intensive and creative training. Intuitive team flow substitutes for set plays and formal structure, and is predicated on focus.

We observed this intuitive flow first hand during two international matches between Australia and New Zealand. Bronwyn Roberts helped us to understand what we saw:

> If you look at Vicki Wilson, as soon as she gets the ball she doesn't even look and quite often her passes are gone; she has a vision of what is happening on the court. Some of those passes they give each other, like the ones Vicki sends someone under the post, part player' hair. She wouldn't do that if she didn't think the players was going to get it. They do miss occasionally, but there is no way she would do it if she didn't think they were going to catch it. It involves a huge respect for each other's ability, not as a person, but as a netballer. It wouldn't flow if I thought, 'My god I am not going to throw to her because she will drop it.' If team members respect each other as players, if they know that when they throw the ball it will be caught, and that it doesn't matter how hard or how difficult it is to catch, then you will have a great, free-flowing team. This is what our team has got.

As Team Manager, Roberts's task is to ensure that the team is able to concentrate exclusively on its court performance, thereby sustaining focus. She proudly boasts a unique heritage within netball. Her mother played on the very first Australian national side and Roberts was herself a member of the national team. In a career which has included stints as state coach in the South Australia league and marketing responsibilities in the national office she is well placed to reflect on how the organization pulls together. Relationships and respect are nurtured over time:

> It's that word team, isn't it? But I believe the real word is actually respect. This is something that you can't create by trying to bond over a weekend of raft-building. I just don't believe that you can go out on a weekend and bond in a

meaningful way. It doesn't work like that. Bonding happens when the team, and by that I mean organization, builds respect over time. You don't have to be someone's friend but you need to have confidence that if you throw them the ball, you know that the job is going to get done. Respect takes time.

This flow state between players enables them to exceed personal best. Liz Ellis says that, 'When you become confident it instils confidence in someone else. The mindset is that we are going to play a perfect game.' Another elite team member, Sharelle McMahon agreed: 'Being put on the team certainly lifted my performance one notch because I felt that I had to lift to another level to be on a par with them.' Jill McIntosh:

> There is a noticeable difference in the performance of some of them in the national league teams compared with when they put on the green and gold. Their performances lift. I think that is because there is a real respect and trust and belief among the players. They know they have done it before and that they will succeed. They have an overwhelming belief that, no matter what happens, even if they have a bad quarter and are down, that they are going to come through and win.

The same sense of mutually reinforced confidence and purpose pervades the organization, and enables organizational best to be exceeded. Former Australia 21 player and Netball Australia marketing team member Karen Miller provides a further illustration: 'You just got on the plane when you had to and you had the gear; we looked like the most professional team out there and that's probably what made us win in the end; all the fine details that went into creating the big picture. Carley Baker is responsible for much of the fine detail:

> My role with the team manager prior to a tour is to attend to every last detail, to ensure that it is all perfect. What size uniforms do you want? How many balls do you want? How many sports drinks do you want? Now I want every player wearing this shirt, this body suit and this bib. All interviews after the match must be done in bibs, with signage on them, no T-shirts, no hats. So much ordering and preparation are required to make

an international event run. But it's informal, very informal, and the players like that.

Organizational flow is dependent on everyone in the team. Wilson explained that when selecting new team members she looks for confident, quick thinking players who are smart both on and off the court:

> We look for people who can contribute something special and fit into the team. Your off-court harmony has an effect on your on-court performance, and if you come to a point where you can't make up your mind you take the one that's happy go lucky.

She believes that peak performance depends on speed, agility, flair, intuition and creativity and affirms: 'We have got a well-educated team; take the creativity out of someone's play and the game no longer becomes open and fast flowing.' Jill McIntosh elaborated:

> If you train with someone often enough you know where they will go in certain situations. You don't know exactly where they will be at a given time, but you know how they think and therefore can judge where they are likely to go. And we can get the ball there ahead of them so they have time and space to react.

Creativity is founded in diversity. 'There is a high degree of diversity in coaching styles,' says Karen Miller,

> Australians like to play a fast, quick game and like a slope pass, whereas in Caribbean countries they have a big, loopy, jumpy sort of game. We don't want a systematic team, like, 'The ball has to go here; oh, my God the ball hasn't gone there, what do we do now!'

Intuition and communal thinking substitute for systems.

The Australian game is developed on creativity and flair and has 'changed heaps since 1985', according to Vicki Wilson:

It's a lot faster; it's a lot stronger. Even this year there is a lot more game sense; a lot more goals have been scored than last year because of the speed of the game. There is an intellectual component to the innovation. In fact there was a time when eight out of ten Australian players were teachers.

Creativity is assisted by 'The strong rivalry that exists between the state and institute coaches, who all have unique coaching styles – this adds to the strength of competition nationally,' explained Sue Taylor. The domestic experimentation engendered by this mixture of diversity and competition has strengthened the national elite squad. Many organizations fear that internal competition will be a waste of financial resources, but they should not. Internal competition strengthens skills, allows the best to come forward, and avoids the waste of the most valuable resource of all – human creativity.

Vicki Wilson believes that 'If you can improve the creativity of your own performance, you will lift the whole team's performance. Then you know when you have really got that rhythm happening that makes you go further.' Vicki remembered that to lift her overall game, 'One year in State training I decided I was going to shoot left handed the whole way through.' She advocates:

Have a go, take a risk, take a risk. I would be mad if you get pulled for a held ball; you have got to have a go . . . I took a risk, but it didn't pay off. If it had come off it would have been sensational, but I will learn from that. Take a risk; why not. It's OK if it doesn't work. You have so many leads coming at you. You have got to be court smart, switched on, with great vision – a thinking player. Creativity on the court is essential. Once you start taking that out of someone's play the game no longer is open and fast flowing. We all have different ideas, but we have a common goal of doing something well.

Game-breaking ideas within the team and within the organization flourish in an environment where, diversity, creativity, risk taking, and the freedom to fail and learn are the norm. A balance of experienced and new players needs to be maintained, both to prevent the repetition of prior failures and to ensure diversity.

In Netball Australia we found the essential elements of all great teamwork, founded in organizational flow:

- Respect for, and trust in, the abilities of other team members, built up over time
- Fast-paced, intuitive understanding of each other's needs
- Confidence and belief in success
- Passing the ball or information, so that team members have time and space to use it effectively
- Being there when needed
- Everyone contributes game-breaking ideas

Team flow, so evident on the netball court, is also manifest within the organization. Players undertake what needs to be done, when it needs to be done, based on an intuitive understanding which derives from community, empathy, respect for each others roles and abilities, close working relationships and a passionate commitment to a shared purpose. The concept of peripheral vision, derived from the netball court, can be applied to organization more generally, and it can be trained for. Organizational peripheral vision implies an awareness of events, actions and others' needs at the limits of the senses. Peak players notice details, from the visitor who looks lost or a torn carpet, to a step missing from a project game plan. And they attend to those issues there and then.

# CONCLUSION

Highly focused teams that are passionate about what they do can consistently achieve peak performance. From Netball Australia we learned to understand the roles that focus, intuition, respect for other team members, intense awareness, harmony, rhythm, calm and poise, play in the achievement of peak performance. The complete involvement of all participants in challenging tasks for which they are fully prepared and confident are essential elements in peak performance, while trust, respect for other players and an intuitive understanding of each other's needs derived from a common focus and longevity of relationships lead to organizational flow experiences – commonly shared experiences of peak performance.

# CHAPTER 4

# Australian Cricket Board – The Story-telling Game

*This is a story-telling game. That's why it appeals to corporate leaders. They may not go to a cricket game, every day, they may not watch every minute's play, but they follow it all the time. It's the cleverness of the game, the subtlety, the strategy and, in particular, the nuances of a Test match which provide intellectual satisfaction. Seeing the sheer majesty of a superb batsman at the crease, coping well with adversity – it's an ethos which is second to none in my view. The Australian Cricket Board is helping to tell the story of cricket. If we continue to do this well, we shall stand the test of time.* – Denis Rogers, Chairman of the Australian Cricket Board*

'He's out!' So reads one of the most famous newspaper billboards in all of sporting history. Understanding the precise meaning of this exclamation is no problem for the last three generations born in the British Commonwealth. These two words can only refer to one man. It's Bradman. The mere mention of his name instantly conjures up a magical aura which compels cricket lovers of all nationalities to wonder why one man was blessed with natural talent and skill beyond reasonable comprehension. Each sporting code has its great players. Their performances, perhaps over a season of play and even over a lifetime, put them on a different plane from the journeymen and women on the pitch. Yet Bradman's feats do not even belong in this category. No sensible person would suggest that any future Test player could surpass Bradman's place in cricket history. Geoff Marsh, ex Test player and ex coach of the Australian Test and one-day international sides has no doubts about the importance of Bradman's contribution to the game of cricket:

The bottom line is that Sir Donald Bradman is the greatest cricketer who ever lived. When I was playing in the Test team, we were a young side and we'd never actually met the 'Don', and all we wanted to do was touch him. We wanted him to come into the dressing room, and just shake his hand and we'd have been very happy with that. However, Bob Simpson, our team coach, asked him to come and have a meal with us. It was the best of nights. I sat next to him. He was drinking red wine, just as I was. And we just talked and talked about the wonderful game of cricket. For him to pass on those experiences . . . it was like being in a dream world.

Non-cricket lovers puzzled by the brevity of the famous 1933 newspaper billboard may now surmise that the phrase, 'He's out,' is commentary on the utter improbability of the event. While batting, the possibility of his dismissal always seemed distant and highly unlikely. Without hesitation, it can be said that the well-worn phrase, 'We shall never see the likes of him again,' truly applies to Bradman. Geoff Marsh confirms that Bradman was not constrained by normal limits:

We had him down for a seminar in 1997. I asked him to come down and meet the players so that they could ask him a few questions. One of the questions I asked was, 'What sort of things did you do when you were out of form?' And he looked at me and he said, 'I can't answer that.' And I asked him why. He said, 'Well, when I played, I was never out of form.' You know, he's a really down-to-earth sort of guy.

In Australia, the Don's legendary playing feats of the thirties and forties, and the presence of inspirational players of the most extraordinary kind, fuelled a passion to both play and dominate the game of cricket.

The origins of the Australian game are firmly located at club level, and local cricket continues to this day to be the bedrock of international success. Rod Marsh, who currently heads the elite Commonwealth Bank Cricket Academy in Adelaide, first kept wicket for Australia in 1971, and went on to make ninety-seven Test appearances. He explained to us the pivotal role of the local club side in the Australian game:

Club cricket, there's no doubt about it, is the major reason for the strength of Australian cricket. It must have been fantastic in the old days, in the Bradman era. He only played fifty-two Test matches, and those spanned twenty years. When he came home from an overseas Test series there wasn't a one-day international programme to play in. In Australia, there might be a Test match series every two years, and only a few Sheffield Shield games, so the rest of the summer he'd be playing club cricket. A young player walks off the street into his local club, and all of a sudden he's playing with Bradman. On his first day, he's playing with Bradman! No wonder Australian cricket's going strong when that sort of thing used to happen.

Marsh also points out that in the modern game Test players still operate at the local club level. Even though the game is now professional, with million-dollar incomes earned by the top Test players, it is still feasible for the Australian captain to find himself at the community roots of the game. Patrick Keane, former ACB Media Manager, believes that the benefit of this type of playing structure is that it offers encouragement to aspire to greater heights in the game:

> When an Australian player comes back into his grade side and trains with his grade club, there are thirty or forty other young players who watch what this guy does and want to be like him. They watch how he trains, and how he prepares. It's a small window on the highest level for them. He is a role model who shows them what the standard is like.

With a larrikin-like smile, Rod Marsh, a Test legend in his own right, revealed to us what the game really looks like from the inside:

> Club cricket is a reflection of life. Just because you're the Australian captain you can't sit on your arse in the dressing room and do nothing. On a Saturday afternoon, if it starts to rain, he helps the rest of the mob put on the canvas. Your team mates won't let you get away with it anyway. And you always want to be at club training, because that's where we all started, and you never miss a club game if you can help it. People from the local area play at the club, people who you went to school

with. The strength of the ACB has to be club cricket, because ultimately, through the states, that is where the delegates come from.

These evocative descriptions of club cricket, although seemingly culled from another era, reveal the foundations of the ACB's sustained strength. Echoing similar sentiments, Sir Donald Bradman explained to us that Australia's long-term dominance of the game can be explained simply by, 'Our mental approach to the game, good climatic conditions and, perhaps most important of all, the opportunity to play.'

The ACB has controlled the development of the game of cricket since 1905, on behalf of the Australian nation. This responsibility includes all the technical and administrative aspects of the game, and fulfils Bradman's view that Australian cricketing superiority begins with maximizing the natural opportunities to play with a bat and ball.

# THE ACID 'TEST'

Australia has the best record in Test-match cricket. The elite Test team has, since 1876, maintained a forty-two per cent win record in all Test matches against England, South Africa, West Indies, New Zealand, India, Pakistan, Zimbabwe and Sri Lanka. In a game which offers a preponderance of draws, no other Test nation can match this win percentage. The Test side has been even more dominant in the last decade, winning forty-eight per cent of their Tests. In the more recent one-day internationals, Australia has a leading fifty-six per cent win record, including two World Cup victories. Their 1999 triumph was the culmination of six straight tournament wins and one draw. Few Australians, however, have a sense of superiority about this, and fewer still would accept that the ACB has anything at all to do with global leadership. Cricket is the national game of a nation which lives and dies by its sporting prowess. Most Australians believe that they can pick the Test side much better than those currently empowered to do so. An obsessive media interest in all cricketing matters has long fuelled a national culture of criticism, sometimes constructive, at other times scornful, of those who control the game from Jolimont Street in Melbourne. To the outsider this might appear to be stress-inducing for the officials of the ACB, yet such behaviour is symptomatic of national ownership. The ACB operates a fiduciary responsibility on behalf of all Australians, who are the ultimate shareholders of the game. Accordingly the ACB's status barely registers in the minds of cricket enthusiasts. Rather than being a peak performing organization, most Australians, if polled, according to David Fouvy, General Manager, Marketing, might score the ACB 'three out of ten'. The superiority of the Australian cricket side is likely to be explained only by way of reference to Bradman's bat or Dennis Lillee's arm. Unquestionably, world-class batting and bowling are the most obvious manifestations of cricketing peak performance, but they are also the product of organization. Denis Rogers, Chairman of the ACB, is entirely untroubled by the lack of popular recognition. He notes simply that the ACB has mastered the art of 'appearing to be losing while we are in fact winning'.

Perhaps not surprisingly, the national office of the ACB is a mixture of cricketing tradition and modern marketing. Suitably close to the world-famous Melbourne Cricket Ground (MCG) – perhaps equivalent to a few hefty throws from the boundary rope to the wicket-keeper – the entrance way leads immediately to the right and a small flight of stairs, at the top of which is a set of doors which cannot be opened without permission given via an intercom. Once allowed through the doors, directly ahead, visitors are greeted with a portrait of Bradman in his later years. You are unmistakably entering a place of legends. Wooden panelling, which instantly communicates tradition, quickly gives way to open-plan office space, decorated with generous splashes of colour, dominated by various shades of green and gold. Marketing posters, signed portraits, bats, jerseys, brochures and fliers spill out of every available space. Some work-stations have been successfully organized so that computers and desk tops can be clearly identified, but for the most part, the national office bristles with cricketing artefacts which prevent any attempts to compartmentalize one area from another.

The formal division of labour in the organization is structured along classic functional lines. General managers in commercial, operations, marketing and public affairs, all report to CEO Malcolm Speed, who was appointed by the Board in 1997. There are some thirty full-time employees who share the national office with the state-elected, fourteen-member Board of Directors. This meets in a separate boardroom which retains the wood panels and historical elegance of another cricketing era. At one end of the boardroom, embedded in the centre of the wooden panelling, is the Australian cricket coat of arms. Along each of the other walls are various Test-match bats, signed by the legends of yesteryear.

The Directors of the ACB meet monthly and stand at the pinnacle of the organization and of Australian cricket. Formally constituted in 1905, its structure mirrors the federalism of the country – representatives from local club cricket constitute the state bodies, which in turn elect the national Board. As custodian of the game, the ACB sees itself as responsible for ensuring that the spirit of the game is both protected and developed. A key element of this is the preservation of the relationship between the ACB and the states. In terms of governance this relationship is hierarchical, but Malcolm Speed has opted to take a different approach:

In an effort to make the federal system work, we bring together the states and the chief executives in regular meetings. Since most of the money comes in at the top, and cricket, particularly at the state level, isn't terribly wealthy, they rely on money coming down from international cricket, which is where the money is generated. So in theory the national body generates income, formulates policy and then assists the states, who implement the policy. The states then have much the same role in co-ordinating the clubs who implement the policy locally, whether in coaching development or marketing.

Despite considerable potential for the message to be diluted, as it filters through this somewhat fragmented structure, two key ingredients maintain co-operation within the cricketing community. The first is simply the powerfully uniting nature of the game. For Denis Rogers cricket brings with it much more than Test series victories:

It's to do with culture. During a game of cricket we spend six hours a day together, over lunch and afternoon tea, and, yes, with the obligatory scones, which should not be dismissed too lightly. As we watch every over of six balls, which takes about four or five minutes to bowl, the rhythm of the game allows for plenty of time to share in other activities and conversation. I wouldn't change that for anything. It builds genuine friendships, not just between players, but between spectators, television audiences and even between administrators of the game. We all love to hear the latest story that comes from the game of cricket.

While the ambience and spiritual qualities of the game are to be commended, Rogers is quick to point out the second ingredient: 'Australian cricket never loses sight of the fact that the prime purpose of its existence, its primary challenge, is to win every international cricket match.' To this end, Rogers argues that, 'Even in the face of fierce inter-state competition the state sides will rest their best players to make them available to represent their country.' Not surprisingly, the whole organization is geared to producing Test players who can perform victoriously in the international arena. Keane explains how this affects the ACB and its affiliates:

Although the states want to win the Sheffield Shield competition, a much more important focus is that they all want to produce the most Test players. The focus is on the national side. Moreover, it's major prestige for a grade side to produce a Test player. Anyone who looks vaguely talented, will have a lot of work and effort directed towards him. The real focus is on how many Test players you can get, which means that there's a real sense of ownership of a successful Test side at all levels. A disproportionate number of our greatest players are actually from the country rather than the city, so the sense of ownership of the Australian team is spread across the entire nation.

To ensure the continued supremacy of Australian cricket by producing a steady flow of players of Test-match quality, the ACB has, over the last ten years or so, sought to create the future by putting together a comprehensive development programme that begins in primary schools and finishes on the most famous cricket pitches around the world. The infrastructure which is now firmly in place more than confirms Sir Donald Bradman's belief that the simple 'opportunity to play' is the basic reason for the continuing success of Australian cricket.

Gerard Clarke, Manager, Development, sees the development of club-level cricket alongside school-based programmes as the fundamental prerequisite for long-term success. Clarke inspires belief in the value of junior development. Formerly a state player with Victoria, Clarke quickly found an interest in cricket administration and, in particular, in creating a strong future for the game. With 5,500 clubs and 13,000 primary and secondary schools throughout the country, it is Clarke's responsibility to oversee the game at the grass-roots. This is a challenge he is more than willing to accept. With enormous conviction, he explains, 'This is *my* story – it is about changing and restructuring people's thinking about cricket.' Clarke takes full charge of this critical aspect of the ACB's work: 'In 1983, the first year of the fully sponsored development programme, we had just one development officer in each state. Now we have about a hundred full-time development officers and about the same number of part-timers.'

At first the ACB used to wheel out high-profile players from past Test sides, but Clarke quickly discovered that, to be effective, a much more professional approach had to be taken:

> Quite often those guys can't deal with the kids in the way that we feel is best for the game's development. They are vital in the promotion of the game, but to actually develop the game from a skill point of view, we found that cricket clinics were best run by people with teaching backgrounds. Even now, to cover all the schools and clubs, we could quite reasonably use another hundred development officers.

The ACB's strategic aim is to build up a huge participation base by exposing children to cricket at an early age. Clarke believes this is the only way that 'we are going to have more good players coming through to be picked up by the elite programmes'. Geoff Marsh, while coaching the national side, is also acutely aware that the quality of the elite squad rests squarely on a good junior structure:

> I believe that the ACB has structured cricket very well. We put a lot of emphasis on having a very strong first eleven and a very

strong junior structure, which the ACB now see as their core business. We are competing against every other sport, so we have got to go out there and make kids feel as though they're enjoying the game of cricket. We do that by giving them all an opportunity to play.

Under Clarke's stewardship the ACB has developed a staircase approach which has a clear line of sight, from the backyard to the Baggy Green cap. (The 'Baggy Green' is the cap awarded to and worn by Australian Test players.) This enables the dream of cricket to be shared with those who aspire to play the game and, perhaps, represent their country one day. The long journey to the Test side begins with Milo Kanga cricket in primary schools. Over a third of a million girls and boys are visited in primary and secondary schools by development officers. 30,000 children aged 5–10 years formally register for the Milo Have-a-Go programme which is an introduction to the club cricket environment. Clarke has broad ambitions for this programme.

> From my point of view, the customer is every boy and girl out there in Australia. The Have-a-Go programme is something I'm very passionate about. At the start it was a battle to get nine clubs to run this programme because it was different to traditional cricket, which could be characterized as the 'Saturday morning turn-up,' when sometimes only a few kids got to bat or bowl.

The Have-a-Go programme is deliberately flexible about playing times, encouraging women in particular to choose cricket as a way to employ their children usefully in the after-school hours. According to Clarke, this 'is also a great way to recruit parents back into the game'. In recognition of their achievements, each child who participates is presented with his or her own Milo which is honoured by the kids in the same way as elite cricketers honour the Baggy Green cap: 'I've seen the enjoyment that the kids get out of it. When we give them the green and gold Milo cap, the impact is amazing. The kids feel so proud when they get home.'

Finding out what type of programme can be soundly implemented involves basic research – one of Clarke's four 'Rs'. Recruitment is an obvious necessity, but the problem of erosion of interest, as other sports or attractions detract from a pure cricketing focus, becomes evident during the teenage years. Retention thus becomes a prime objective along with the final 'R' – restructuring. Game-breaking ideas in the form of the Milo Super 8s create sufficient attraction to see participation from over 160,000 teenagers. The ACB has found it necessary to rethink and, in some cases, quite dramatically, restructure 'the product' in order to be at the head of the queue for the 'first-choice athlete'. Clarke explains the origins and intention of the Super 8s initiative:

There are eleven kids in the traditional game, but Super 8s is a shorter, modified version of the game. It has been a huge success with kids, parents and teachers, since changes in school times have created a need for some form of cricket that can be played in less than two hours. Sections of the community are saying that they want a faster game, because they haven't got that much time to spend – they want to be able to get in, have a game and get out within two hours, and they also want to bat, bowl and field in that time!

Super 8s has in turn forced the ACB to adopt such developments at a more senior level so that the initiative attracts broader support. Super 8s contests at an international level have recently been staged in Kuala Lumpur. Cathay Pacific has also mounted the Hong Kong Sixes. Both these tournaments saw participation from elite Australian players. Clarke believes that taking these new ideas about the game to essentially non-cricketing nations is part of a process which 'is looking to restructure or change people's thinking'. The purpose of the Super 8s initiative at the secondary-school level is to ensure the retention of a broad cricketing base that can then be channelled into the local club structure. To achieve this, Clarke sees the need to sell the right product. 'We've got to play when *they* want to play, not when *we* think they should play and, more importantly, we have to take into account *what* they want to play.'

These development programmes are designed to act as bridges between schools, the community and the club structure of the game. Further along, national coaching programmes identify the talented players who are able to perform in the national schools' cup and the Under 17 and Under 19 Championships. Both state-wide and international youth teams are given the opportunity to compete at a level that mirrors the stresses and pressures of the professional game. Specialist programmes in fast bowling and spin bowling serve to underscore the massive commitment that ACB makes to developing the best players. Many of the specialist programmes rely heavily on great players of the past who bring with them skills and stories that are both informative and inspirational.

The final element in the ACB development portfolio is the Commonwealth Bank Cricket Academy, founded in the 1988–9 season. Following the retirement, in the mid-eighties, of a number of Australian Test stars, the national team suffered several defeats at the hands of the English. Ever mindful of its stewardship of the game, the ACB approached the Australian Institute of Sport in 1987, and suggested that they jointly establish an academy which would draw on the technical resources of the Institute, while the association with the number-one sport in Australia would provide a high profile for the Institute.

The best youth players with elite potential in the state coaching programmes are tagged for entry into the Academy using a nation-wide database. Although most of these youth players are already well known to Rod Marsh, Academy Director, each year, twenty or thirty hopefuls will apply direct. Along with the under-eighteen and under-nineteen championship players, these applicants are judged on their suitability. Finally, fifteen or so will be chosen and provided with full-time scholarships. The intent is simple. Rod Marsh:

> We try to accelerate their progress from where they are currently, say the under-nineteen level, to elite status, and along the way give them the knowledge and skills they need to actually go and play first-class cricket. In fact, we overload them with experience – our competition programme is fairly intense – it includes an international and a domestic tour.

Even though the amount of funds available from the AIS is small in comparison to the Aus $60 million revenue generated annually by the ACB, the technical advantage, according to Marsh, is quite significant: 'Cricket has access to all their departments, including all the experts we can find. We have a swimming coach, a running coach, sports psychologists, nutritionists and a bio-mechanist. The Academy now has the best that cricket can offer.'

Additionally, many of the Test greats, past and present, spend time at the Academy, passing on 'the good oil'. 'Work-load diaries' record to the last detail the activities of the players on a season-by-season basis. This means that pace bowlers such as Glenn McGrath are followed by the Academy beyond their scholarship days. Marsh's reach is comprehensive: 'We know exactly how many balls he's bowled at training and in matches. In fact, through the national pace bowling programme we have these statistics on all our pacemen. It's driven from here.' The Academy has been so successful that the Board has sanctioned its activities to include 'remedial' work for Test players who need extra help in certain areas of their game. This includes sending individual players overseas to experience specific playing conditions.

Finally, the work of the Academy has become so renowned that players from overseas have applied and been accepted. In a three-year period over seventy players from New Zealand, Zimbabwe, Malaysia, India, Sri Lanka, New Guinea, Bangladesh and Hong Kong have been through the overseas programme. Although this might appear to be potentially self-defeating – assisting the competition to improve themselves – the ACB takes the high ground. Rod Marsh defends this policy with a combination of business acumen and a belief in the overarching importance of the game:

> From a commercial point of view it's been worthwhile, but more importantly we believe we've got something to offer. We're happy to share the Academy with overseas countries because the important thing is that the game of cricket progresses. Because Australia is one of the leading cricketing nations, it's part of our duty to help the game of cricket develop in emerging countries.

Creating the future also involves putting in place alliances and networks between institutions, from schools to cricketing authorities overseas, and commercial sponsors. Inspired administrators such as Rod Marsh and Gerard Clarke are only the most obvious elements of Australian cricket's drive for global success. One of the results of looking after the infrastructure of the game is the concurrent growth of administration that this requires. Malcolm Speed joined the organization from a different professional sports background. Coming from the less-well patronized code of basketball, he is well placed to reflect on the organizational strengths of the ACB:

> Cricket historically throws up some good solid administrators who are well and truly tested through the club and state structures before they get to the national stage. These administrators are very thoughtful, diverse, intelligent, dedicated and experienced. By the time they get through to the national body they have earned their stripes, for sure.

Speed's appointment itself appears to be something of an enigma. The ACB seems to represent, at least to the public, a tradition of conservatism that would eschew an external person in the key role of CEO. Although Speed was 'quite surprised' at his own appointment, he very quickly realized that the image of tradition was not, by any means, the complete story. Indeed, in the years following the Kerry Packer inspired World Series Cricket (WSC), innovation and experimentation with game-breaking ideas became the norm for the ACB. The appointment of Speed was, in fact, typical of an organization which had long realized that constant change would have to be addressed by re-energizing the traditions of cricket, and that that would have to include new managerial talent.

Unquestionably, WSC was the catalyst which set in motion the modern game which now includes, at the international level, an integrated menu of Test matches and one-day games. Bob Parish, who was on the Board for thirty-six years, and is now the honorary ACB historian, played a leading role during the WSC era, and in the changes to the game that ensued. His tenure on the Board, which included stints as chairman, spanned the period 1977–9, when the media tycoon Kerry Packer contracted many of the world's top Test players to play a special brand of international one-day, limited overs cricket. Parish was the man who, in 1976, negotiated a television contract with Australian Broadcasting Corporation (ABC) for Aus $71,000 each year for three years. That year Kerry Packer offered Aus $1.5 million for sole television rights over the same period. Parish's hands were tied, as Packer's approach occurred after the ABC agreement had been finalised. In frustration, Packer started his own team, thus splitting the cricketing world.

World Series Cricket created a remarkable interregnum in the ACB's overarching control and promotion of the sport. The one-day game, or pyjama cricket as it is sometimes called, which was heavily promoted by WSC, reignited mass interest in a game which had not changed significantly since the turn of the century. However, in the long run, WSC could not be sustained without strong grass-roots development, which was the preserve of the ACB. At the same time, the ACB was well aware that revenue streams from the state-based Sheffield Shield competition and Test matches simply could not support the professional game. Bradman in particular, according to Parish, had long argued that a shorter game would have to be embraced in order to maintain cricket's pre-eminent position in the culture and psyche of the nation. Bradman's leadership on this question is of no surprise to Parish, who has long held that the Don's playing feats, while clearly inspirational on a global scale, over shadowed his supreme contribution to the ACB's administration of the game. Importantly, Parish and Bradman were at the centre of the negotiations in late 1978 which saw a 'peace treaty', enabling total control of cricket to return to the ACB. In May 1979, when WSC proposed to the ACB the continuation of one-day internationals alongside Test matches, Bradman grasped the initiative. Bob Parish:

In a small sub-committee this was unequivocally accepted by Bradman, without any argument. So we then went to the full Board, and it went through unanimously. No one argued with Bradman's support of the WSC proposal, he just turned over the page and said 'It's a good result.' That's the way it's recorded in the minutes. I think everybody was tremendously surprised at Bradman's reaction, but nevertheless that's the way he ran it. He influenced a lot of people to go along with his thoughts and the net result of it is that the ACB now controls and promotes the game.

Twenty years later, Bradman's views have not changed. Defending his position, with characteristic purpose, he told us that, 'It was time to make the game appeal to the public. The game had to change. People wanted a more exciting game than what was being played at the time.' Bradman's key role in returning control of the game to the ACB proved to be a watershed. It marked the moment when innovation came to dominate the Board's activities – never again would it be caught out. Parish believes that in the aftermath of WSC, 'It is the ACB which is now the initiator of new ideas.'

## ON THE FRONT FOOT

The legacy of WSC is now apparent in the current activities, structures and policies of the ACB. Ex Coach Geoff Marsh was the all-important conduit through which the ACB's work contributed directly to the players' on-field performance:

> In taking cricket into the year 2000 and beyond, the ACB is very, very positive. It is run by a good mixture of business people who all have a huge passion for the game. They are very flexible and very good listeners – if there is a problem, you can go to them and they will sort it out in a very positive way. They are an extremely professional unit.

From a technical point of view, the ACB, through the national office, assists the team directly by overseeing the *Players' Handbook* which is issued to all Test-match players. It contains detailed information on fitness regimes, dietary habits, training schedules for tours and motivational mantras which demonstrate how players can focus on 'taking control of the 1% things'. Recently retired captain of the Australian Test side, Mark Taylor, said of the handbook that, 'It does certainly have its uses,' but players are presumed to be capable of making their own judgement regarding the details. Steve Waugh, current captain, told us:

> It's important to a lot of the players, but I've never used it. I have my own personal diary which I've been using for years. Either way, it's important to have one. People who aren't on schedule or who don't look after themselves or don't do the right thing are generally pretty sloppy in their cricket. It's an overall attitude you have to have these days.

Waugh's comments are in part a response to the amount of professional cricket played at the elite level, and the necessity for players to pace themselves and look after logistics of playing and travelling. It is not unknown for the players to be on the road for well over 300 days each year, including overseas tours. Such a schedule is symptomatic of decisions made by the ACB, regarding the development of the professional game. As a forward-thinking organization that is prepared to break with long-held traditions, the ACB makes no distinction between Test cricket and the one-day game at the international level. The revenues generated from the shorter version of cricket need to be distributed to the states and, ultimately, to the club sides. Denis Rogers explains:

We should not be concerned about the delineation between Test cricket and one-day cricket, other than to say that they're different. In Test cricket you have to get twenty wickets to win, in one-day cricket you score more runs, but for us, they cohabit happily. They are both important to Australian cricket. When we do our promotions we show players with coloured uniforms and players dressed in whites side by side. We don't discriminate by saying that one-day cricket is more important than Test cricket. What we say about Test cricket is that it's full of drama, it's serious, it's six hours a day for five days. There are nuances and subtleties which can also be strategic. We say that one-day cricket is colourful, entertaining and explosive, and it makes commercial sense. Even though its origins can be traced back to conflict with WSC we don't carry any baggage about that at all.

Rogers drives the Board by holding one-on-one meetings with each member, to establish, 'a level of intellectual rigour second to none, in order to resolve today's contemporary sporting challenges'. Vigorously embracing the one-day game has proved to be one of those challenges. Rogers also aims to get the best out of the Board through his establishment of a forum for debate where 'progress is made through disagreement'. This high level of engagement is also expected in the national office. Rogers insists that operational issues are kept away from Board meetings so that only the larger strategic concerns are dealt with at that level, which, he argues, means that policy issues can be addressed 'with fresh minds and fresh vigour'. In turn, this allows the national office to manage and implement Board policy. This 'clear dichotomy',

Rogers explains, can only work if the people employed are out-standing: 'All my life, I've only recruited the best, and this was the same brief given to the CEO, Malcolm Speed.' The unmistak-able focus of this approach is, according to Rogers, to 'generate revenue that enables Australia to keep focused on winning. The administration in Australian cricket will leave no stone unturned to create an environment where players are given every opportu-nity to win.'

For players to be paid a professional sportsperson's salary, more one-day international cricket has to be played, since this form of cricket produces the necessary revenues. Malcolm Speed astutely recognizes that the marketplace changes rapidly and continues to confront challenge after challenge, beyond the playing of one-day cricket. Moreover, he acknowledges that in order to maintain the position of cricket as the number-one playing and spectator sport in terms of gate attendance and, even more importantly, television viewing, the ACB has to develop 'well-thought out strategies' which will effectively lead to healthy revenue streams. These income streams are split into television rights, match attendance, sponsor-ships and licensing. The need to maximize these revenue-generating possibilities has led to the intensive marketing of cricket. Indeed, if there is one area that the ACB has developed unswervingly, it is the sponsorship and selling of the game. Malcolm Speed:

> When you look at old photos of Test matches, there is not a corporate sign to be seen. Now, if you go to a cricket ground, the perimeter is covered in corporate signs. I think if you com-pare the progress that has been made in marketing, over the last twenty years, compared with most other sports, cricket has really picked up in providing better entertainment.

This is a far cry from the first days of television coverage, which Bob Parish sold to the ABC network 'for the magnificent sum of £25'. Sponsorship money was also less than spectacular, prior to WSC. Parish recollects that 'The first Benson & Hedges contract I signed in 1973 was for Aus $50,000, and I thought we were made.' Sharing the dream of Australian cricket through sponsor-ship alone, now brings in close to Aus $12m, with television rights more than double this figure. Gate money and licensing net close to Aus $15m. These activities are now the preserve of the marketing group, headed by David Fouvy, who joined the ACB in November 1993. The ACB only stopped contracting out its marketing in 1994.

Fouvy has the dual responsibility to build revenue and a brand image for cricket. This has led to the development of separate, yet mutually reinforcing, brand wheels for Test cricket and one-day Internationals. Each wheel contains different brand attributes, benefits, values, personalities and core essence. Prior to 1993, the selling of the game was usually based around the next game to be played by the elite squad. The new initiative from Fouvy's group takes a brand focus rather than a gate focus for the first time in two decades of Australian cricket. David Fouvy:

> There are a number of brand drivers. First, how the elite teams perform on the field. Australians adore winners, and this is something we have been able to tap into with respect to the Australian team performance since the late 1980s. Another driver is how well we do the job of promoting cricket at the grass-roots level, how accessible it is. Finally there is the cohesion between all the programmes.

In keeping with the aim of making cricket available to all those who want to play, Fouvy has been careful to position the game as one that is very portable, and can be played for fun almost everywhere. Advertising campaigns on television emphasize that the very spirit of the game resides in the schoolyard, on the beach and in the backyard, as children and adults enjoy trying to emulate their heroes. These evocative images, which lie at the heart of the 'Go Aussie Go' campaign, are specifically designed to be both inspirational *and* aspirational, so that each image of backyard cricket is mirrored by one of an elite player carrying out the same action. The sharing of the dream is powerful and clear. Additionally, key inspirational players such as Sir Donald Bradman, Dennis Lillee, Ian and Greg Chappell, Allan Border and many other legends of the game, form a marketing tool of unrivalled potency to assist in the building of the brand. They help to establish cricket as the game to both watch and play.

Some of these marketing and promotional initiatives aim to recast the core traditions of the game. Chairman Rogers confirms that loving the traditional game can also include 'freshness that challenges sacred cows in an educated way'. Fouvy's team has challenged several sacred cows along the way. In the spirit of entertainment that is more evident in one-day internationals, Fouvy's division came up with the notion of musical interludes which could be used to introduce incoming batsmen or bid them farewell when they were dismissed. A dropped catch would be followed by the famous Homer Simpson exclamation, 'Doh!' The Press, who took an immediate dislike to this Board-sponsored initiative, raised the issue to that of a national crisis. Under siege, Fouvy was forced into making an astute observation:

Here was this bastard child, hated by everyone, even though it was simply light entertainment. But all of a sudden people were saying that's against the *tradition* of the one-day game, 'You can't do that.' I was left thinking, how many years do you have to have before you get a tradition? Apparently less than twenty is the answer. It was an interesting experiment. It showed me that you have got to harness this passion for the game, but in such a way that you don't kill it.

Despite the occasional setback, the ACB is still receptive to game-breaking ideas which challenge traditional ways of thinking. Fouvy was instrumental in one of the most startling innovations in one-day cricket – the impetus behind the initiative came purely from a marketing perspective. During the 1994–5 season Zimbabwe, a relative newcomer to international cricket and a team with little profile in Australia, was scheduled as one of the three teams play-ing in the one-day international series, then known as the World Series. Fouvy's concern from a marketing perspective was that the proposed line up of teams might lead to a reduced level of con-sumer interest in the annual World Series. His solution, which was duly submitted to a subcommittee and then the full Board, was to introduce a fourth team which was a second Australian team. This team was simply called Australia 'A'. This would gener-ate increased public interest and be a further opportunity to show-case the depth of Australian cricket. Moreover, it would also provide a stimulus for those cricketers on the verge of international honours, by creating a new arena in which their skills and ability would be exposed to competition. To Fouvy's amazement the Board approved the idea:

'Australia 'A' was a brave move. I was pushing hard, and was frankly surprised when they went for it. They haven't got many decisions wrong. This decision added a new dimension to Australian cricket.

The search for new ways to promote, sell and share the dream of Australian cricket flourishes in the ACB. Fouvy and other senior figures give great credit to Malcolm Speed for embracing and driving new ideas and direction. He is the important link between the Board and management. David Fouvy:

He's very open and is prepared to consult in the development of a joint vision. More importantly, he is not biased in any way. Although new to cricket administration, he has worked in other sports. This, together with a legal background and a logical approach to issues, makes for excellent leadership.

Denis Rogers also acknowledges the impact that Speed has had on Australian cricket, noting that, 'In the last two years I've no doubt that he's been vital to what we've been able to achieve and will achieve.' Malcolm Gray, past Chairman of the Board and President-elect of the International Cricket Council, taking a global view, pays the ACB CEO the highest accolade of all: 'Speed, in my judgement, is excellent. He is the best cricket administrator I have seen around the world. He is a thinker who is resilient, unshakeable, hard working and energetic.'

Malcolm Speed is now keeper and holder of the dream. This might be remarkable, given his relatively short tenure with the organization, yet his pivotal role reflects a strong community that quickly enables inspirational players to establish their credentials. Denis Rogers calls it the 'cricketing family', which comes together to support and assist any and all contributions to the wider aim. The concept of the cricketing family is frowned upon by the media, but Rogers is unwilling to back off: 'I still think it's key, and I won't step back from that point of view.' Even though the national office is relatively new, in terms of many of its employees, it has considerable continuity with little turnover. Fouvy's team, for example, which has a 'real camaraderie', has all been appointed within the past few years, while veterans such as Parish and other long-serving staff and Board members help to preserve identity, continuity and trust. Those who, for whatever reason, step outside the stated purpose and focus of the ACB, are unlikely to remain.

The elite squad has its own long-held and powerful identity. It is a sanctum that only the privileged few can enter. Geoff Marsh: 'There is a huge spirit amongst past and present Australian cricketers. It has a real family thing about it. One of the reasons is the passage of different eras. Ian Chappell, Allan Border and Mark Taylor – there is a huge spirit about each of them.' A strong integrating factor is the team's method of celebration, which has stayed the same across the years. At the conclusion of a Test match victory and, particularly, a series win, the dressing-room door is locked and the players (and players alone) sing, 'Beneath the Southern Cross'. Geoff Marsh explains that, 'You're only allowed to sing it once, and it's got to be a very special moment if it's sung twice.' Much of the energy in the Australian team revolves around symbols and artefacts. Steve Waugh, known for his passion for tradition, takes his rituals seriously. Geoff Marsh marvels at the ceremony that Waugh engages in when it comes to the Baggy Green:

> Steve wears the same Baggy Green that they gave him back in '86' – it's been through all the parties. The next day in the dressing room, Steve will be sitting at the basin washing out his Australian cap because someone has poured beer all over it, but he washes it, hangs it up, dries it and then next day he'll go out and bat with it and field with it. Steve's a traditionalist – he loves the game with a passion and all those little traditional things about cricket.

After a recent Ashes series victory against the English, there was a bet within the team as to how long the players could wear their caps. Marsh remembers that, 'Some of them wore their caps for more than four days. Justin Langer went to bed with his cap on.' Marsh believes that this is in stark contrast to the England side, who 'wear faded caps which look terrible – we just couldn't believe it, pride is a big word in our side.'

Perhaps understandably, this level of commitment leads to considerable mental anguish and disappointment when a batsman is dismissed. David Fouvy has learned not to request promotional duties from such players, even if they appear to have time on their hands due to early dismissal. In a 'story-telling game' there are, inevitably, some 'real corkers' which communicate what is at stake at the international level:

> With David Boon I don't know what was worse, seeing him out for a duck or seeing him out for 50. In short, when he came into the dressing room, you needed to get out and give him some privacy. Allan Border was similar – no matter how many runs he got, he was always unhappy to get out. One time, Michael Slater was so affected that he tried to flush all his gear down the toilet, his pads, box, gloves, everything.

Although difficult to confirm, there are strong rumours that many players, when selected for the Test side, have their allocated number tattooed on their posterior. Colourful though these stories are, they represent a community determined to excel. As a past captain of the side, Mark Taylor believes that they are part and parcel of an organization that 'just keeps beating itself'.

## CONCLUSION

The ACB has a clear idea of what it wants to achieve and how it will do it. Sharing the dream of cricket and providing opportunities for everyone to play the game easily translates into a passion for winning at the international level. Moreover, the Board recognizes what it has to do to produce the elite players who can sustain peak performance. Inspirational players and past legends of the game promote cricket through myriad activities. Sponsorship revenues and the continuing pre-eminence of the game in a sports-crazy country enable the ACB to maintain a constant stream of talented players who have access to highly developed programmes, from junior cricket to the elite level. The pervasive feeling of family and community encourages risk, innovation and game-breaking initiatives. Players, both on and off the field, are constantly provided with challenges which spur them to better themselves. The organization is at its best when it has earned the right to tell yet another story which adds a new ring to the contours of the cricketing soul.

# CHAPTER 5

# New Zealand Rugby Football Union – Any Colour as long as it's All Black

*Passion. Passion for the game. I think there's no one in this organization who doesn't have a genuine love and passion for what we do. Passion makes this place tick, along with good leadership and good governance. And the All Blacks are the pinnacle of that passion. They are the glue.* – Evan Crawford, Manager, Rugby Development

The All Blacks. Few brand names in the sporting world carry so much power. For over 100 years, revered and respected by common acclaim, the New Zealand All Blacks have been the dominant force in world rugby union. Only a small number of sports teams can trace their lineage back to the nineteenth century and none can claim a seventy-two per cent win record over this astonishing length of time. The game of rugby union is played throughout the world, with local club sides forming the backbone of the Test-playing nations. England, Ireland, Scotland, Wales, France, Italy, Canada, Argentina, South Africa, Australia and New Zealand annually wage titanic struggles for championships in their respective hemispheres, yet the New Zealand All Blacks set the standard for the game.

For more than a century New Zealand's national pride rose and fell with the fortunes of the team that wore the black jersey with the silver fern, but in 1995 this linkage nearly broke down. The fine line between sport and entertainment had been breached in the early nineties, when both codes, rugby league and rugby union, were eyed as potential money-makers by media moguls who had little time or understanding for the subtleties of national culture and rugby traditions.

Rugby union in New Zealand was largely a provincial affair, with a representative national council of twenty-seven members (reduced to nineteen in more recent times) which met infrequently and tried to administer the game with a hard-working national office of two or three full-time workers. Current chairman of the New Zealand Rugby Football Union (NZRFU), Rob Fisher, recalls that, 'half the time you couldn't even see who was speaking at national meetings.' While the structure of the organization was less important when the game was being administered on a purely amateur basis, the professional era required a far greater degree of strategic intent and large-scale operational ability. The impetus for change came from two directions. Most important was the greater development of professional rugby league, played passionately up and down the eastern seaboard of Australia and in the north of England. A less fluent game than rugby union, rugby league retains an avid following that, in the early nineties, was beginning to translate into television rights, sponsorship deals and a professional game in the form of a new Super League.

Lured by the prospect of lucrative late-career deals, many of the star players at Test and provincial level began switching codes, thus potentially depriving the rugby union game of role models for the young school children who for generations had formed the backbone of the All Blacks' international success. This was also a period when the 'joy-stick generation' was emerging, where physical contact sport was played out on computer screens rather than on the nation's parklands and pitches. The amateur game, which in terms of stature and status had had an unchallenged place in the hearts and minds of New Zealanders, was in danger of being lost. The NZRFU also faced the further threat of professional initiative from within its own code.

In 1995 the World Rugby Corporation (WRC), apparently backed by Australia's charismatic media baron, Kerry Packer, threatened to sign a significant number of rugby stars, All Blacks included, to its own professionally based international competition. Although the WRC initiative was doomed to fail, like World Series Cricket two decades earlier, the impact of this intervention was both dramatic and traumatic. Unable to react to the new situation with sufficient coherence or strategic clarity, the council, which had successfully built the All Blacks into a fearsome winning team and a durable brand, had sufficient guile to vote in favour of its own extinction, to be replaced by a smaller board of nine members and a growing professional national office of fifty people, which by 1998 was handling annual revenues of some NZ$50 million.

Initial backing from Rupert Murdoch through News Corporation enabled the NZRFU to maintain its position as the regulator and steward of the game, although, from 1995, the elite players were paid. With the recognition that business acumen would be essential in the new era, the character of the board inevitably changed. Kevin Roberts, who, in 1995, was the chief operating officer of the Lion Nathan brewery, a major sponsor of All Blacks rugby, played a key role in establishing professional rugby by acting as a broker between the competing interests of the Packer and Murdoch camps. Appointed to the new board as an external member, Roberts immediately brought a range of skills which helped facilitate organizational transformation. Board Chairman Rob Fisher is in no doubt as to Roberts' importance to New Zealand rugby:

> Kevin has a fearsome intellect, and an ability to think much more laterally than anyone else around the board table, myself included. And he has a remarkable clarity of thought. I don't know too many other people who can say, 'Guys, here are the six things that we need to do,' and out of his head, from a complex set of discussions, lay them out. I might have thought of six, but by the time I get to articulate them, I'm struggling to recall what the first two were! He does it without writing anything down, so he just has that rare clarity of thought. And he's visionary. Of course, he absolutely loves the game and the All Blacks, so you put all that together, and you're well served.

Fisher has evidence he can point to directly. In 1997 Roberts, together with CEO David Moffett, was instrumental in negotiating a major sponsorship deal with the adidas organization. This included the supply of state-of-the-art sports kit for the All Blacks designed especially for the 1999 Rugby World Cup. The overall dollar value of the sponsorship, rumoured to be over NZ$80m, including bonus payments for championship victories, spread over five years, effectively secured the future of New Zealand rugby union. Peter Ciulionis, Director of Finance and Administration, is in no doubt as to its importance:

> Are we happy? I think it's an absolutely brilliant deal. It's going to make a huge difference to rugby. It's a big exercise, managing an influx of money like that. Where do I want the money to go? I think it can go into the amateur grass-roots side of things and, professionally speaking, we also need to preserve some funds for the best players, not for those who are already past their best.

Ciulionis neatly describes the two levels which New Zealand rugby has to consider simultaneously – amateur development and resourcing the elite players. Either way, the newly constituted board was aware that if the All Blacks were to remain all-conquering, the game would have to be rebuilt, from the bottom to the top.

In order to excite the nation, the new, 'greatest imaginable challenge', facing the board required a far more sophisticated plan than just parading the boys in black once more. Accordingly, the board embarked on a wholesale restructuring of the relationship between itself, the provincial rugby associations and local clubs. In simple terms, the focus is the creation of significantly wider opportunities to play, and identify with, the game. To achieve this the newly constituted board and its operational staff, while continuing to provide the necessary technical, regulatory steward-ship of rugby, set in motion formidable developmental pro-grammes at all levels of the game. Without a systematic approach to rebuilding, the broad base upon which the All Blacks had estab-lished their long-held supremacy risked rapid erosion. Moreover, according to its stated strategic intent, the union endeavours 'to ensure rugby is the most exciting entertainment product for all New Zealand and [for it] to be recognized as a leading sports brand worldwide'. The union's inspirational dream is nothing less than to maintain rugby's position at the heart of the nation.

The new organizational structure, or 'family tree' as it is usually referred to, naturally places the board at the policy level, with the national office, clustering around three functional directors. These are Jack Ralston, for commercial and marketing, Peter Ciulionis, for finance and administration and, finally, Bill Wallace, who heads up the largest group, rugby services, which includes managers for rugby development, referee development and managers for the amateur and professional game. The directors, including Communication Manager Jackie Maitland, all report to CEO David Moffett.[1] Together, they are the 'tight five'.

## A HOUSE OF BRANDS

As part of the fallout from the move towards professionalism the NZRFU, rather than the club or provincial sides, contracted to pay the salaries of those players deemed good enough to earn a living playing the game. While accepting responsibility for professional payments, the Union, by default, clearly needed to establish viable competitions, such as the Super 12, in which contracted players could ply their trade. Despite the obvious significance of these game-breaking ideas, CEO David Moffett continually points out that:

> The professional part of the game represents only 0.1 per cent of the people involved in rugby. The game in total has not gone professional. It is still the largest amateur sport in this country. What we have got is the splitting of rugby union into two. One arm looks after the professional part of the game and another arm looks after the amateur activities. The professional game generates the funds which are then, in part, redistributed to the amateur game, which in turn secures the future of rugby.

Without question, the All Blacks are the premier brand upon which the fortunes of the game rest. The sacrosanct black jersey is the uniting link between the amateur and the professional game. A run of defeats, as in the 1998 season, is treated as a national crisis with the potential to undermine the very roots of rugby, which will inflict considerable damage to the confidence level of the country. Prior to the professional era, the All Blacks were a microcosm of New Zealand society. Bill Wallace, Director of Rugby Services, notes that, 'We had this incredible ability to have the doctor, the farmer, the shearer and the unemployed, all playing together as equals.' As a consequence of this, Wallace argues that

The All Blacks brand is owned by New Zealanders. They are the stakeholders. That's the thing that has been profoundly illustrated to me so many times. We get heaps of letters and phone calls, and until you've actually read them or listened to them, you truthfully don't realize how passionate New Zealanders are in their belief that *they* own the All Blacks. So you carry this very heavy responsibility. You know that it is extremely important that this brand remains a valuable icon in the national culture.

Recently, the NZRFU set out to codify the brand values associated with its most famous charges. Inevitably, the values which capture the essence of the All Blacks brand are those of respect and humility, combined with power, tradition, commitment and masculinity – values which form the basis upon which any and all professional relationships, internal or external, are formed. Former coach and player Laurie Mains describes what these values actually feel like:

Nobody in this world knows what it means to be an All Black, if they haven't been there themselves. Even someone who has been on the periphery, such as a selector, can never fully understand this. If they have not pulled the jersey on, they can't actually feel what it is. I wasn't a great All Black, I only played fifteen games or so, and yet that jersey just did something to me. The day I pulled it on was something I'll never forget.

Over the years the jersey has gone through many changes. Each time a new design is about to be presented to the New Zealand public there are claims that traditions are being sacrificed. However, Kevin Roberts, back-room architect of the latest version of the Kiwi icon, rejects such ideas: 'Down through the years captains in every era have pulled on a different style jersey, but the *common* denominator is that every one of them remains an All Black.' Chairman Rob Fisher, who, the photographs in his office attest, has spent many years in and around the game of rugby, was reminded of the power of the jersey during a sports seminar which was being addressed by a New Zealander who had played in the National Football League in the United States. His pre-eminent position as speaker, rested on his winning of a Super Bowl ring, the pinnacle of achievement in the gridiron code. Rob Fisher explained what happened:

> I was chairing the session and it was most agonizing, because he couldn't speak, he just absolutely choked up. One of the players put his hand up and asked a question, which enabled him to get started. But he froze because he was in a room full of All Blacks. Despite everything he'd achieved in the world of sport, he couldn't handle it.

Jonah Lomu, currently the most famous rugby player in the world says of the impact of the black jersey: 'It's like putting an "S" on the front.' Echoing sentiments familiar to many players, Lomu describes a close-knit community:

> There is a saying that once you are an All Black, you are always an All Black. When the guys who are former All Blacks turn up, they are still treated as All Blacks. It doesn't matter what year you played, you still get the respect. It carries on.

As the game has become more commercialized, the issue of projecting the All Blacks brand in an appropriate manner has seen the NZRFU reconstitute the way in which the dream is shared. Sponsorship dollars provide critical lifeblood for the game, but nonetheless the NZRFU has recently developed a strict set of guidelines which are designed to protect the All Blacks brand from any long-term damage. No partnership is contemplated if it contradicts the core values of the brand. In this sense, although the All Blacks create significant leverage for the NZRFU, they are never for sale. Jack Ralston, Director of Commercial and Marketing, who was lured away from the Nike organization in 1997, explains how the national office deals with these all-important brand issues:

> We look for people who have the same values as the All Blacks. It's one of the things we are adamant about. We used to have sponsors that didn't quite fit with the values of the All Blacks. We've shifted and repositioned some sponsors too. For example, McDonald's have moved from the All Blacks, which we didn't feel was the right fit, to a more appropriate brand. McDonald's agreed with us.

Prior to the professional era, building the All Blacks brand was largely a subliminal process, but with NZ$15 million dollars of sponsorship revenue generated annually, the development of the brand was quickly subjected to new pressures, forcing the NZRFU to examine what the All Blacks actually stood for. Jack Ralston gives a fascinating insider's view as to how the organization learned how to defend its brand values systematically:

> In the early days of professionalism there were no strict brand disciplines. For instance, if a company had an advertisement that they wanted us to approve, it was virtually done by consensus. It was held up in the office and everybody commented on whether they liked it or not! On my second day in the job, this is what happened. An advertisement was held up and I said, 'Well, does it fit our brand values?' Everybody looked bewildered, so we had a think-tank to put together some basic values, and the advertisement didn't measure up. Even though we liked the colour and the copy, when you ran it past some values it didn't measure up.
>
> So we spent a lot of time early on developing these very strong brand values against which we now measure any possible sponsor. And we'll only associate with people that fit. Recently we had very heated discussions with a company that wanted to associate the All Blacks with the James Bond theme, using Jonah Lomu as the front person. It absolutely didn't fit with our values, so we had to stand and put our hands on our hearts and say, because it doesn't fit our brand values, we're not going to do it.

Not surprisingly, the imagery, affinity and performance of the brand resonate across all functions and activities of the organization. The team has its own management structure, headed by Team Manager Mike Banks and Coach John Hart, but interaction with the board and operational staff, according to Banks, is now, 'running a lot closer together than in the past'. This is a delicate balancing act, since for many years the All Blacks flourished as an independent unit, operating as a 'subsidiary company' with a high degree of autonomy, in terms of accountability, from the board. The point of contact with the parent body is now provided by the Manager of Professional Rugby, Cameron Harland, who faces the challenge of maintaining the traditions of the All Blacks brand while handling a complex set of competing professional pressures, including management of all the professional teams under the 'Union house'. Harland is himself a product of the NZRFU's dash to embrace the future. Before taking on the NZRFU's professional liaison duties, as a twenty-something executive, Harland had already served on special projects reporting directly to CEO David Moffett, successfully managed the bid to have the 2003 Rugby World Cup hosted in New Zealand, and developed the NZRFU's all-important perspective on brands all the while acting as chief strategic planner for the organization.

Harland states bluntly that, 'The success of this organization is about the All Blacks winning. Everything that we do drives towards that.' He is able to articulate precisely what he has to do to ensure on-field success – as budget manager, he has to ensure, that the All Blacks have the resources to operate both efficiently and effectively:

> My job is to make sure that John [Hart] can do his job, which is to coach, and Mike [Banks] can do his job, which is to manage. It's also to make sure that the players do their job, which is to play. I'm directly in the firing line in terms of making sure that John and Mike and the players are looked after. So we need to make sure that any of the other issues that they have on their minds are removed. For example, I ensure that their contracts are sound and that they know what their future is with the NZRFU. We also deal with their worries about what they're going to do after rugby – who will take them on board?

These activities are far more problematic than might be imagined. It is not simply a question of looking after the last detail, although contractual issues naturally require this. Harland has a far greater level of responsibility. The emergence of professionalism for the elite rugby players means that seemingly trivial decisions relating to players and teams carry significant impact with respect to overall policy coherence. Important issues such as player retention can be influenced by equity considerations between players, different treatment of elite players at different levels of skill, and continuity of policy with respect to team selection when considering players who have been lured to play for overseas clubs. What appears to be a simple liaison role is in fact project-based management with strategic significance. Alliances have to be contemplated between the NZRFU and rugby union organizations in other countries. The loss of elite players, or 'player drain', is one of the major concerns of the NZRFU. Losing players overseas subverts the sharing of the dream, as inspirational players are no longer available to represent the game. Fostering a strong sense of community within the rugby family is therefore a fundamental objective.

The stability of the community, including both the amateur and professional game, is complicated further by the potentially competing needs of several brands which have only recently become part of the NZRFU's operations, and by the inspirational dream of keeping rugby at the heart of the nation. Providing players with the opportunity to compete in tournaments outside international Test matches is a vital part of the NZRFU's strategy to robustly support the elite squad. At the same time, the NZRFU also needs to appeal to thousands of rugby players who will never make the professional grade. Cameron Harland:

> Yes, the top of the heap is the All Blacks, but, we've only got fifteen guys who run out for them! There are at least 135,000 people in this country who play rugby, most of whom are never going to play for the All Blacks. We would hope they won't stop playing rugby just because they know that they're not going to wear the black jersey.

This translates into broadening the base of the game. The most important development in the world of rugby that addresses this need has been the advent of the Super 12 competition. Regularly lambasted in the Press and by every pundit imaginable, this critical initiative was put in place both to support the professional game and to attract a broader spectrum of spectators. As the *Brand Book*, which describes each of the portfolios under the NZRFU's care, says, Super 12 is about 'entertainment, flamboyance, colour and razzmatazz'. Deliberately lacking the symbolism of All Blacks rugby, these games, which are played between franchise clubs owned by the Unions in South Africa, Australia and New Zealand, are designed to appeal to non-traditional fans, including teenagers and families, and with a particular emphasis on women. With bonus points for high scoring, the Super 12 Competition produces fast, risk-taking rugby which is full of extrovert play and flair. Semi-final places in the competition have been dominated by the Kiwi teams and, more importantly, every Super 12 final has been won by a New Zealand franchise. These events have a very special flavour, which illustrate the NZRFU's success in adding to its brand portfolio.

The 1999 final was played at the Carisbrook Stadium in Dunedin, New Zealand, one of the world's most celebrated rugby grounds, between the 1998 champions, the Canterbury Crusaders, and the Otago Highlanders. Super 12 rugby is little short of a revolution. Prior to the game, passengers disembarking from flights into Dunedin are piped into the airport, reflecting the region's Scottish ancestry that is deeply imbedded within the brand values of the Otago Highlanders rugby franchise. The taxi ride from the airport reveals the passion for the game ingrained in Kiwi culture. Throughout the length of the journey balloons, ribbons, flags and banners display the Highlanders blue, gold and red colours. Cars, lorries, letterboxes, houses, shops are all adorned. Even the city centre clock has a Highlanders scarf tied around it!

The Super 12 Competition uniquely combines provincial and international pride, since players compete both for the nation and for local supporters. The passion is intense – all 41,000 tickets for the stadium were sold out within thirteen hours of coming on sale. This game, featuring, according to the NZRFU Chairman Rob Fisher, 'the world's best two provincial teams', will be watched by 100 million people around the world. Rugby-playing nations throughout the globe carefully scrutinized TV coverage of the Super 12 in the build up to the 1999 Rugby World Cup, since these two teams provide fifteen of the twenty-four-strong All Blacks squad.

This is a big occasion for the NZRFU. The president, inspirational former All Black Andy Dalton, David Moffett, directors of the NZRFU and Rob Fisher, both chairman of the Union and current chairman of SANZAR, the alliance between the New Zealand, Australian and South African Rugby Unions, are all gathered together at a hotel, as are representatives of the alliance partners and key sponsors UBIX and Ford. Symbolic of the significance of this event to the nation, Prime Minister Jenny Shipley attends the game and the pre-and post-match functions.

The NZRFU contingent, dignitaries included, leave by coach for the pre-match function in the Otago Rugby Union boardroom. Here, national and local officials, current and from times gone by, together with their families, enjoy waiting for the upcoming game from a vantage point in the main stadium while the crowds and the atmosphere build outside. David Moffett, in his carefully balanced scarf of gold, blue, red and black, reflects quietly on the joy of experiencing the drama of the build up to the match just four years after he was instrumental in the implementation of the Super 12 Competition. Already the low-cost, outdoor 'scarfies' seats are awash with the gold and blue of the home side supporters, intermingled with the black and red of the invading Crusaders. Painted faces, and gold, blue, or red and black hair portray unmistakably the partisanship of the fans. To leave absolutely no room for doubt, parents and kids alike carry banners or flags proclaiming their support, or brandish their mock Crusaders' swords or Highlanders' axes to great effect. This is an occasion to 'dress up', and an opportunity for the good-natured crowd to indulge in an afternoon's enjoyment.

Pre-match entertainment, consistent with the Highlanders brand, is in evidence everywhere. By finishing top on points the Highlanders have earned this home-town advantage. Thousands of balloons are released into the stadium and float skywards. And there is the usual mock intimidation of the visitors, as the Highlanders' evocative song, is sung and resung by 30,000 partisan voices. The words appear on the score-board, although few need to read them. The atmosphere is electric. The Crusaders team runs onto the field to a crescendo of applause, and a sea of red and black banners and flags appears. As the time of kick-off approaches, the Highlanders are piped on to the field by a full Scottish pipe band to an eruption of approval from the supporters. The rituals are complete, the game can begin.

Bone-crunching tackles, followed by awesome break away speed, strength-sapping scrums, brilliant set plays, precision shots on goal and roar-inducing tries all combine to invoke the intense concentration and involvement of the 41,000 fans. Here is a brand in the making. The game lives up to the eager anticipation, and the outcome is in contention until the very end. The Crusaders claim victory for the second year in a row. Red and black flags and banners prevail; home fans move away quietly and Dunedin is deserted that night. Gold and blue banners and balloons hang forlornly, and the party is over for another year.

With cups awarded, congratulatory speeches made and media interviews given, it is time for the after-match functions. Along with the prime minister, players from both teams, national and local rugby officials, sponsors, spouses and partners, children and babies mix in the easy harmony of an extended family of hundreds. Satisfaction in achievement or wry resignation betray the players from both sides more readily than their smart team blazers. Victor and defeated players alike converse about competitions to come, now that this challenge is over, and through their concerted efforts the position of the inspirational dream of rugby in the psyche of the New Zealand nation has been strengthened once more. In only a few days, players from both teams will be members of the All Blacks family as preparation for the World Cup begins.

Away from the roar of the crowd and the entertainment of the Super 12 final Bill Wallace understands that, if the Union is to create the future successfully, it must continue to generate new revenues which can be driven down to the all-important club level. From a technical point of view the Super 12 franchise format has seen the development of new structures which encourage and stimulate innovative administration. Bill Wallace:

Infrastructure. We will live and die by our infrastructure. The Super 12 is a fascinating study in itself. We decided to go the franchise way, even though no one had actually done it for rugby before. Here's how it works. We said, 'Here is the franchise of that brand, it's on a risk or return basis and we'll charge nothing. You take all the gate, it's all yours and we'll provide you with the players and the coaches, all paid.' The franchise clubs are accountable to us under their contracts, so there is a bottom-line responsibility there. The Super 12 clubs appoint the rest of the management and do the marketing, so their responsibility is to build the brand. Typically, in any arrangement such as this, we communicate frequently as a franchise group. We put coaches on incentive programmes and all the players are highly motivated because they only get paid if they get selected. In the first year the Wellington franchise made $900,000 profit from zero and kept the lot. They then distributed it to their unions. A little union like Poverty Bay got $20,000. That's trickle down. This is what we wanted to achieve.

Servicing the Super 12 brand also necessitates constant review and reflection. At the end of the season, Wallace and a small group from the NZRFU hold debriefing sessions with all the players. Questionnaires and open-ended notes are made available and collected to ensure the widest possible feedback on all matters relating to the conduct of the season. Separate workshops are arranged where major problems can be tackled head-on. Some of these sessions deal with post-career advice and skill-building for life after the paddock. Even though the Super 12 competition is still in its infancy, the supportive community focus provided by the NZRFU has given the five New Zealand franchises a solid basis for success. In recognition of this important addition to the NZRFU's portfolio, visitors to the offices in Wellington are immediately greeted by the five franchise jerseys displayed together behind the reception area. It is a reflection of the era that these flashy, brightly coloured icons of a new generation are flanked by All Black jerseys, which remain the most powerful image for sponsors.

Even though sponsorship interest is inevitably largely focused on the All Blacks, Jack Ralston has had little difficulty in marketing the Super 12 brand. It is a high-profile competition with an international flavour, which expands opportunities to share the dream with sponsors and the public at large. Moreover, its unique brand values led Ralston to look for a different type of sponsor for the Super 12. This caused McDonald's to move their sponsorship from the All Blacks to the Super 12, where they could appeal to the broader section of the population newly attracted to rugby entertainment. Ralston's aim is to build on New Zealanders' natural passion for the game:

There's a whole raft of extended identities that have fallen out from this exercise. As a result we can now legitimately appeal to both sexes. In a nutshell, we had to define clearly the values for our core products, the All Blacks and Super 12. We talk of products in a marketing sense in this office, but we don't use that publicly. We talk about teams and competitions.

The search for clarity and focus is far from being an academic exercise. The extensive deliberations around brand identity have seen sponsorship revenues and television rights totalling close to NZ$40m during 1998. This is a far cry from the early nineties, when annual income barely scraped into seven digits. Now the future of the professional game depends on this financial structure.

In addition to the All Blacks and Super 12, the NZRFU maintains the National Provincial Championship (NPC), which is embraced by the premier clubs in the nation. Although the Union does not control the club sides who compete for the NPC and the Ranfurly Shield,[2] NPC rugby is still seen as fundamental to the brand portfolio. Coming from the heartland, the NPC fosters local pride and unrivalled fervour. The *Brand Book* distinguishes the NPC in the following manner: 'NPC rugby is played in every major town in New Zealand. It is the rugby of old – raw, gritty and real. It is the fundamental backbone of our game.' Ralston attracts sponsors who reflect these values, where, 'It's the people, the passion and the pride that's associated with being back on your own turf. For the NPC we clearly delineate those things.' The Super 12 and NPC competitions, attracted over 1.2m spectators in 1998 divided roughly equally between them, while almost half the nation could claim to have watched at least one Super 12 game on television. Traditional Ranfurly Shield games evoke passionate tribal instincts, similar to those of Super 12 finals.

Apart from the three major rugby brands, the NZRFU also stewards several other teams. Most notable is the national women's rugby team, the Black Ferns who, in 1998, thrillingly captured the World Championship title for the first time. The New Zealand Maori Team held an undefeated tour of England, Scotland and Tonga, while the New Zealand Sevens Team won Commonwealth Gold in the 1998 games in Kuala Lumpur, as well as winning several other high-profile Sevens tournaments. Perhaps most significant of all, in early 1999, the New Zealand youth team took the Youth World Cup in Wales.

The NZRFU has firmly embraced the challenge of the professional game by developing a number of highly successful brands which have broadened the appeal of the game. The audience is larger, the revenues greater, and the rugby experience is more varied and robust.

## FROM SMALL BLACKS TO ALL BLACKS

The success of the youth team in particular, is indicative of the NZRFU's massive commitment to grass-roots rugby. Coach John Hart is firmly wedded to this enduring principle. He argues forcefully that, 'For rugby to continue to flourish we can never lose sight of the grass-roots requirement to cultivate the game and to encourage people to participate.' Historically, the strength of the game has been located at the local level, and the great players are forged here. Laurie Mains, John Hart's predecessor, explains the system:

> We have got huge drawing power from within the provinces, which nurtures talent for international rugby. At club level, competition in the first, second and third divisions keeps tossing up players. Carlos Spencer, Christian Cullen and Jonah Lomu all came from the lower divisions. While playing for a small club, someone in second division snatches them out of third division, and gives them a promotion. Then someone in first division drags them out of the second division. Nowhere else in the world has got this foundation, this structure that discovers, nurtures and develops players.

Additionally, one of the most recent initiatives aimed at improving elite development further is the Institute of Rugby, based at Massey University and co-sponsored with the New Zealand Sports Foundation. Cameron Harland has no doubt that the Institute is 'the single most important commitment that this organization can offer professional rugby. Each year we focus on twenty young up-and-coming guys, so we're talking about development of the young elite.' The cohort group go through nutrition education, media training, alcohol abuse recognition, budgeting and, finally, career advice. The purpose is to prepare potential All Blacks to a level of professionalism worthy of the black jersey, including exposure to off-field duties which the players are likely to encounter. Harland notes the meticulous planning that goes into the programme:

We really work hard to provide the right environment for these guys. This includes preparing them appropriately for the professional game. As future role models they have to be able to handle themselves in the public glare, so we established a basic code of conduct for off the field as well as on it.'

On more familiar territory, the team from the Institute is put through its paces against international opposition. During the 1998 season victories were recorded against the England and Tonga touring sides.

Little of this preparatory work with elite players has any meaning unless it sits inside a broader framework of player development, beginning with club and school rugby. Until the professional era responsibilities for administration of the game were clearly understood and well segmented. In simple terms, the NZRFU looked after provincial matters and the All Blacks, while the provincial associations dealt with the local club sides. At board and national office level it has, however, been recognized since 1995 that the benefits of the professional game must go well beyond a handful of stars at the top. Channelling funds into the amateur game has seen the unprecedented development of programmes and initiatives designed to create the future of rugby in New Zealand.

The NZRFU has created a fully integrated programme known as the 'rugby stairway', which can take the youngest players of the game, aged five, from Small Black rugby to All Blacks. There are seven intermediate steps along the way, each one with its own distinctive characteristics. The size of the field and length of playing time gradually increase as the children progress from Junior and Super All Black categories to teenage levels at school, alongside club and colt rugby. Simultaneously, the skill levels are also amplified at each step. The penultimate sixth step, before the All Blacks themselves, is the NPC and Super 12. Manager of Rugby Development Evan Crawford co-ordinates this extensive programme. He can count on over fifty regional development officers (RDOs) to work in conjunction with the provincial associations, who pay a portion of their salaries, and formally retain responsibility for club and player development. Some top-up money is also received from the Hillary Commission, a government-sponsored body which provides funding and policy direction for all sports played in New Zealand. Recently, the Union has employed an additional three national RDOs who help to deploy the non-stop activities of the RDOs more effectively.

The RDOs' brief is to work primarily with the provinces, to deliver the development programmes. Evan Crawford:

> The RDOs' primary role is retention and recruitment of players, coaches and administrators. The provinces sign a contract which advises the RDOs of the strategic direction and the job specification that we have outlined for them. They help write the programme and deliver it. When the Small Black kids have their weigh-in with the RDOs, the parents who are going to be coaches take a simple course that talks about coaching ethics. The RDOs also give them free resources, and as much assistance as they can.

To this end, Crawford has in his possession a plethora of coaching manuals, diaries, pathways, handbooks and guidebooks. Brightly coloured coaching guides, invariably carrying the distinctive golden McDonald's arches, containing introductions to training methods, injury prevention techniques and plain skill-building, can be found all around his office. Apart from being intrinsically valuable in their own right, these documents exist for a more urgent purpose. A drop off in the number of people playing rugby necessitated the development of a strategy to re-energize the nation's interest in rugby union. Although attracting new players and keeping them would seem to be the most appropriate response, it is also vital to maintain the commitment of young players as they progress up the rugby stairway. Creating the future for rugby union rests heavily on the ability of coaches to provide support and ongoing technical advice for emerging players. Crawford's problem, however, begins with sustaining continuity of coaches:

> It would be fair to say that the direction we've taken in the last two years in development is geared less towards recruitment and retention of players and more towards recruitment and retention of coaches. The belief is that if we get coaches and we educate them, we will attract players. At the same time, the players that we have already got will be better catered for. In the past, it was just, 'go out there and get as many kids playing the game' as possible. We did that, but we didn't have the

people on the ground to coach and help them, therefore the playing numbers dwindled.

Crawford confirms that, although the Union has over 8,000 coaches it loses half of them each year, which means another 4,000 have to be recruited just to maintain existing coverage. This unsustainable drop off led Crawford to concentrate on developing resources aimed at making the coaching role as attractive as possible:

> So what we're trying to do is educate them. We're trying to provide them with user-friendly resources so that anyone, mum, dad, sister, anyone, can take and adequately coach a little junior team. If they get a taste of it and like the experience we can encourage them to progress through, and become more advanced coaches.

In order to be pro-active with grass-roots rugby, the NZRFU also set up a Provincial Advisory Group under the auspices of ex-All Black great Brian Lochore. This reviewed player progression from club rugby to higher provincial levels, and reported in 1998. Historically this might have been seen as 'provincial turf', but the NZRFU's resourcing of the game through professional revenue has created a greater responsibility, and increased opportunity, to develop secure pathways for player enhancement and progression to the elite level. A club and junior rugby manager now oversees this aspect of the NZRFU's grass-roots work.

The developmental aspect of rugby, in terms of coherent policy towards coaching, player attraction and progression up the stairway, has no realistic counterpart in the pre-professional era. In less than four years, the NZRFU has systematically identified what it needs to do to create the future of New Zealand rugby.

Less well recognized, but still vital to the NZRFU's inspirational dream, is a commitment to playing the game a certain way, with flair, and in an expressive, free-flowing manner. As rugby became ever more professional, the Union had the foresight to establish a referee development programme with a view to maintaining both a particular style of play and the quality of officiation. According to Keith Lawrence, Manager of Referee Development, 'The Board and David Moffett recognized that refereeing could no longer remain an adjunct to the game. It had to be part of the mainstream.' Beginning in the early nineties, funds allocated to this aspect of rugby increased from a few tens of thousands of dollars to over NZ$1.5m in 1998. Lawrence can call upon five full-time regional referee development officers, who also work closely with coaches in the field, thus providing a coherent infrastructure. At the elite level Lawrence points out that, 'If you are going to have a really good NPC or Super 12 Championship, you need more than one good referee at that level.' As well as cultivating good referees on home turf, the NZRFU has been at the forefront in bringing officials in from overseas:

> One of the interesting things we have done is to encourage visiting referees from the UK, South Africa, or wherever. Over time we have been able to get across the Southern-hemisphere psyche of the game. We've looked after them very, very well, showing them all the sights of NZ, made available our best training facilities, and we've involved them in our referees' meetings, just so that they can have a presence. Generally speaking, they come around to our way of thinking. We don't do this necessarily just to suit the All Blacks, we do it because we have a really strong belief that rugby, if it is to be sustained, needs to be played in a free-flowing positive fashion. Within New Zealand, we try to encourage our referees, throughout the grades, to take on this philosophy.

From the most unexpected of quarters, referee development, the NZRFU has found an intriguing, if not powerful, way to express the flavour of one of its inspirational dreams, to have the game played the way it should be played as an 'entertaining product, recognized as a leading sports brand worldwide'. Through its international links, it is also able to share the dream with those who manage the game on the field for its foreign competitors.

## THE UNION MAKES US STRONG

The developmental picture of the organization begins with a recent personnel initiative. Given the riches available, the NZRFU has properly understood the importance of retaining the services of those inspirational players who in years past brought a nation to its feet. Without exception, every single person who works for the NZRFU, either in Wellington or out in the field as an RDO or unpaid coach, understands the magic of the All Blacks, but without the continuity provided by those best placed to communicate hard-earned lessons, there is a danger of losing the sense of community which the All Blacks themselves have built across the generations. 'Once an All Black, always an All Black,' is a phrase well known to every New Zealander. With this simple statement in mind, the Union has astutely made key appointments to ensure that the *organization* benefits directly from the All Blacks' memory and experience.

Andy Dalton, currently the president of the NZRFU, was an outstanding, inspirational All Black captain from 1981 to 1987, and now plays an important role as a figurehead for the NZRFU Dalton states:

> I attend functions from club level to board meetings to the international arena. This way I am able to promote rugby to players, supporters and the public at large. On behalf of the NZRFU, I also host visiting officials, sponsors and visiting teams and personally address special functions and events.

This largely ceremonial position, that purposely does not carry any job description, puts Dalton in the position of visible representative of the NZRFU's values. Sean Fitzpatrick, who was captain from 1992 until his retirement in 1997, is widely recognized as most probably the greatest All Black captain of all time, and one of the greatest players in the history of the game. He gained a reputation for being a consummate professional, who, better than any other, maintained the spirit of All Blacks rugby. In his new role as consultant he is uniquely placed to transfer his experience back into the NZRFU's activities, in a variety of organizational settings. He brings a perspective that is both inspirational and aspirational:

> What's the magic of the All Blacks? I loved the All Blacks because we were so successful. We created a wonderful environment to be involved in. We were the best at our job, the best rugby team in the world, ninety-nine per cent of the time. As

we ran out on to the field, we knew we'd worked harder than anyone else. We had a real resolve to make sure that we were going win.

Fitzpatrick now approaches the organizational challenge before him, from a player's perspective:

My primary objective is simply to create a good environment by accessing the necessary resources so that the players can be successful. Second, I'm responsible for creating a line of communication from the players to the board. I use my career experiences to connect with the new breed of professional player, which includes assisting to set up a Players' Association.

Fitzpatrick considerably enhances organizational continuity from field to office. Maintaining the presence of inspirational players as the NZRFU's activities rapidly expand transfers legacies from one era to the next, while fostering a strong sense of community in the organization at large.

Sustaining a robust community requires more than habitual exhortations from managers or coaches. 'How then, do the All Blacks constantly set up personal challenges for themselves?' was the question we asked of rugby superstar Johan Lomu. His response was crystal clear. 'All the players – we hate coming second-best to ourselves.' This formulation neatly re-engineers the sports mantra of exceeding personal best. It also lies at the heart of the NZRFU. Personal responsibility and an overwhelming passion to improve and 'do better', sum up the attitude and actions of the staff at national office. The search for self-improvement on the rugby field is matched by those who manage the affairs of the Union. It starts with the CEO, David Moffett:

We want people in here who are going to be self-starters, motivated to actually go off and do it. People here understand that we are not going to be just reactive. I encourage that. I don't want to run this business, I want my people to run it. We foster a culture of hard work, commitment and passion. Passion for everything we do, but specifically passion for the All Blacks. There are no half measures. If you're not passionate about the All Blacks, don't come and work here.

Moffett has been credited with creating a self-regulating 'tight unit'. Plaudits come easily from those who work closely with him. Jackie Maitland, in dealing with a demanding media, has to work extremely closely with Moffett, whom she describes as, 'a particularly good CEO'. Evan Crawford sees Moffett's preference for encouraging staff to be pro-active as critical to his own development: 'He allows people like myself and Bill Wallace to run with the ball.' Jack Ralston sees this particular inspirational player as the catalyst responsible for many of the successes associated with the organization:

> I think you need to know the important part that Dave Moffett has played. He has the ability to get down to what needs to be done, rather than get lost in the woods. He has terrific vision of where this game needs to go, and is a true agent of change. You can't underestimate what he's done in pulling the whole group together, and in identifying the right organizational players. That's the story here, David's ability to attract the right people.

Given the relative infancy of the 'new' NZRFU organization, in conjunction with the board Moffett has emphasized strategic planning activities in order to create clarity of focus. Building new brands, solidifying older ones and setting up new development programmes has all been carried out at breakneck speed. The constant updating of strategic documents, with mid-year summits and the like, enables the NZRFU to take into account external pressures and actively attempt to make 'first plays' in the 'industry'. Executing projects as planned and then taking them as far as possible introduces discipline to each aspect of the NZRFU's affairs. The 1998 annual report displays a level of accountability and reports on progress that would cause most corporate employees to grimace. Six key measures of success are each addressed by a total of twenty-five strategic objectives against which progress is matched. This, and a sense of strong engagement, enables a level of intense and sustained peak performance to be achieved. Jack Ralston:

> Everybody has input, everybody is listened to, everybody is a valuable unit in here. It's the little things that count, like the

Monday morning work-in-progress meetings where we all find out what's happening and where we are at, so that we are absolutely accountable for what we do. This makes our teams very fluid. We know each other's jobs pretty well, so that we take responsibility for the total result, not just our component of it. We love breaking down walls.

The atmosphere in the national office changes when All Black Test matches approach. Jackie Maitland immediately feels the heightened expectations as she deals with reporters and photographers all demanding accreditation for the game. Jane Dent, Media Manager, also says, 'From my point of view, it's frantic – the place is really buzzing. The phones and the fax run red-hot.' David Moffett's core passions shine through when an All Blacks game is on the line.'

When the All Blacks are playing we always send them off a fax which everybody signs. In the office we've got banners everywhere, you know, we get right behind it. There are no half-measures. I've got total commitment to the All Blacks winning.

John Hart, as Coach, is on the receiving end of the NZRFU's obvious dedication to the All Blacks – he carries the burden of a nation's expectations. Among many initiatives which he has taken to the board, he has successfully persuaded the NZRFU to resource larger touring parties, which enable him to field a New Zealand 'A' side. Developing and showcasing the depth of talent in New Zealand rugby also helps to prevent the elite squad from being over-played. Hart recognizes clearly the strength of the organization behind him: 'The Union has been through a lot of change. It got tipped upside down overnight, so they had to change people and processes very quickly. I have a huge respect for what they've done.' Hart's own contributions to the All Blacks and, by proxy, to the NZRFU relate for the most part, to the technicalities of rugby, and will not be rehearsed here. However, his philosophy regarding the basic principles of human interaction match closely those of the organization's administration. In keeping with the theme of personal growth, Hart notes simply that, 'Although it has been hard for some of them, I try to get the players to express and take responsibility.' Jonah Lomu feels that the All Blacks team relishes Hart's management style:

> The players have really enjoyed it. It gives them a bit of time and space to think about things we are going to do. Training with John gives you the chance to learn new skills. That's an attribute he has, giving the players the opportunity to have their say and a chance to grow in their part in the sport. Everybody is trying to reach the same goal, and that's to go out there and win the game.

## CONCLUSION

In less than half a decade the NZRFU has helped to usher in the professional era, and in doing so has developed into a formidable PPO. The speed at which the NZRFU has been able to establish brand identifies and equity, together with the development of all aspects of the grass-roots amateur game, is breathtaking. How have they achieved such a rapid transformation? In terms of its overarching purpose, the organization quickly realized that, following the advent of professionalism, the maintenance of the inspirational dream – to keep rugby union close to the heart of the nation – required the sharing of new dreams, additional to the traditions and long-standing values of the All Blacks. The NZRFU is now a burgeoning house of brands. Although the greatest imaginable challenge remains All Black supremacy, particularly in the World Cup tournament, the NZRFU is also able to point to its other domestic and regional brands as evidence of its success. The focus now involves relentless brand building alongside extensive player and organizational development. Through these activities, the NZRFU is creating the future, today.

Finally, the whole organization desires not to come second best to itself. Administration and players alike are 'locked' into a zone that is entirely their own.

*

Kevin Roberts, as a member of the board of the NZRFU, did not participate as an author in the research or writing of this chapter.

# CHAPTER 6

# Women's Hockey Australia – The Colour is Gold

*The night we won the gold medal in Atlanta, we came off the dais and because of all the security problems they wouldn't let us go up to our parents. Mum and Dad fought their way down from the grandstand, where they could stand right on the edge of the barrier. My sister Katrina (who is also on the team), and I had to get plastic chairs to stand up on so that we could just reach them with our outstretched arms. I have never seen my Dad cry and Mum was hysterical. It was a big thank you for everything, for both of them, for everything they had done for us throughout our lives. Buying hockey sticks, paying for fees, paying for trips, taking us to trains, waiting in cars, driving us home from training – it was a huge moment for them and us. I will never forget that night, on Friday 1 July 1996* – Lisa Powell, Hockeyroos, Defender*

The driving rain on a late June evening in Perth forces a handful of spectators to seek protection under the canopy of an otherwise empty Bentley hockey stadium. The heart of the game resides here. Night and day the facility hosts a whirl of bustling activity, with games, drills, practice and meetings. School children, national athletes and veterans alike constantly come and go, interacting, playing and learning. The stadium complex is hockey heaven, and exudes a friendly communal warmth.

For the few remaining observers who are not accustomed to dealing with inclement weather, bone-chilling conditions such as these are a substantial shock to the system. Shoulders are drawn closer to ears, and arms and hands are either thrust deeply into pockets or pulled ever tighter around waistlines. A veterans' game has long since been completed, leaving just a handful of players,

who, seemingly oblivious to the unrelenting rain, continue to practise what appear to be set plays involving rapid passing across the
field, ending with a shot on goal. The crack of stick on ball, which
echoes loudly around the floodlit stadium, is interspersed with the
odd shout or mock whoop of triumph, as the ball crashes into the
back of the goal from time to time. By some measure, meaningless
to others or not, these goals still seem to count to those on the
pitch. One of the players who is apparently unaware of the marked
deterioration in the weather, continues to pound the synthetic turf
inexorably. She is Rechelle Hawkes, Co-captain of the Australian
team.

It is literally only a few days since she returned with the rest of
the Hockeyroos from yet another gold-medal-winning performance at the World Championships in Utrecht, Holland. For
Hawkes, winning gold is something of a habit. In 1998 she added
a Commonwealth gold medal to four Champions Cup gold
medals, two World Cup gold medals and, finally and most precious
of all, two Olympic gold medals from Seoul in 1988 and Atlanta
in 1996. A silver medal in the Sydney World Cup in 1990 and
fifth place at the Barcelona Olympics in 1992 barely detract from
the fact that, in the last decade, Hawkes and Hockeyroos have
utterly dominated the game of women's field hockey. Since the
appointment of coach Richard Charlesworth they have achieved
an astonishing win record of eighty per cent in close to 200 games.

But for Hawkes there is no let up. Not yet satisfied with her
cache of gold, the opportunity for self-improvement, and to exceed
personal best, appears to offer her a far greater sustained challenge
than the quest for gold:

> Training is enjoyable when you push yourself to the limit. You
> see the rewards afterwards. I've always loved training, being
> able to see how hard I can push myself and feel the improve-
> ment. If I am not improving every time or getting something
> out of it, I get *really* annoyed. I guess that is something within
> my personality. I can't go through the motions of training with-
> out getting something out of it. This is self-imposed pressure.

Playing for the Australian team that she loves and is 'totally
wrapped up in,' presented opportunities that are in stark contrast
to what might have been. Thinking back on her very first selection

to the national team, Hawkes reflected on the divergent paths that lay before her:

> The defining moment for me was at eighteen years of age. I was studying at the time, baby-sitting two kids when I got a phone call from Women's Hockey Australia. It was the secretary from the Hockey Association, who had tracked me down at someone's house and he said, 'Rechelle Hawkes, you have been chosen for the Australian women's hockey team,' and I said, 'What!?' and he said, 'Yes, you have been selected to play a series against Germany.' I was in total disbelief, because I hadn't even made the state team at this stage, and I was selected straight into the Australian team. I took some convincing. I remember thinking at that time that this was a new direction, a turning point for me. I could have ended up having kids of my own in the next year or so. Equally, without the hockey path, I could have also ended up baby-sitting five days a week.

Hawkes, along with 160,000 women in Australia who play hockey at various levels, is living the dream that began in 1910, when the All Australia Women's Hockey Association was formed. Membership was set annually at one guinea, and the ruling committee was made up of three members from each state who elected the president annually. So began the strong tradition of state involvement in the grass-roots development of hockey. The initial rules of the Association set out in 1910 ran to all of fifteen points printed on five pages measuring two inches square. The Women's Hockey Australia (WHA) has always guided the growth and popularity of the game and, as this is an amateur sport, the professional Sydney national office now in existence co-ordinates a huge volunteer force responsible for administration of the game at state level.

One of the WHA's objectives ever since its foundation has been to provide women with the opportunity to participate in a structured competitive sport, and its annual report states that it currently seeks to 'raise the profile of women's hockey nationwide as a healthy, recreational and social team sport.' In the early 1980s an additional element was added – that of preserving the WHA's high profile in world hockey. The aim is global domination of field hockey. Finally, the success of the organization means that it has made a major contribution to developing the leadership role of women in society. Nowhere is this more apparent than in the national office.

Upon entering the Sydney premises it is immediately clear that activity flows smoothly around any objects, human or otherwise, that might impede progress. Full-time employees, board members and volunteers constantly cycle through the office. Stick and ball might be absent, but there is a strong sense of shared purpose. A sudden collective cheer, signifying the equivalent of scoring an 'office goal', would not seem out of place. Although the tempo is high, it is not frenetic. Calm, co-ordinated activity with no obvious locus of control creates an impression of flow.

Perhaps with an eye on sponsorship priorities, at first take the national office appears to be focused on the Hockeyroos. Trophies and symbols of international success are never far from the eye, yet they are not ostentatiously displayed. Even a brief conversation with the women in action reveals a commitment to the game of hockey itself above the more limited considerations of elite success. Their passion is evident, almost contagious, especially when the subject of being the best in the world is raised.

Unquestionably, the managerial ambience is one of friendly informality, yet with sponsors and government money involved, formal accountability, not to mention democratic rationale, necessitates a degree of formality and procedure that we failed to encounter in any of the other case studies. Even though the WHA gets by on a slender budget of less than Aus$3 million, the yearly business plan runs to some forty pages. Each committee is held accountable to measurable objectives, with cost estimates of expected activities, the source of revenue and finally an explanation of variance if so required. With annual performance monitoring of office staff, the operation is run as tightly as the Hockeyroos defence. Pam Tye, the current WHA president, is well aware of the formalities that are demanded of the WHA by external bodies, and deliberately spends time in the office helping to establish informality, heaping plenty of praise on deserving staff, and demonstrating passion and interest in the tasks undertaken. It might also include 'sitting down and having a Scotch with the president'.

'Brenda Cawood, our general manager, who works very well at keeping lines of communication open, is key to what happens in the office,' Tye observes. Cawood is the crucial conduit who ensures that trust and loyalty exist between the board, the states, and the elite programmes in Perth. Her inspirational contribution to the WHA is not as a fixer or deal-maker between the constituent parts of the organization, but as a constructive catalyst who opens up channels between potentially partisan interests. Cawood believes that risk and game-breaking ideas developed between herself and the board are the result of dialogue and policy debate which has a positive, constructive flavour. A significant example of this is the formation of the Telstra STIX National Hockey League, an initiative primarily stewarded by herself and last incumbent president, Meg Wilson.

Within the office, Cawood holds informal weekly management meetings with a view to keeping the organization 'happy and harmonious'. This creates a flow of information which ensures that each area is able to work through to resolve the inevitable task interdependencies. Another value of this process is that it constantly reinvigorates the dual focus between development and the elite. Tracey Edmundson, Media Manager, knows that the best opportunities for increasing media coverage come from having a successful national team. This inevitably provides the organization with a wider turning circle in terms of delivering good value for existing sponsors, and attracting new ones. Success is all the more critical given that hockey has to compete for coverage and sponsorship with several other high-profile sports in Australia, such as Australian Rules, cricket, tennis and rugby league. While Edmundson needs to extract every possible advantage from the Hockeyroos' success, Marg Ryan, Coaching and Technical Manager, has to focus on the development and technical accreditation of officials at the grass-roots. Coaching and umpiring are the sinews of the game. Securing board support for an umpire development officer is as important to Ryan as celebrating the latest Hockeyroos gold medal. Even though Ryan was manager of the Australian team in the early eighties, she strongly believes that, 'The WHA mission is to provide sport and recreation for women and girls in Australia. That's what I'm interested in, to be able to have them exercise and enjoy recreation. I don't care whether they're elite, I just want them to play the game.' To this end she runs the National championships, reviews the Intensive Training Centre Coaches in the states and develops the national officiating programme. She is literally responsible for how the game is played.

Another equally vital element of the developmental focus of the WHA, is getting young girls into the game of hockey. This responsibility belongs to the development manager. Fortuitously, when the position was advertised in 1995, one of the applications came from an occupational health and safety officer working with Australia Post. Sharon Buchanan was an inspirational choice, not least because she happened to have captained the Hockeyroos to gold in the 1988 Seoul Olympics. Buchanan is the player who was rightfully associated with the emergence of Australian Field hockey supremacy. In a stunning performance, her two goals in the Olympic semi-final, against a hitherto dominant Dutch side, are widely held to be the turning point in the fortunes of WHA. While other players have since sustained WHA supremacy Buchanan's performance that day made such dreams possible. Describing the first goal she scored, Buchanan's memory of the occasion, to this day, remains vividly clear:

> I knew Tracy was going to pass to me and so I instinctively got into position to receive the ball. When it came I had the opportunity to pass or shoot. Passing was the easier option but there was no question in my mind about what I was going to do. All through training we had practised this shooting position, so I had all the confidence and focus I needed to make the shot. There was never any doubt in my mind that I was going to score. This was the chance I had always wanted.

Returning to the hockey family, Buchanan also brought with her a natural love of the game, outstanding professional abilities and a passionate commitment to the developmental side of hockey. Additionally, as Australia's first women's hockey celebrity, who is often called upon to do hockey commentary for television, Buchanan's public profile is a powerful vehicle for sharing the dream with young players. To this end, and as part of the WHA's extensive developmental programme, the secondary-school based Telstra Buchanan Cup was established, enabling both the organization and chief sponsor to take advantage of her fame.

Her past glory as a player and her role as Development Manager, allow Buchanan to bridge different WHA activities. In particular, she keeps a close personal contact with many former team mates. This provides an extra perspective for the national office, without distracting from Buchanan's main role, which is to create the future by building hockey from the ground up. Sharon Buchanan:

> We have a number of different competitions. Even at the minky, primary-school level, we have a state-based competition, run through either schools or clubs for the youngsters. We also try to link the schools and the clubs through extensive coaching visits. Then we have three under-sixteen tournaments for ages twelve through to sixteen. A state competition and two invitational tournaments attract about twenty, ten and eight teams respectively. Then we go into under-eighteen, over twenty-one, junior and senior squad competitions and then finally the Telstra STIX National Hockey League. We've also got what we call the 'Let's play Hockey' programme which has been put out by our sponsor, Telstra. That programme goes to the schools of Australia, where certificates and stickers are presented to the participants.

Buchanan's poise and grace lift those around her. In a very real sense she stands at the heart of the hockey community. She is able to access a respectful, perhaps even deferential, audience when pushing for support for her development agenda, but she does not expect resources to be forthcoming simply because she is an Australian icon. Support for the development programme occurs for exactly the same reason as for the other portfolios.

Daphne Pirie, a member of the board of directors, described to us the ties that unite the organization:

> Respect of each other, love of the game, plus a determination to succeed. It's not much different from being a player. In an organization such as this, either on the board or in the national office, you still attack the job in the same manner, you set yourself goals just as you did as a player. It makes no difference if we are talking strategic plans, budgets or whatever, you still have to see the bigger picture, which is what we had to do when we were playing. If we could have our time over again we would all still rather be out on the paddock than in the boardroom or office. Our collective memory keeps it together.

Sharon Buchanan, the most recent person to make the transition from playing to managing, expresses similar sentiments:

I know my developmental perspective for the organization is very different from a lot of others, but even so, the first thing that really comes to mind for me is our overall success, so we need to do all these other things too. If we don't do them well, we will no longer be successful. Now, we just have to keep improving all the time.

The national office is where partisan interests and tensions are distilled. Each portfolio pushes its own agenda to the limit, but never to the point of losing sight of the broader dream. The duality of development and the elite is also one of the distinctive dilemmas that Dr Richard Charlesworth, National Coach, has to face.

Why would an organization dedicated to the development of opportunities for women have absolutely no qualms about turning to a man to ensure that it remained successful? In the first instance, after several years as national coach, Brian Glencross had already successfully taken the Hockeyroos to their first Olympic gold medal in 1988. When the position was advertised in 1993, the WHA was a very different organization from the time of his appointment in 1980. It had become a much larger professional outfit with pretensions to global leadership, and women had been deliberately deployed, mentored, resourced and placed in positions of responsibility and authority. Even so, the new national coach would be appointed to help achieve the overarching dream of the Association, and as having the top national team in the world was an essential part of that dream, the best coach available would be employed, regardless of gender.

As the national coach, Dr Richard Charlesworth has yet to see any colour in tournament play other than gold. Brian Glencross, now high performance manager at the Australian Institute of Sport (AIS), argues that, 'He is unique, he is probably the best coach in the world'. Charlesworth's background is eclectic to say the least. A stand-out hockey player with 227 caps for the Australian men's team, he won a gold medal in the World Championships in London in 1986, but despite four attempts Olympic gold eluded him, silver being his best result in Montreal, 1976. He is a medical practitioner and was, for several years, a Member of Parliament.

In the eyes of the WHA he is peerless. He commands complete respect. Sharon Buchanan, who was coached by Charlesworth in her last year as a player, has such a belief in him, that she feels,

> He could coach just about any sport and be successful. He demands so much of himself and you know he will demand the same of you. He's just got that competitiveness which is fantastic. You would lie down and die for him if that enabled someone to score a goal for us.

When Charlesworth accepted the appointment as women's national coach, the WHA knew that they had snared the best coach in Australia. Charlesworth:

> I sort of fell into this you know. I never thought I would be doing this job if you had asked seven years ago when I was in Parliament. I made a decision in about July of 1992 to get out of politics, because although it was a very interesting job, it was a terrible life. About two or three months later a couple of players on the national team rang me and asked if I was interested. I hadn't been involved in hockey since I finished playing in 1988, and indeed that was probably a very good thing, because I had had nothing to do with it and I was quite fresh. I thought about it and thought, oh yes, that might be an interesting thing to do, so I got involved. I was accepted and given an opportunity.

Charlesworth's philosophy clearly matched that of the WHA, who were looking for someone who could take the Hockeyroos to the next level.

> I suppose I had an abiding belief that we had never really developed a team as a sports team could be developed. Our state teams and our club teams developed in a unified way, and I felt that that should be possible with the national team. It is extraordinary how poorly prepared teams are in terms of team work and integration in tournaments like the soccer World Cup. What you have is a complex integrated team which requires all sorts of judgements and decisions to be made by people in a split second. It is a very hard thing to tie together. In hockey

we need the sort of understanding and unity that you can only develop by really working at it. I believed that we could go a lot further in terms of that in our national team. I don't think we have ever done very well at this in the past.

There were other reasons why the new national coach felt that the Hockeyroos were a good bet to succeed. First, Charlesworth saw that women who were good enough for consideration for the national side were generally younger than the corresponding men, and were in a different stage of their lives, usually without large financial commitments and firm career expectations. In consequence, he argues, 'Their focus was much more performance orientated – they were simply better athletes, faster and much more willing to train hard.' Second, it was possible for women's hockey to recruit more 'first-choice athletes' since the number of team sports open to women was significantly smaller than those available to men. Men could choose to concentrate on rugby, cricket, Australian Rules or soccer, while women had a choice of two codes – hockey or netball.

The WHA head hunted Charlesworth primarily because, by reputation, they knew he was a supreme inspirational player and an innovator who would maintain and amplify the team's natural instinct for flair and attack. His well-known quest to challenge and improve both himself and others also sat well with the WHA's never-ending search for both administrative and technical advantage. Put simply, the WHA wanted game-breaking ideas from Charlesworth to ensure their global dominance of the code – the Hockeyroos' record since 1993 obviously speaks for itself. In explaining to us how this remarkable record was achieved, Charlesworth shared much more than a coaching manual. His philosophy of team performance is a compelling example of managerial style. It begins, however, with the individual player exceeding personal best:

Everybody gets carried away with the score. I like to develop different attitudes in the players. One of the most critical things that you have to do is develop an attitude which is analytical and clinical. We keep a lot of statistics to help us look closely at everything that happens. Each person gets an efficiency rating for every game they play, so we know that if they got the ball forty-five times and they turned it over fifty times, that is not good – or if they only turned it over twice and they were penetrating on fifteen occasions then that's very good and their efficiency is ninety-five per cent or whatever. Although somewhat an arbitrary figure, it means something.

This enables players to look behind the result. They can be honest in a way that is not threatening. It is all about improving. If you improve yourself, you will beat the opposition. We actually don't go out there to win, we go out to play well, and winning is the byproduct of that. The focus is on how we play, rather than the outcome.

For Rechelle Hawkes, the training regimes which accompany this style of coaching are heaven-sent. Fitness, skill levels, detailed analysis and constant execution of plays are taken to a higher plane than in other teams: 'factors which separate us from other countries who are simply not as intensely prepared as we are'.

Personal responsibility for performance is strongly reinforced by Charlesworth's insistence on playing the game using all available resources. Unlike every other hockey team and almost every other sporting code, the Hockeyroos do not employ, and will not countenance, the notion of a bench. This means that there is no 'first eleven', plus others who substitute with lesser skills and ability. Charlesworth explains the reasons behind this:

That was a conscious decision that I made six years ago. Every time I had a bench, implicitly or explicitly I was saying, 'You are not good enough to start.' Players start to believe that. If I say to them, you are all going to play, then those people believe that they are good enough *and* they surprise you *and* they play with more skill *and* better than they did before. This is important for a number of reasons that are very practical. The game can be very hot and difficult anyway, so using all our players allows us to play at a higher tempo which other teams simply can't sustain. It also lifted those people and made them believe that they were good enough. It unified the group.

Although this perspective is very much in line with the overall development of people within WHA, we suggested that the notion of 'bench strength', particularly as it applies to basketball, was a sound concept. 'It's all bullshit in my opinion,' was the swift and non-debatable response. If we had any further concerns about the validity of Charlesworth's approach, they were more than dispelled by Jenny Morris, fullback for the Hockeyroos:

> Everyone knows that when they go to a tournament they will play. It creates heaps of team spirit because everyone knows they are going on to the field. We don't even use the word bench. It took us ages to get used to that. There is no such thing as a bench, or substitutes or reserves – as much as the media still like to talk that way.

Charlesworth means what he says. Alyson Annan, arguably the best hockey player in the world, had less time on the field during the 1998 World Cup than several other players. The constant interchange of players has other benefits too. With European teams dedicated to marking each player, their game plan is severely disrupted if the best player in the world isn't there to mark. Changing positions also allows the coach to interact with the team as the game progresses.

Many of Charlesworth's innovations and game-breaking ideas, based around flair and flexibility, have simply left the opposition floundering. It even includes completely changing a player's game. Lisa Powell turned out for many years as an attacker, but after losing her place, Charlesworth suggested that she should re-establish herself in the side as a defender, thus adding some pace to the team where it was least expected. In less than six months Powell fought her way back into the team. When these initiatives fit together the players experience a heightened state of flow. Rechelle Hawkes:

> There is intensity. There is the running off the ball, helping each other, communication, confidence, and everyone wants to get involved. All eleven on the field want that ball, or are helping someone to get it. It feels as if we are on a roll. We feel like we have got this invincibility. Everyone is so confident in the team and in themselves, we believe that we can really overrun a team.

Sentiments such as these are also indicative of the strong community that has been built around the team. For the 1996 Olympic

Games in Atlanta, the WHA was able to obtain the necessary finances to bring the team together in Perth for several months. This helped to create significant bonds, as the squad was able to knit together socially. Ann Konrath, who works in administration for the national coach, described to us how, in the lead-up to a major tournament, rigorous training schedules are balanced with more recreational activities:

> Sometimes, after training, the whole team will come over to my house for a meal, or we might all go out to lunch. In the very hot weather some of the players who live here offer their homes because they have a pool. They are a fun, committed, hard-working group.

The self-confidence that travels with this team, wherever it goes, has its origins in Charlesworth's ability to develop the whole person. Peak performance requires a fundamental merging of both conception and execution of task. Success on the hockey field provides a powerful metaphor for organizational life. Richard Charlesworth:

> Once the ball is in play, the opposition rarely do what you expect them to do. In every situation, something else happens. In preparation for this, we have to make the players better decision makers, and give them the authority to do it. Give them the opportunity. Help them to make that critical decision for themselves and the team. Increase their capacity to decide. In the end, they have to play, you cannot do it for them.

Shirley Davies explains that the emphasis on maintaining individuality runs through the entire coaching system:

> Under our elite system, there is an intensive training scheme whereby a coach is appointed in every state so that the national coach at the top can feed into the elite coaches in every state. This structure ensures that people are being coached along the same lines, but without pushing away their flair. And there will be other coaches watching players in the states. They will gather information from their elite coach so that anyone who has the talent in the states is automatically picked up. The Intensive

Training Centre (ITC) coach is responsible for developing these elite players, whether they're the talented under-sixteens, or the talented under-eighteens.

Our three national coaches will develop a pattern of play, but although there is a common thread they're all encouraged to do it their way, so that the flair comes through. We don't want to have the national coach saying 'Everyone does it this way, or that way.' You've got to give people the opportunity to develop their own style. Otherwise you'd have a system where people wouldn't be able to use their own creative talent on the field. If you want people to react in particular ways then you've got to give them the ability to be able to do it.

In the organization as a whole, everyone has their own 'Rick' story. Veronica Newman, whose board jurisdiction includes finance, spent her first two years in the position of being constantly challenged with requests from the national coach. According to Newman some of these experiences were 'intense' to say the least, yet she credits Charlesworth with developing a financially sustainable elite structure around the team, with excellent administration, assistant coaches and support activities which, crucially, include a stress psychologist. She is also mindful of the way in which his proposal to use 'Direct Athlete Support' money, 'enticed the players to go to Perth to prepare months ahead, as full-time athletes for the 1996 Atlanta Olympics'; Newman praises the results: 'I don't think that I've ever seen a hockey team so well-prepared for a competition, both mentally and physically. It would have to be one of the best teams that I have ever seen. In the end we put it down to the creativity of the coach.'

Charlesworth sought out Newman after the gold-medal-winning game in Atlanta, to thank her for her work. This was seen as something 'quite special'. In similar vein, the unexpected photograph of the Olympic team on the dais in Atlanta, signed with thanks and sent by Charlesworth, to Tracey Edmundson, Media Manager, 'keeps the dream alive' for her. Jenny Morris remembers well a game in England where she got 'whacked in the face' with a stick. She endured blood, injections and stitches, and 'Rick helped me get through the pain, without allowing me to wallow in self-pity.' The stories of respect and admiration go on and on. Charlesworth is unquestionably a mighty inspirational player who stands at the centre of WHA's current sustained period of peak performance. Pam Tye: 'He's such a perfectionist. He's a very questioning person, whereas perhaps other coaches are not, or not to the same degree. We want him to continue challenging us. I like that.'

Indeed, in order to keep the Hockeyroos at the pinnacle of performance Charlesworth generates a constant stream of organizational challenges from Perth, which are processed by the board and the Sydney national office.

Despite fielding competitive teams for many years, in the past the amateur nature of the game precluded the development of a truly elite squad. Moreover, with the game firmly anchored in Europe, both cost and absence of opportunity served to undermine active consideration of an aggressive programme of international competition. Beating England on their home turf, in 1959, was the catalyst which first prompted a growing passion and intensity for top-flight success. Organizationally the WHA was less than prepared for an expansion of its role. Shirley Davies, a former player for Australia and current board member, recalls vividly that back in the seventies, at her first council meeting some two days were spent dealing with matters arising from correspondence, but there was a growing thirst for more. Although creating the future took time, the WHA had inspirational players prepared to chart the necessary course. Shirley Davies:

Within the Association there was a growing number of teachers and lecturers who brought administrative skills from their own careers into our board structure. More important was the ability to look at the sport and know what we had to do to change. By the early eighties we had an excellent group of people with a deep feeling for the sport who were committed to advancing the cause of women and Australian hockey. Over about a decade, we went from a completely amateur group to a professional entity. The big vision was to see women's hockey established as a very well managed business that could achieve success at a national and international level.

A further catalyst was the disappointment of not being able to attend the boycotted Moscow Olympics in 1980. This fuelled a desire to be competitive in Los Angeles in 1984. Participation in the Olympic tournament enabled women's hockey to access funds and elite programmes developed in conjunction with the Australian Institute of Sport (AIS), which was established in Perth at the Bentley Stadium at that time. Key administrators were acutely aware of the opportunities that had been created by the Australian government's commitment to sport, channelled through the Australian Sports Commission. As Shirley Davies explains, 'You get recognition by being the best in the world,' something which now appeared to be within grasp, but this dream could not be achieved without clear planning.

Meg Wilson, who took over the presidency of the WHA in 1986, was the key inspirational player during this period. A member of the Australian team during her own playing days, her presidency lasted a decade, coinciding, not by chance, with Australia's rise to dominance in world hockey. On the field of play, the Australian penchant for attacking flair in the face of the dour defences of the European teams had already shown fruit with a fourth place in the 1984 Los Angeles Olympics. National Coach Brian Glencross was starting to manufacture a winning formula, and Wilson's organizational agenda straddled both the elite squad and the grass-roots programmes located within the states. 'You've got to have a strong base so that many players get their basic skills right, from minky to junior and even social levels of play. From this base, talented players can be developed and fed into the elite system.'

Developing the game during the eighties was as much an organizational issue as it was one for the coaches charged with the responsibility of lifting the game on the field. Meg Wilson knew what was needed and, more importantly, what had to be done to make it happen. Of measured character, she is a reflective thinker who prevails through relentless determination, born out of a combination of passion and astute analytical ability, together with an uncanny knack for being able to coax others into doing things for which they would not normally consider themselves eligible. We were immediately made aware of Wilson's penchant for influencing events when she 'suggested' that rather than use the convivial Bentley Stadium offices under the stand, for her discussion with us, she would prefer to use one of the external observation booths, where she could keep track of the fiercely contested hockey game below.

Exposure to international competition, according to Wilson, is the key to maintaining an elite squad that can compete on an ongoing basis. With limited funds available to travel overseas, the women's game needed to develop a strong profile which would make Australia an attractive place for other teams to tour. As a past player and Australian selector, Wilson was well placed to develop a network of international contacts which were 'activated' the moment she was elected president of the WHA. Soon after her domestic elevation she became the first Australian woman ever to represent her country on the Federation of International Hockey (FIH). Wilson then set about getting Australian officials placed on FIH committees:

I was the logical person to use the power of the FIH. That involved getting Australian women on to the development committees, umpiring committees, and on the jury for appeal, as well as getting an Australian umpire appointed at the Olympic Games. I also got an Australian person on to the technical bench – where the power resides. So Australian women were being recognized all the time. Once you've done all this, you can plan for your next bid.

Wilson's agenda was to bid for, and successfully host, the 1990 World Cup in Sydney. For this she needed money and an administrator with the consummate skills necessary to pull off such a major event. It was a bold initiative, but not out of place, as by the late eighties the Australian team was beginning to challenge the Dutch for world supremacy.

Against the expectations of many, the Hockeyroos won Olympic gold medal at the 1988 games in Seoul. The dream was well under way and, fortuitously, an opportunity to share it was about to present itself. Watching the magic-making gold medal celebrations in the Olympic stadium was an executive from the Telstra Corporation, who immediately saw the potential of a long-term association with a winning hockey team. Meg Wilson was not about to let slip a chance to share the dream with a major sponsor who would be able to provide funds for long-term development, which would in turn enable the WHA to bid successfully for major international tournaments. Using an uncharacteristically forceful voice, Wilson sought to impress upon us the significance of the Telstra initiative:

In the end, when you get to a final, it's national success gets you a sponsor, and there's no doubt that success breeds success. You have to seize that success and make the best of it. Seize it. Go with it, or you will have lost the chance, you'll lose the momentum. That's what it's all about.

The momentum created by the gold medal, and the extra cash injections, came to a head when the FIH duly awarded Australia, and Sydney, the 1990 World Cup. The WHA then needed to demonstrate that they could be 'very good at managing'. A well-run World Cup would pave the way for teams to visit Australia on a more regular basis. This was a central feature of Wilson's determination to build a lasting dynasty.

Since the early eighties, the infrastructure of the WHA had grown alongside the programmes and operations associated with AIS in Perth. As new council members from each of the states are elected onto the federal body, Wilson ensured that each was given extensive responsibilities and portfolios. One of the emerging council members was Pam Tye, from Sydney. As early at 1986, Tye had put together a budget for hosting an international tournament. This kind of initiative ignited Wilson's belief in seeking out and mentoring women who had the passion and drive to elevate the profile of the WHA. Her long-term development of inspirational players as an essential element in creating the future is heavily underscored by Pam Tye's career path. Her personal growth and development as an outstanding administrator were clearly not accidental – her organizational exposure was meticulously planned. Within a very short time of her initial election to council, she was given enormous responsibility in the form of running the 1990 World Cup, which in turn gave her the necessary skills and profile to become a member of the board of directors, and finally to be elected as president of the WHA in 1996. The final piece in the jigsaw was securing her position in FIH upon Wilson's departure. Meg Wilson:

We went through a deliberate process. In the business of getting our people known, we deliberately made Pam the chairperson of the organizing committee. You don't get people into top positions in a federation in international hockey unless they already have some kind of profile. As a result of running the

World Cup, Pam was well known, and when I wanted her to replace me on the FIH Board, I was able to do it because the ground had been prepared already. You absolutely must ensure that you are well recognized in areas such as federations, international sports commissions and the Australian Olympic Committee. You establish the kudos of the people in your organization so that your association can progress.

Pam Tye who readily recognizes Wilson's key role in driving the organization forwards over the year:

Meg, in her leadership style, targets key people within the community she feels can assist in driving where she is perhaps incapable of doing it. She will focus on people and get their support – she has done that consistently over the years. In fact, I wouldn't be on the international scene if Meg hadn't had the foresight to realize that she would have to have a woman come through the ranks to replace her. In her development of people in the right places within the managerial structures of WHA she has made an enormous contribution. And I don't think many people realize how strong and clear thinking she was for the future.

The growth of the WHA necessitated a more formal review of its structures. The Bradley report, written in early 1991, reflected the expansion of the sport and the growing need to address the developmental side of women's hockey at state level, while ensuring that the elite programme could deliver a world-beating national side. Rather than rely on infrequent general council meetings and a small cadre of executive officers to run the WHA, Bradley devised a five-member board of directors and president, nominated and elected by the states. The board is ultimately answerable to the council of sixteen state representatives. Several policy and operational committees were also established, with each of the board members allocated responsibility for their overall management. On the policy side, portfolios were created in development, international, marketing and promotions, finance, coaching and umpiring. Operational committees were established for selection, umpiring, indoor hockey, technical and coaching.

At the start of the eighties the WHA was an amateur body

staffed almost entirely by volunteers. By the end of the decade the transformation to a thoroughly peak performing professional association was almost complete. Pam Tye saw the last vestiges of the old regime before Meg Wilson began moving the organization forward in the mid-eighties, and by the nineties she was at the centre of activity designed to extend the supremacy of Australian women's field hockey on the world stage. As a school principal, authority comes easily to Tye. She is never lost for a controversial word or three, and positively delights in 'close-to-the-bone' remarks that will guarantee her close attention. Typically not pulling any punches, Tye tells how it used to be and what she wants to see now:

> In the early days it was a very amateurish organization, with the national body not as strong and developed as it is now, and the relationship with the states was not very well defined. Although I see my role as president is to provide an opportunity for the continued development of our elite players, the development of the game at the grass-roots level is equally important. We need a very strong, broad base from which we can operate, and I believe we are not doing our job if we fail to consider the development of younger players through to elite players. Our core business is our players.

From a public-relations point of view, Tye, with tongue in cheek, argues that, 'If we are not seen in the media and on television as successful, then they are all going to play netball and we can't have that.' The constant balancing act between development of the game at state level the need to drive the achievements of the elite programme and the Hockeyroos, calls for a double focus. This is Tye's greatest challenge:

> I don't want to 'lose' representatives from the states because, from our perspective, we must always consider what's happening at this important level. We must provide them with the resources and the information that they require, but we've also got to develop a greater understanding within our states of what the national body is doing, its relationship with international people and the importance of elite success, particularly with the Sydney Olympics in 2000.

Overall Tye believes that 'after "Bradley" we have developed further and become a lot stronger'. Confirmation of this comes from Rechelle Hawkes:

My observation of the organization is that there is constant development in their professionalism. They are all passionate about hockey and they love the game and always try to do their very best to promote hockey. I have seen improvement in the last three or four years which I hadn't noticed before. It is important that they all have a real passion for the game. The administrative push for hockey to be at the top, together with the developments in the junior game all speak highly for WHA.

Unquestionably, by the time of the 1996 Olympics in Atlanta, a combination of sponsorship money, greater exposure and experience in tournament logistics, and the continued professionalism of the elite programmes was clearly evident in the superior support systems and preparation of the national team. Planning and attention to the last detail set the Australian team apart from their international competitors. Hawkes's reference to the concept of 'improvement' carries with it a subtle nuance that is extremely perceptive. The WHA, without question, is the most self-critical organization in this study. Members of WHA rarely express satisfaction with current performance. Invariably, descriptions of processes, procedures or activities are couched in terms of how the next iteration will improve on current, sub-optimum results. The push to exceed personal best is utterly relentless.

Seeking to better one's own performance frequently leads to game-breaking ideas. Pam Tye, ever mindful of the continued strength of the European Federation, which is reflected in the prestigious and hard-fought European Cup competition, feels that the WHA is now strong enough to widen its field of influence by establishing an Asia-wide competition that would include teams from New Zealand, Korea and China. Sharing the dream of women's hockey encompasses building and developing the game elsewhere.

## CONCLUSION

The national team is based in Perth. The national office is located in Sydney. The state associations are voluntary. In a moderate sized corporation the revenue streams would barely pass for expenses. The sporting culture in Australia is, for the most part, male dominated. In most circumstances, these would not be attractive odds to pick a winner. But it has happened. The Hockeyroos have sustained peak performance for more than a decade, displacing along the way the powerhouse sides from the European Federation.

Key inspirational players such as Shirley Davies and Meg Wilson initially began to lay the foundations for international success. This is an organisation that has targeted and developed its people like no other we have seen. Opportunities have been carefully maximized by finding those talents who are willing and able to maintain the momentum for success. In a very deliberate fashion, those with a flair for administration have been plucked from the state associations, given resources, charged with responsibilities and then promoted to positions of authority – Pam Tye is the most obvious example of this process. Shirley Davies moved from player to council, to the board, to handling the critical portfolio of the elite programme. Almost every senior administrator in the organization has been 'pulled' through on a calculated line of career progression. The organization creates its future by putting its people at the right time in the right place. This system of mentoring has enabled the WHA to sustain peak performance.

It is no surprise then, that the organization boasts a continual influx of inspirational players, none of whom put themselves above the dream. The tension and balance between elite success and grass-roots development continues to be handled astutely by all those who face the dilemma daily. Some personnel have two decades of tenure, but this continuity has not served to slow down the rate of change. Administrators and players alike constantly strive for improvement, better ways to do things and game-breaking ideas that others simply cannot match. In this, Coach Richard Charlesworth occupies a special place next to greatness.

There is, however, one development on the horizon which will sorely test the ability of the WHA to maintain its pre-eminence.

From 2001, women's hockey will be merged with its male counter-part, to become Hockey Australia. Pressure from FIH affiliates and the Australian government have combined to alter the field of play irrevocably. Typically, almost all senior administrators in the organization support the move, arguing that they will be able to maintain the focus which the WHA has unswervingly served. Pam Tye:

We have the ability to open our eyes and look down the track, to ensure the provision of opportunities for women to have highly successful careers in sport, to experience the exhilaration of an organization that is well run. Amalgamation will not alter the dream. It will add to it. What more can I say?

## CHAPTER • 7

# The Chicago Bulls – A Bulls' Market

*I have been blessed to have been a part of, and to have witnessed at close range, the Michael Jordan era, the wonderful players who surrounded him and all the championships that we have accomplished together as a team. I've been more blessed than any professional deserves, and the scary thing is that, when you're as blessed as this, you face the challenge of the future. There never has been, and may never be, a sports team that has faced this kind of challenge – who will have to fill such a void – like the Chicago Bulls will have to, when Jordan retires. We will never see the likes of him again.* – Stephen Schanwald Vice-President, Marketing & Broadcasting

It is a regular season game day, and the Minnesota Timberwolves are in town. In the early afternoon the cavernous $200-million-dollar United Center, the custom-built facility operated by the Chicago Bulls and the National Hockey League team, the Chicago Blackhawks, since the 1994–5 season, is empty and silent. In preparation for the evening's event, the seemingly unnatural tranquillity is occasionally punctuated by the clatter of workers erecting court-side tables, TV equipment and the like. Outside, game day or not, hundreds of fans throng excitedly around the Michael Jordan sculpture that 'guards' the entrance to the building, photographing their hero in majestic flight to the basket. It is an evocative image, frozen in time, preserving the legend.

An hour before tip-off and the United Center, aided and abetted by 22,000 partisan Bulls fans, has undergone a dramatic transformation. Cacophonous sound from the relentless pre-game entertainment show echoes around the concourse areas, magnetically drawing remaining spectators to their seats. Sensory overload and hyped anticipation distinguish those inside from the world outside. These are precious moments for all those who have been fortunate enough to share in the remarkable Jordan era that is soon to draw to a close.

Deep below; the Press room, thronging with 200 of the world's newspaper, radio and TV personnel, is buzzing with talk of the impending game, deadlines and the scoop that will grab tomorrow's sporting headlines around the globe. Further down the corridor is the Bulls' locker room. It is modest in size, but adjacent to it lie the generously expansive lounge and weight room where the team spends much of its pre-game preparation time. In contrast to the frenzied, court-side celebrations above, the Bulls' locker room remains insulated and unruffled. Luc Longley, the giant Australian import, stands awkwardly next to his locker, ruminating about an injury that has kept him out of the game, leaving him wearing, unlike the rest of the team, a three-piece suit:

My diagnosis is that I have a bruise on the head of my femur and other various bone bruise injuries, which have come and gone, and come again. Bone bruises can take a while to heal. I was told to treat them like a fracture and there is nothing you can do about it. I was probably a bit ambitious coming back – I felt pretty good, but then the next day it was a bit sore, so we are going to take as much time as we need to get it right. Hopefully that won't be very long. We will have to see how it goes, but I suspect I will be playing in the play-offs.

He is clearly unhappy with the situation he finds himself in. Tony Kukoc and Bill Wennington, after a brief pre-game workout on court, sit quietly in one corner of the locker room discussing the upcoming game. Dennis Rodman, the last to arrive, is greeted with smiles. Nothing is said. Prior to the last-minute team talk, and as game time approaches, Coach Phil Jackson, looking deep in thought, strides purposefully in and out of the locker room.

Perhaps thinking about his upcoming retirement, another Bulls player takes time out to reflect on what it took to create the Bulls dynasty. Michael Jordan:

I think we have been very fortunate. We've been together a little bit longer than some of the other teams. We know how to go out and deal with the situation. The team knows how to compensate, you miss key players and other players step forward. This has enabled us to survive without key players, and hopefully we can continue to do that for as long as we need to. I think that's part of being a championship team. I am very happy with the way we have achieved things.

And so it was to be on this night. Jordan drained 41 points as part of a 107–93 victory over the Timberwolves, leading the team to yet another play-off berth and, inexorably, towards a sixth championship ring. Despite the turmoil created by his impending retirement, in the locker room after the game, a sharp-suited Michael Jordan was at ease with himself. We were anxious to ask him about his personal philosophy towards the game of basketball. Our assumption was that his considerable influence, and his attitude, might transfer across to the organization itself. Earlier in our research, the great New Zealand rugby All Black Jonah Lomu, told us that he hated coming second best to himself. This concept of exceeding personal best appealed to us. Indeed, we found it in all the organizations we studied. So, one of the key questions we posed to Jordan was whether he hated coming second best to himself. His initial reaction was one of surprise – this was one question he had not been asked before in an endless round of pedestrian interviews. After raising his eyebrows, inducing a rare furrowed brow, he recovered quickly and shot back: 'I don't mind coming second best to myself – at least I have got the first two spots wrapped up!' We got the message! Truly great inspirational players have no peers. For Jordan, a performance second best to himself is of sufficiently high calibre to be ahead of all the rest. That has been the story of the Bulls throughout the nineties.

## RUNNING OF THE BULLS

The Chicago Bulls have every reason to feel smug about their organization, yet little or nothing is taken for granted. Like the game itself, the physical structure of the organization is supremely orchestrated. The Bulls' offices are a short elevator ride away from the ground-floor entrance to the United Center complex, and the obligatory security desk which screens workers and visitors alike.

The reception area bristles with basketball lore. A row of refurbished, wooden-slated bleachers from the old stadium, in addition to being a place to sit and wait, offers an evocative link to the past. On the walls action-laden photographs, enlarged, mounted Press cuttings announcing victories, hoops, nets, signed basketballs and singlets all celebrate the dizzy heights of the Bulls' history. In this space, it is simply not possible to keep one's eyes steady. In an adjacent corridor hangs the now famous shot of Dennis Rodman, hurling himself in horizontal flight as he attempts to retrieve a basketball which appears hopelessly destined for the court-side seats. Most intriguing of all is the floor. Wooden boards replete with court markings encourage fanciful thoughts that could not be sustained elsewhere. While sitting on the bright-red bleachers, it seems entirely possible that a Jordan or a Pippen might emerge from around the next corner, expertly dribbling the ball past the reception desk. Just maybe.

Past the reception area, the front office has all the relentless intensity of a full-court press, in a closely contested play-off game. Despite the obvious pressure of game day, smiles come easily here, reflecting a close-knit community that is fun-loving, respectful and professional. Building a team as successful as the Chicago Bulls requires more than pure basketball skills. Irwin Mandel, Vice-President of Financial and Legal, and salary cap co-ordinator, credits owner Jerry Reinsdorf, General Manager Jerry Krause and Coach Phil Jackson for their respective abilities to utilize the draft and salary cap to the best advantage. Mandel argues that long-standing relationships between these three organizational players have ensured that drafting and trading has taken place with a long-term view in mind, and that they have not tried to invade the technical parameters of each other's expertise. 'Loyalty, sincerity and trust', according to Mandel, ensure that the owner does not second guess the player choices and trading decisions of the general manager, who in turn will respect the tactically imperative requirements of the coach. Mandel is the final deal-maker:

> I try to understand the salary-cap rules as best I can. I work very closely with the general manager. We are always trying to think ahead: how much salary cap room do we have now; how much are we going to have in the future – what is the right thing to do salary-cap-wise? The general manager will always

talk to me if he wants to make a player move. I have been with
the Bulls for twenty-five years, and never once has the Bulls'
general manager, said to me, 'Is this a good move basketball-
wise, is this player better than that player?' I have never been
asked that in twenty-five years, nor should I be. The owner
shouldn't decide that and neither should the vice-president
financial and legal. That is not my job, but he will always say
to me, Irwin, how can we do this salary-cap-wise, does this
make sense?

What did make sense was perhaps the most important draft pick
in the history of pro-sports. It is well known that, in the 1984
draft, Jordan was passed over by Portland who, with the second
pick, wanted a centre rather than a guard. Chicago duly moved
up from their third-pick position and Michael Jordan became a
Bull. Some elements of luck can be observed there, but the critical
philosophy of long-term development began with an ownership
change the year following the drafting of Michael Jordan. Additionally, Mandel stresses that Jerry Krause employed a strategic
approach to picking complementary players from the draft, whereas
other NBA organizations saw their activity merely in tactical
terms. By moving up in the draft, Mandel argues, Krause was able
to obtain key players such as Scottie Pippen and Charles Oakley:

> The public and the Press like to know what the Bulls are doing.
> But Jerry Krause doesn't inform the public or the Press about
> his plans. He cares about getting the best team, and he won't
> tell you anything, on the record or off the record – even if you
> swear to him that you'll tell nobody, he still won't tell you what
> his plans are. His reason is that if he had let it out that he
> wanted Scottie Pippen, and that he was trying to move up to
> number five in the draft, then another team that wanted Scottie
> Pippen might move up to number four, so Jerry Krause played
> that very secretively. Nobody knew he wanted Pippen, and right
> before the draft he moved from eight to five to get Scottie
> Pippen. He was very aggressive and he made it happen. It boils
> down to this. Who do we love? We will do everything in our
> power to get the guy that we love. You make it happen. You
> do everything in your power and that's what the Bulls did to
> get Scottie Pippen.

Mandel also credits Bulls owner and Chairman Jerry Reinsdorf, who took over the Bulls franchise in 1985, for establishing a streamlined organizational structure which allows for quick and responsive decisive making. Directly under Reinsdorf are three vice-presidents, Jerry Krause for basketball operations, Steve Schanwald for marketing and broadcasting, while Irwin Mandel takes care of financial and legal issues. There are seven departmental heads who are responsible for thirty-two front-office staff, and an additional twenty or so assistant coaches, trainers, medical staff and media announcers. Together with the on-court players, the organization gets by with less than seventy people. Irwin Mandel:

> The Bulls in my opinion are set up very, very well. I really like the way we are organized. Jerry Reinsdorf gives his three vice-presidents a great deal of leeway, a great deal of independence, responsibility and jurisdiction. I cringe when I see an organization that has too many layers. One of the brilliant things about Jerry Reinsdorf is that if I need any answer I can go to him direct. There are no layers in between, we can make our case directly to Jerry. We don't have to go to a president, a vice-chairman and then a chairman, which causes things to get lost in translation. Since Jerry is a decisive person, we get to make our case directly and quickly. There have been some teams in the NBA that have had many owners and those owners have appointed executive committees which decide things. To me that is not good. In my opinion it is much better if you have got one guy who gives the final ok, and he gives it to people who he has a lot of confidence in. A structure like this gives you a much better chance of success.

Keith Brown, Senior Director of Sales, underscores the speed of decision making in the organization, noting that formal channels are less important than the cogency and leverage of a good idea:

> A service rep, a sales rep or an intern might come up with an idea for a way in which we can improve our game entertainment, or a way to be more efficient in a particular area, and we will do it. Unlike a lot of organizations that I have observed, from idea to implementation can take literally minutes. We don't have to go through an arduous or cumbersome chain of command.

If there is something that I think will make my department
or any area of the Bulls more efficient, I can go to my vice-
president, and we can debate the pros and cons, and if we like
the idea the decision is made right there, it's done. Even if it's
a decision that involves a substantial investment. If we like an
idea we can pick up the phone and call our owner, Jerry
Reinsdorf, who is extremely accessible, and Jerry will give you
a 'Yes, go ahead it's a great idea,' or 'No it's not,' and things
get done very quickly and very easily. There isn't a lot of red
tape or paperwork. Our management structure is well defined
and pretty streamlined.

Another critical aspect of the organization is the continuity of its
staff, in particular the senior executives, most of whom joined the
Bulls either before, or at the start of, the winning era. Keith Brown
shoulders the burden of receiving and sifting through the thousands of job applications that arrive at the Bulls' front office every
year. Although not impossible, tenure with the most famous franchise in sports history is a tough nut to crack. Apart from a small
number of positions where specific skills are required, only interns
are hired – college graduates who, if lucky, might be considered
for one of the few full-time positions that may become vacant or
be newly created. The business is currently built around a cadre
of well-established people who collectively set the entry criteria
for those lucky enough to be considered as employment prospects.
Keith Brown:

We came in at entry level and have grown with the organization.
That experience and consistency certainly contributes a tremendous amount to the business success that we enjoy. Now, when
we hire, we look for good people of good character, people
who are happy and are fun to be with. They will be intelligent,
hard-working, enthusiastic, and willing to learn the business
from the bottom up. They have to be good solid citizens with
a strong sense of humour and a great work ethic. Those intan-
gibles are every bit, if not more important, than job skills. Chemistry too, has an awful lot to do with success of this community.

Mandel notes that the stability of the staff is vital to the Bulls'
success. Sitting in his office, where some of the largest and most

talked about player contracts in the history of professional sports have been put together, he animatedly drives home the point:

> This is an important thing that I'm going to say. Most of our people have been here for twenty or twenty-five years. Our ticket manager has been here about twenty years. Our PR director has been here about eighteen years. I've been here twenty-five, our controller has been here thirteen years. Our marketing vice-president has been here thirteen years and our sales director has been here about thirteen years. These are experienced people. Every person is a damn hard worker, has a great attitude, is capable, and working to the very best of their ability. If you ask other people in NBA, I think they would say that this is one of the best-run front offices in the league.

Steve Schanwald is unequivocal about the value of the Bulls' staff and, in particular, how the future of the organization rests squarely on personal development:

> Our philosophy has always been to promote from within. People know that they have a chance to grow within the organization. Growth is very hard, it's one of my biggest challenges as a manager because we have a small staff and the turnover is very low, with a lot of competition for jobs. I always tell people that my goal is to help you grow internally but if I can't help you grow internally my commitment to you, in exchange for your commitment to me, is to help you grow externally. I have no aversion to, and in fact take great pride in, seeing somebody go on to bigger and better things outside the organization.

The flow of activity in the front office benefits substantially from the continuity of employees. Traditional forms of managing collapse when established staff and new entrants have the necessary commensurate skills, and can routinely access the inventory of accumulated organizational knowledge. For Schanwald, it is not a matter of leading or delegating. Using a familiar on-court sporting metaphor, he argues for personal responsibility:

> With good people you let them do their jobs. Give them an overall philosophy. Then you give them the ball and you let

them run with it. That's the only way it can work. I don't have the time to be looking over people's shoulders. We've hired our people, we've agreed where we want the organization to go and how we're going to get there. And now, everybody just runs with the ball.

Co-ordination of administration and game-day preparations in the United Center are the most tangible examples of what Schanwald is referring to. Tim Hallam, Senior Director of Media Services, and a twenty-year-plus veteran of the Bulls, has seen the bad and the good times, and is uniquely positioned to witness how the place truly operates. Hallam, more than anyone else, has been the conduit through which the world has gained access to Michael Jordan. He is not one to stand on ceremony, and has a gifted comedic reaction to anyone who tried to grandstand or bluff their way through to the Bulls locker room. The public, pressure-cooker atmosphere he has inhabited for the last decade or more has forced Hallam to ring-fence his internal operations to ensure maximum focus on getting the job done. In this, the organization is a source of strength:

> There's a lot of trust in allowing you to do your job, so from that standpoint, from an ownership or management style it's very conducive to building the right frame of mind. You can see how it operates – the people here who are laughing and walking around smiling all the time, are also doing a hell of a lot of work. It has to do with the atmosphere here. People are friendly. Probably ninety per cent of the people in this building are here because they enjoy sports of some form or another and wanted to get into sports marketing and public relations.

This work-place environment enables the Bulls to pull together, as a team, without formal governance or explicitly identified roles. Organizational processes are transparent and transferable between people. This state of peak flow is critical to understanding how the Bulls sustain peak performance. For Hallam, the thrill of working with the Bulls is the way in which the community comes together, separates and coalesces again:

You can illustrate this by looking at the night of a game. For example, you have media services and you're worrying about the players, the locker room, the interviews, the brochures and the game itself. You also have marketing, you're worried about the handouts, the music and the promotions. You have another group of people helping out with the giveaways, you have the ticket manager and his people worrying about all the departments that may come up with lost tickets or what have you. Everybody is out of formation, in their own formation. But we're really *in* formation. They may not be *visible* formations but we're still following the same goal. We've all got our little different formations doing spins and loops, getting the job done. It's like a school of fish at times. We are in formation but at times it seems as if there is no formation – which is the beauty of it. And when needed, at the snap of a finger, we can all go back in the formation, which is fantastic. I think that's probably the key to this whole place.

This type of transparent activity produces an atmosphere conducive to creativity, which the organization also sought to encourage by establishing the position of manager of creative services, a role currently filled by Jim Hopkins. Unlike many other sports organizations, who farm out all promotional materials to external agencies, the Bulls do all their brand imaging in-house. Hopkins is responsible for game programmes, season guides, flyers, brochures, invitations, posters and giveaway promotions, as well as submitting designs for championship rings. In short, Hopkins, working very closely with Steve Schanwald, manages anything that gets across the image and messages associated with the Bulls. He argues forcefully that internal control leads to greater spontaneity and, of course, creativity, to the point where ideas can be changed on a daily basis. Game-breaking ideas are the result:

This is a young, dynamic and forward-thinking organisation. Everyone is open to new ideas and, more importantly, is supportive and ready and willing to share ideas with one another. As a grass-roots organization, we don't lose control of our message, which might well be diluted or changed by going to an outside agency.

As a relative newcomer to the Bulls, Hopkins wryly shared with us the following telling observation that every reader can surely identify with:

> It's a lot easier to get out of bed in the morning, you know, when you're going to work for the Chicago Bulls, than it would be if I had to go work at the post office. I mean, I could sort the mail here, and it would be a lot more fun because I'm doing it for the Bulls. That helps a lot I think in making everyone a little bit more excited and maybe work a little bit harder.

The veterans translate this in a slightly different way. They argue that trust and the ability to rely on each other without the pretence of formal regulation or performance management review at every twist and turn is at the heart of the 'running of the Bulls'. Perhaps surprisingly, Tim Hallam believes that it 'probably has nothing to do with winning', and that it is more likely that this community has been forged at a much deeper level of commitment. In reflecting on life with the Chicago Bulls, Hallam offers both an explanation for peak performance and a powerful charter for personal conduct:

> I walk into work every day. It's friendly, it's informal, yet respectful. You respect people's questions and jobs that they have. You're genuinely curious about their life, their family and their children, as well as what's going on with the Bulls.
>
> I've been here long enough to see Irwin's kids go from three years old to college. We've seen people struggle through deaths, personal problems, divorces and at the same time we've all laughed ourselves silly. We've enjoyed ourselves and we've frequently worked ourselves to exhaustion. We've all had crises in our own areas that we've got hammered on and pulled out of. We've enjoyed the top of the mountain, and some of us have started at the very bottom. We've seen growth in every aspect of the organization and ourselves.

Sara Salzman, Director of Community Services, who is in her eleventh year with the Bulls, shares similar sentiments. She observes that strong loyalty, pride and tradition enable everyone to feel part of the organization. 'We feel like we belong,' is her simple yet profound statement. Such feelings of community are amply fuelled by the championship rings which are presented to all those employed in the organization. This is made all the more meaningful by the fact that the entire cast of the Bulls, along with spouses, is flown by chartered plane to away games in the championship finals. The organization pays for five-star accommodation, meals, tickets and transportation. Marketing retreats are also held where work is interspersed with play. Salzman believes that these and other special functions help to build a genuine camaraderie which bonds people together. More importantly, she argues that these community-based 'getting-to-know-each-other' activities encourage peak-performing qualities: 'We have very high goals and drive for excellence in ourselves and others. I don't think there are any real weak links in this organization. In this community there is a lot of grit and a lot of drive and determination.'

Despite the self-imposed pressure, the tight deadlines and the expectations of constant first-class results, the ambience of the organization remains decidedly informal, creating what one director told us was 'a chance to grow and a chance to learn'. Even on game day, as we witnessed, there is a complete absence of formal meetings. In a very relaxed way, people talk all the time, sharing key information, and enjoying each other's friendship while getting the job done. With significant intrinsic fringe benefits and generous levels of pay, coercive comparisons between people, which can serve to undermine organizational community, are largely absent. Until Jerry Reinsdorf took ownership of the Chicago Bulls, the franchise had never made a profit. Since that time, a profit has been realized each year and staff now receive a ten per cent bonus on gross salary, plus US $1,000 cash. Keith Brown:

> One of the best things about our offices is that everyone is good fun, you can say anything to anyone. There is an awful lot of joking and teasing. Everyone is comfortable and on a first name basis. It is not an environment where you are looking over your shoulder, thinking that big brother is watching you. It is a very casual atmosphere. People who are happy work harder and better. Our owners pay very well, including bonuses and good benefits. We are paid fairly, and treated well. Other teams like to keep salaries down, but they end up losing good people.

# BRANDING THE BULLS

The Jordan era has seen a corporate marketing strategy put in place which assiduously builds the brand of the Bulls. There is no question that the 1984 drafting of the most gifted athlete to grace a basketball court provided a strong product to sell, but Irwin Mandel argues that a job still had to be done, and that the presence of Jordan did not by itself guarantee a meal-ticket for the rest of the business. He credits Jerry Reinsdorf, in the first instance, for being very marketing-conscious. At Reinsdorf's insistence, and in order to maximize potential revenue, the marketing department quintupled in size. Irwin Mandel:

> I give Steve Schanwald a lot of credit – Steve is a brilliant marketer. So, at the same time that the team was improving, so was our marketing. In spite of how great our team is, I really respect Steve Schanwald, who gets the maximum dollars that there are to be gotten. If we had a less capable marketing department we would still make money and we would still do well but we would not do *as* well. What his department does, is maximize revenues. They do that beautifully – my guess is that there are very few teams in sports that have as capable a marketing department as do the Bulls.

Steve Schanwald joined the Bulls in 1987 when season tickets sold numbered less than 5,000, yet that year they began their several-hundred home-stand sell-out streak, still alive at the conclusion of the 1998–1999 season, and slated to continue for several more. Whatever the popular image people around the world have of the Bulls, Schanwald is probably responsible for it. The branding of the Bulls in the Schanwald years is probably one of the most successful marketing operations in modern times. Building a successful sports team is one thing, but sustaining it requires encouraging long-term customer habits that roll into revenue streams which can then be deployed in the interest of team development. Steve Schanwald has made this possible. The office he works from positively drips with an astonishing array of Bulls memorabilia, taken from the championship-winning years. It is also appointed with personalized mementoes from sporting icons across the world. Pele, Muhammad Ali, Wayne Gretzky, and, inevitably, Michael Jordan, lead a jaw-dropping gallery of dreams.

Schanwald is an inspirational player who exudes confidence and pride in his organization and its people. Unlike his airiness, Schanwald has to keep both feet firmly planted on terra firma. The pressure associated with the Bulls' territory could easily unhinge the best of professionals, but through all the hoopla of six NBA Championship victories Schanwald has retained a measured sense of purpose. His purpose is simple – to share the dream that *is* the Chicago Bulls. Each year the department sets out its strategic marketing plan for the upcoming year. Following a review of the previous year, discussion turns to the philosophy to be deployed in each area of the marketing product. Schanwald leads his team through the new goals and, step by step, how those goals are going to be achieved. Customer service begins with the administrative equivalent of the Bulls' famed triangle offence – intense marketing strategy to sell over one million seats per season is amplified with the development of long-term corporate partnerships, and finally investment in the local community through the community service function.

Marketing is responsible for ensuring that season tickets are sold to capacity and that current holders continue to patronize the product. Schanwald's vision is clear:

> We tell all of our staff that everybody has to contribute in an active or passive way to a successful sale of season tickets. I want that to be the focus. I want people to understand that being able to market season tickets successfully is the lifeblood of any sports organization.

'Steve is ambitious and hardworking – it sets a tone,' Keith Brown observes, 'he always wants to push the envelope, to do more in better ways. This kind of thinking permeates the organization.' As with 'the basketball department', a term used by Steve Schanwald, exceeding personal best in the marketing department is a natural goal. For Brown, 'it boils down to not resting on your laurels'. Game-breaking ideas are constantly thrown into the cauldron to ensure that, whatever the result of the game, the entertainment package wrapped around the total product is the best it can possibly be. Staff visits to Disney and NBA marketing meetings fuel the imagination, added to which, the Bulls' marketing machine is in constant overdrive, supplementing, developing, and raising hybrid ideas. Given that the fans are in the building for over three hours and that the game is only forty-eight minutes long, entertainment becomes critical. The Bulls squeeze every last ounce of magic out of every available second to enthral their customers. A relentless, mesmerizing sustained stream of audience-relevant promotions, audio-visuals and cameo acts accompanies every game. Although the formula is familiar to many North American sports arenas, the Bulls simply do it better. Much better. The aim is to inoculate against the ultimate failure of the core product. Keith Brown:

> Our mission is to maximize the sales potential of the product by attracting people who aren't die-hard basketball fans. Our marketing philosophy is to make winning and losing as moot an issue as it can possibly be in terms of its impact on attendance and fan enjoyment. What you see here can be truly unbelievable. People who are attending a game for the first time can touch the magic. You will see grown men, women and children crying or literally trembling because they are so excited just to be here.

As a direct result of Schanwald's marketing strategy, for well over a decade the Bulls have been able to cap their season-ticket holders at 15,000, with the remaining 4,000 being withheld as 'street seats' and for special corporate and group bookings. Finally there are 3,000 corporate seats in advantageously located suites. The level of sustained interest in season tickets is remarkable, and has been the prime reason for the selling out of the United Center year after year. Even more remarkable is the 25,000-strong waiting list to apply for a season ticket! This enviable state of affairs is not lost on the Bulls' marketing chief:

> We promote that list extensively. We promote our sellout streak, if nothing else to let season ticket holders and others know subliminally that they possess a valuable commodity, and that once the cycle turns down with us, as it inevitably does for all teams, they will want to hang on to that ticket because, as soon as they give it up, there's somebody standing in line waiting for the chance to get it. Once they give it up, it's gone forever. Our

hope is that people will recognize this and that people will give us time to rebuild and that they will therefore hold on to their tickets.

As far as the 'floating seats' go, Schanwald is determined to ensure that he gives people a chance to sample the product. Although all games are extensively televised, he wants to grow new fans who can attend games at the United Centre, 'especially the younger fans, and to create and instil habits in people that will be difficult to break. Sports marketing is about creating habits in people.' Certainly, the television broadcasts are a critical component in opening up the Bulls product to a huge audience. They have helped to produce one of the most staggering statistics we have encountered in this study. In the city of Chicago and the state of Illinois alone, the Chicago Bulls have an active database of over 500,000 fans who have expressed the desire to purchase a ticket to a Bulls game. In preparation for Jordan's retirement, Schanwald is ready to move: 'When seats become available again, as they inevitably will, these are the people that we will market directly to.'

In all of these considerations, Schanwald has resisted the view that the price of a ticket to a Bulls game is infinitely inelastic, and that black-market prices of $1,000 and over, for a place at court-side, suggest that massive revenues can be generated by hiking the costs of seats at the United Center skywards:

> One of my great worries is ticket pricing. As you continue to raise your price the double-edged sword is that you've got more revenue, but at some point you will trigger a reduced fan base. The team owner's philosophy is to strike a balance. My greatest worry, in fact, is the escalation of ticket prices. This should not become an elitist sport.

Rather than drive up ticket prices to create short-term advantage, the Bulls' marketing plan takes a more long-term approach. Creating equity in the product is achieved by building loyalty, in the first instance, among season ticket holders in a very personal way. As a member of the marketing office, Keith Brown is directly responsible for making a season ticket more than just a passport to a basketball game. Like everyone else in the organization, he is driven by long-term considerations, rather than simply the desire to capitalize on current successes. As well as continually and aggressively seeking out new fans, thus adding to the incomparable database, Brown also cultivates and nurtures those who are already in the fold:

> This is unique to sports organizations. We have four full-time service representatives whose sole job is to meet face to face each year with every single Bulls season-ticket holder. They actually go to their place of business or home, knock on the door, walk in and say hello. They let them know that we appreciate their support of the Bulls. They ask if they have any questions or problems that they might be able to help them solve, and let them know that they are available to them should they ever need something from the Bulls. We always hand deliver a gift to them at this time. We also correspond with them regularly, affording them the opportunity to buy tickets to other events. And throughout the year we send them other gifts and promotional items, including a monthly magazine.

Brown is well aware that without the gifts, the magazines and the personalized visits of the service representatives, the Bulls would still easily sell out the United Center game after game. Yet he sees the salaries of the representatives and the costs of the promotions and gifts as investments for the future.

> By cultivating some good will, by letting them know they are appreciated, by giving them something back, by being pro-active by serving them, we are creating what we hope is a good long-term relationship. If we become a team that wins only fifty per cent of its games and the guy is debating whether or not he wants to renew his tickets, and is on the fence, we hope those little things will push him our way.

Creating long-term loyalty is also central to corporate partnerships. Despite the obvious advantages of being able to market one of the most recognized and revered athletes in the history of sport, when dealing with sponsors, the organization has resisted the temptation to focus purely on its most obvious talent. Greg Carney, Director of Corporate Partnerships, knows what his clients initially think about when they are toying with the idea of an association with the Bulls, but he quickly steers them in a different direction. For Carney, sharing the dream with corporate sponsors goes beyond current players:

> We focus so hard on customer service and treating the people who we work with right. When I sit down and talk with clients, the first thing they want to talk about is Michael Jordan, Scottie Pippen and Dennis Rodman. It's hard to get people out of that thinking – what I intend to work hardest on, is our brand, our logo – the Chicago Bulls. If you want to do a promotion, do it with the Bulls' logo, don't do it with Michael, Scottie or with Dennis. The first thing is the logo. We've worked so hard to build equity into it, to make it recognizable. Now, you can take the logo and put it on anything and people know what it is. I can say, 'This is going to be beneficial for us, because the logo is beneficial for you.' That's really the strength and value of what we do. It's that branding. The Bulls' logo is always going to be there and that's what we want people to recognize. At the moment, the Bulls logo uniquely conjures up images of Michael Jordan, and championships. And that's just fine.

As with ticket sales, Carney looks to engage a family of sponsors who will be committed to the Bulls for much longer than the current run of success. The guiding vision is to reap the benefits of the association with Jordan without being completely reliant on a one-dimensional strategy to attract the interest of potential sponsors. Just as the Bulls try to make winning or losing a secondary issue in the purchase of a game ticket, they address corporate partnerships in precisely the same manner.

> We're all realists. We know that one day it's going to come to an end. It's our hope that we've created first-class relationships that are strong, that we've delivered value over the years, and that the benefits to their company will continue until the next great player comes along and plays in Chicago.

At any one time the Bulls maintain somewhere between 200 and 250 corporate partnerships. Each one is important to the Bulls, regardless of the money attached to the relationship, be it a handful of dollars or a US $100,000 promotion. Sponsorship deals are always integrated with basketball, and Carney is adamant that the building will never host a straight advertisement. Each sponsorship promotion is directly linked to the entertainment package experienced by the fans, which in turn increases recognition and association with the Bulls brand. This co-ordination between 'punters and partners' calls for consistency and fit between what the sponsors might like to do, and what is deemed to be appropriate within a pure basketball context. Getting the right theme to a promotion, rather than merely signing big money corporate deals, is a principle that Carney will not break. Nor will the organization attempt to deliver something that is out of its range. Rather, it will over deliver on what it knows is possible.

> Sometimes we've walked away from dollars because potential sponsors have wanted to do something that we've tried before and that we know doesn't work. If it doesn't work for us, then it's not going to be mutually beneficial. Hopefully we have the expertise to come up with something different. That's the fun, creative part of my job.

As with the season ticket holders, the Bulls go to extraordinary lengths to cultivate their corporate partners. Once on board, they can expect a smorgasbord of delight. It starts with receiving, as a matter of course, monthly mailings, in-house magazines and promotional items, and quickly moves to the more substantive area of block bookings for home games. Special clinics are organized where sponsors and their families alone have the opportunity to meet the players and obtain autographs and memories to last a lifetime. Each year a different mix of sponsors is flown out to Los Angeles to an exclusive resort for 'golf, relaxation and good food', while sponsors' birthdays and other anniversary dates will always be remembered with cards and phone calls. If during the season the pre-game entertainment is going to profile a specifically family theme, sponsors with families will be invited. Every last detail is painstakingly taken care of. Throughout all this, Carney knows as intimately as possible the industries that have created a partnership with the Bulls:

> This morning I went from cars, to hot dogs, to credit cards and telecommunications. We have to be creative all the time. I sit

in meetings with eight or nine people throwing out ideas and just think 'Wow!' We are always looking for game-breaking ideas.

Before the marketing department became active, the only promotion the Bulls had to offer was a waste-paper basket, so in the early days it was not difficult to dream up exciting new ideas. In more recent times the Bulls have been able to innovate using themes based on players' personalities. One of Carney's favourite promotions was a cup with a picture of the controversial Dennis Rodman on the side with yellow hair. A cold drink turned his hair red. This gimmick was so effective that McDonald's, despite being one of the most image-conscious companies in the world, hired Rodman to do a series of similar promotions.

Now, Dennis Rodman and McDonald's, I ask you. You'd never think those two would come together. They did commercials with him with different types of hairdos with four different sets of cups. Each week the cup changed to a new colour. It was really fun. This is the magic of being able to bring something different to the table, being able to produce new ideas effectively.

The Rodman cups demonstrate how great ideas create multiple benefits. In this case, the Bulls were able to forge an association with one of the strongest companies in the market place. Carney argues that these game-breaking ideas provide the leverage for revenue generation which 'helps the organization put a quality player on the court'.

The sale of season tickets and development of corporate partnerships are undoubtedly driven by business necessity, although these activities are far from exploitative. If ever a sports franchise had the opportunity to capitalize on the good fortune of obtaining the services of a legendary athlete, the Bulls have been better placed to use that opportunity than any other in history. Corporate citizenship, however, is seen in a much deeper philosophical light. Steve Schanwald:

All our creative promotions and publications are designed to speak to the tradition of the organization, and to reflect well on us as a company that does things in a first class way. We also wish to be good neighbours, and to perform good service in the community. Accordingly, we have a director of community services. It's very important to be active and involved in the community, to give back to the community, to be an organization that cares about more than just its profit, its bottom line, and so we work very hard at giving back to the community.

Sara Salzman, as director of community services, can count on complete support from both Jerry Reinsdorf and Steve Schanwald. Even though she is aware that the perception might be that all she does all day long is 'give things away', Salzman also notes that her eleven-year-old department, one of the oldest in the NBA, is still in the business of sharing the dream, and as such connects directly with the concept of passive revenue generation:

> I hope, passively or otherwise, that everything we do will subliminally stick in people's minds and maybe one day down the road, people will think, 'The Bulls did something good', and I am going to support them. We are grooming young fans, doing nice things in a feel-good type of way.

As with direct ticket sales and corporate partnerships, Salzman is rigorous in applying the highest of standards when it comes to dealing with her constituents. Everyone who comes into contact with the Bulls asking for assistance will receive an answer. And the number of requests is staggering. Two to three hundred written requests and one hundred and fifty phone calls each day, tens of thousands by the year, more at play-off and championship time. Many requests, particularly the thousands that are addressed to Michael Jordan, cannot be met easily, although Salzman's department always tries to compensate with something appropriate. Each year, more than US $800,000 is raised for other charities that receive autographed Chicago Bulls memorabilia.

With demands such as these, the organization had to respond with a formal institutional initiative. The CharitaBulls was established as a separate organization in 1987, to serve as a vehicle to improve the quality of life in the greater Chicago metropolitan area. In 1994 the CharitaBulls donated US $4.5 million to establish the multi-facility James Jordan Boys' & Girls' Club and Family

Life Center. Over one million dollars has been donated to the Chicago Park District Programs to restore 140 damaged city basketball courts. Tens of thousands of dollars are regularly donated to Special Olympics basketball tournaments, computers for local libraries, school programmes and scholarships. Dozens of organizations in the Chicago area benefit from the community services initiatives undertaken by the CharitaBulls. In 1998, the Bulls donated US $3.5 million to Chicago public schools.

Special dinners, raffles, auctions, local three-on-three basketball contests, player appearances and straight corporate sponsorship programmes are some of the many vehicles used to raise both awareness and the money necessary to make a difference. A network of former players, mascots and Bulls announcers ease the demand on current players by making appearances on their behalf. The strong youth and education orientation of the CharitaBulls' work sits well with the over-arching theme that can be found at the heart of the Bulls' sustained sharing of the dream. Sara Salzman believes that, outside of NBA Championships, 'focusing on the community, and doing long-lasting work that will have an impact in perpetuity', is the mission and principle by which the Bulls live. Although charity work is undertaken by most sports franchises these days, we have seen nothing before, during or since, that matches the work of the CharitaBulls.

## CONCLUSION

The Chicago Bulls was our last port of call. In truth from the outside, it initially appeared to be an organization in flux. After five championships rings and a shaky start to the campaign for a sixth, all the talk in the media centred around Jordan's impending retirement, Jackson's desire to move on at the end of the season, and intense contract negotiations with Pippen, Rodman and probably others as well. We were challenged by the common perception that the only way to understand the Bulls' sustained peak performance in the 1990s could be summed up in just two words – Michael Jordan. More troubling still, as media speculation intensified to fever pitch in the spring of 1998, was the prospect of having our 'access denied' at the last minute. This would have been entirely understandable. We also frequently speculated that PPO theory, now well stabilized through all the previous case studies, might be severely tested by an organization in disarray.

Instead, we found in Chicago massive evidence of organization. It is strongest in the very place where, intuitively, we expected it to be weakest. As we celebrate the undoubted magnificence of the greatest athlete of our times, the picture is woefully incomplete without a thorough understanding of the organization behind him. This is an *organization* that wins championships. We did not find panic or a frenetic group of people perched dangerously on the edge of a precipice. Rather, we observed calm, confidence, clarity, and a community with an almost complete disassociation from the wild speculation swirling outside the confines of the United Center.

As all of the inspirational players have lived, learned and grown together, so the organization has been able to maximize fully the business opportunities created by the Jordan era. On the day he was drafted, the Chicago Bulls were already planning how to move the organization beyond his retirement. Accordingly, they have developed their brand image, creating direct, long-lasting relationships with the ticket-buying public, with strategic corporate partners and, finally, with the Chicago community. Yet as the opening quote from Steve Schanwald explains, no other sports organization is likely to face the retirement of a player such as Michael Jordan. Beyond the notion of a franchise or marque player, Jordan has helped define the game of basketball as a global entertainment. The gutting of the Bulls' team following his retirement, inevitably, but only temporarily, suspends the team's sustained contention for the NBA Championship.

# CHAPTER 8

# The Atlanta Braves –
# The Eagle has Landed

*There's a great sense of pride, here. You really have to pinch yourself every now and then to remind yourself that you're living through, something that is very, very rare in any sport – to be at the level of success that we've been for the last eight years, and with a reasonable expectation of continuing that success for the next four or five years, considering our team and the popularity of Turner Field. You really don't see our run coming to an end anytime soon.* – Bob Wolfe, Senior Vice-President, Administration

Many people in the Braves organization had little love for the old Atlanta-Fulton County Stadium. Hank Aaron might have slugged his 715th home run there, thereby eclipsing Babe Ruth's improbable long-standing record, and it might have hosted a World Series victory in 1995, but the day it was razed to the ground, few seemed to mind. Most, like the President, Stan Kasten, were glad to see the back of it. Perhaps the old stadium was for ever tainted with pre-1991 memories of lost games, dwindling crowds and an organization which had lost its way. Somehow, the Braves staff were able to divorce the greatest winning streak in baseball history from the very stadium where the feat began. They disliked the cramped offices, the lack of atmosphere and the poor facilities. Quite simply, this peak performing organization had outgrown its home.

Since the turnaround season of 1991, when the team went from worst to first in major league baseball, the Braves have won eight consecutive divisional titles, five national league titles and the World Series in 1995. Their total attendance in 1990 was 980,129, whereas in 1997 that figure had climbed to 3,464,488, an increase by a factor of 3.5. No other team in the history of baseball has matched this level of sustained peak performance. More than anything else, their new home stadium, Turner Field, symbolizes this hard-earned change of fortunes. It trumpets both a successful ballclub *and* an entertainment brand second to none within the sports industry, which competes intensely with other outlets for the disposable dollar.

Turner Field was the original venue for the Atlanta Olympic Games held in 1996, yet the Braves did not simply inherit an Olympic stadium. The reality is a little different. Stan Kasten and Billy Payne, who was the President and CEO of the Atlanta Olympic Committee, had the strategic vision to fulfil the needs of both organizations by contracting for the specs for the stadium to be drawn up in such a way that when the Braves took ownership, its conversion to a ballpark would essentially be a reconversion. As far back as 1989, when Atlanta city leaders were talking about putting in a bid for the Olympic Games, Stan Kasten suggested to them the idea of an Olympic stadium that could be converted to a baseball park later. Around this time the Atlanta Falcons, of the National Football League, had a new stadium built for them – the Georgia Dome. This left the Braves as the sole tenant in Atlanta-Fulton County Stadium, a thirty-year-old facility that wasn't ideal for either football or baseball, but was plausible for both. Given that the city had assisted the football team, the Atlanta Braves began busily investigating their own options. Bob Wolfe, Senior Vice-President of Administration:

> That's when Stan started laying the seeds for Turner Field. This was *before* the team on the field took off with any level of success. By the time the city won its Olympic bid, we had already hired architects to start plans for an Olympic stadium that could be converted to a baseball park. It was really a baseball park that could be used temporarily as an Olympic stadium. We had invested in those plans even before the city succeeded in the Olympic bid – we were well ahead of them on that. Once the city got the bid, a deal was put together that ultimately provided the Braves with Turner Field. Knowing that in 1997 we were going to open up the baseball season in Turner Field affected our planning year by year.

Sharing the dream of a new baseball stadium with the Olympic community ensured that the Braves and the city got a new park for a fraction of the real price. Virtually custom built for the Braves, Turner Field is now the new field of dreams – the 'rarest of diamonds',[1] where making magic on the ballpark's opening night took some shrewd planning, boosted by a large slice of luck. The intention was to keep the opening ceremony fairly elegant, without being too glitzy. The evening began with a relay of the home plate from Atlanta-Fulton County Stadium to Turner Field. Bill Bartholomay, Chairman of the Board, who had once owned the Atlanta Braves, and sold the club to Ted Turner back in the seventies, carried the plate out of Atlanta-Fulton County Stadium and handed it over to a group of young children who lived in the neighbourhood. The kids then brought the plate over to Turner Field and handed it to Hank Aaron, who was waiting behind the centre-field wall. As the fence opened up he came walking out with the plate. Amy Richter, Director of Advertising, describes the scene:

The whole stadium went crazy – he is just an icon, a baseball legend. He walked towards second base and was met by Tom Glavine. The past and the present came together – the two people who have helped make this organization what it is. They sat the home plate down to complete the Turner Field diamond. We then had the Georgia Massed Choir sing the national anthem, as they had during the opening ceremony for the Olympics, thus recognizing the ties between the Olympic Games and the opening of Turner Field. As they sang we let loose an eagle, an American bald eagle, from the top of the ballpark. While the choir sang, the eagle, with its huge wing span of seven feet, circled around the field and landed at home plate on the last note of the national anthem.

It was the perfect ending to a perfect night, the culmination of an incredible six months spent getting this facility ready. It was surreal, and one of the most magnificent things I have ever seen. The look on Ted Turner's face, President Jimmy Carter and all the other dignitaries who were in Ted's box – they were like kids when they saw this eagle landing at home plate – they were like little kids getting a puppy for their birthday.

The move from Atlanta-Fulton County Stadium to Turner Field, a baseball theme park of a type that the industry had not seen before, was indeed a game-breaking idea, symbolic of a first-class organization spreading its wings.

## THE ANATOMY OF A PPO: CREATING THE FUTURE

Ted Turner bought the Braves franchise in 1976. Fortuitously, a year later, he met a young Stan Kasten, at a Braves–Cardinals game in St Louis, where Kasten was celebrating his graduation from law school with a tour of major league baseball parks. Impressed with Kasten's savvy, Turner appointed him in-house legal counsel for the organization, a role which quickly became a baptism of fire. In 1977, during a seventeen-game losing streak, Turner, who was at this stage flirting with micro-management of the team, went the whole way on a road trip to Pittsburgh, when he decided to replace the team manager, Dave Bristol, and take over the dugout duties himself! Stan Kasten was just out of law school and employed in a legal capacity to 'watch over Turner', who at this time was under suspension for making comments at a World Series party the previous year. Kasten takes up the story:

> In my first week on the job I got home to my little apartment, I turned on the TV and damn, what did I see? Ted's running the game from the dugout – in the middle of this suspension. I called our counsel from our outside law firm and I said 'Are you watching the Pittsburgh game?' He said, 'No, I just got in, why?', 'Maybe you want to turn it on' I said. 'Why, what's up?' he replied. I said, 'Ted's taken Bristol out of the game and is calling all the plays. I'm not quite clear on this yet. I just turned it on myself.' The next day I was a twenty-four-year-old trying to explain to the world what my client had just done and why this was a good thing. Ted was gone that day, as Commissioner Bowie Kuhn banished him upstairs. Ted's tenure in the dugout lasted only one game. He lost to Pittsburgh, 2–1.

Of course, this colourful event is now firmly entrenched in Braves folklore, but it also helps to explain the origins of the current management style of the Braves organisation. Turner's attempts, in the early days of his ownership, to manage the team game by game, gave way to Kasten's vision of creating the future from a tradition of development.

Kasten is one of the top sports administrators in the US. In 1979, at the age of twenty-seven, he was appointed president of the Atlanta Hawks basketball franchise, later adding the Braves to his portfolio. His office in the CNN building in downtown Atlanta is a working office. Sat behind a large desk littered with work in progress, Kasten is articulate, passionate, and thoroughly engaged in the conversation about how the Braves turned everything around. He has told the story many times before, but is anxious to provide the full explanation – this is not just another rehearsal. Scattered in the midst of his narrative are several friendly, yet revealing, anecdotes (none of which can be reproduced for public consumption), which provide essential colour and understanding. With his good humour and genuine love of conversation, Kasten is riveting to listen to. His insights are many and valuable, particularly in the area of Braves history.

From the seventies through to the mid-eighties, although the Braves won a divisional title in 1982 and a couple of second-place finishes in the following years, the organization was suffering from the disease of 'short-termism'. Kasten was responsible for altering, root and branch, the direction which the Braves had followed for many years. The team had the highest payroll in baseball, and were placed last in the league, an embarrassment about which he drily notes: 'You almost can't do that if you are trying to.' To compound the problem, the Braves did not have the excellent minor league system which is so critical in professional baseball. The philosophy up to this time had been based on a short time-frame, driven largely by the fact that the organization was, very much, a TV entity. The result was that each year, management pursued the best team for that year, necessitating a never-ending, frenetic search for viable free agents. Kasten saw the problem:

When things work and you spend two million bucks on a great pitcher (which today would buy you nothing), you get one great year out of one great player. But if it doesn't work, that money is gone, you've lost the draft pick that you had to give up to sign the free agent, and the money which could have been spent building up your minor league is also gone. Doing this from year to year is not good, but if you take that same two million bucks, and you immediately plough it into development and add minor league teams, minor league instructors and scouts, the same two million bucks down the road might produce ten great years out of ten great players. Remarkably, the formula is not secret, it can be replicated anywhere, and has been from time to time.

The problem for Kasten and any pro sports team is, how long can you continue to lose before the media and fans eat you alive? Ted Turner, an owner who had already learned the hard way, gave Kasten the precious gift of time. Frequently, many teams begin with a long-term plan, but lose two games in a row and, in time-honoured fashion, projects are abandoned and the general manager is fired. Turner allowed Kasten to do it his way. Musing on the short-term outcome of this strategy, Kasten realized that:

It means for the next two to three years, every day in the newspapers we are going to be idiots, we don't know what we're doing, we're clueless. And I understand that, if you're a fan or a shareholder, all you care about is how's that team or organization doing today. You don't care how good you're becoming in the minor league systems, and so I understand, I really do. But we have an owner who said, just get it going your way, just do it.

Turner clearly deserves much credit for investing in time. This new direction also found favour with the General Manager, Bobby Cox, who arrived the year before Stan Kasten. He responded immediately to Kasten's philosophy of replacing the yearly quick fix with building up the minor leagues, by expanding the multiples of what could be obtained for the money that had been sunk into free agents. Kasten and Cox, hand in glove, simply turned the dial all the way in the direction of minor league development. Minor league teams were bought and at the same time, scouting and coaching were expanded. Chances were taken with young players who previously would have been sacrificed in favour of free agents.

Despite the obvious importance of investing in the future, Kasten still expresses surprise at the results:

> We stopped giving away those drafts, and started developing. It meant being a couple years more in the basement, it meant a couple years more of being the last-placed team. But I didn't know that our success was going to be so incredible. I thought we would succeed, and we'd become a good team, able to compete every year. I didn't think that we would win seven straight divisions, I didn't know that, I didn't know that we'd have the greatest pitching staff maybe in history. I couldn't know that. But we couldn't have done it unless Ted had given us the chance, or if I didn't know that Ted wasn't going to fire me the first time we lost two games, and of course I knew that very well.
>
> I have been with Ted for twenty years now, and I tell everyone the blame for everything stops at my desk, because I have complete authority to do anything I want. He's never turned me down on anything that I said I needed, ever, in twenty years. On the other hand, if Ted feels strongly about something, that matters to me because he is one of the world's smartest people. That still doesn't mean we don't disagree, but if I feel strongly about doing something he's never, never contested me, and I can't tell you how rare and important that is. If you don't have that, you go off course very quickly. So that was the most important thing for us. The singular, most important distinction when I came on, was that Ted allowed us to change our philosophy and gave us the time to do it – that was the one way the infrastructure could work.

Stan Kasten's vision of sustained peak performance on the field also carried over into the heart of the organization itself. However, unlike many corporations which seek to start afresh by removing existing staff and replacing them, Kasten had a different approach:

> The main challenge for me in my first sixty to ninety days was really getting a hold of who should stay and who should go. There were a lot of rumours from the outside – some people often got a lot of blame from the newspapers which affected my mindset going in – one guy in particular, who I thought must be at fault. After ninety days I learned that on the contrary

he was very good; he knew what he was doing, and had a plan – maybe he needed to be deployed a little bit differently. He became a star in the industry. The first thing a lot of people told me to do when I walked in, was to get rid of this guy, but although we did replace some people, we kept almost everybody there. We focused them, and gave them the challenge of building from the bottom up, and it was a lot more fun for everyone. It gave them some breathing room, because everyone would like to do it that way if they were ever given the chance – start from scratch, go from the bottom up.

Bob Wolfe, Senior Vice-President, Administration, who started with the Braves in 1980, has continued the theme of player development. Loyalty to staff and providing opportunities for everyone to grow through constant challenge have been the principles by which the Braves maintain what Wolfe calls 'a first-class organization' – sentiments echoed by all the staff. In return, Wolfe implicitly receives the confidence of the Braves staff, and carries it with consummate ease. His relaxed style flows unobtrusively yet effectively throughout the front office. Records show that almost all administrative staff in director-level positions came into the organisation at entry level and worked their way up. The management ethos includes a conscious effort to hire or promote from within – although not always possible, this is the Braves' initial intent. Low turnover and high retention rates mean that most of the staff have had the experience of running the organization when the team was not successful. This has helped to establish an organizational memory which maintains a balanced perspective on the Braves' current sustained run of success. Bob Wolfe notes that:

> The people who we have hired since 1991, good employees as they are, have no perspective on what it's like to be in last place for five years running. It is valuable to know that side to be able to enjoy the success that the team is having now. This franchise moved here from Milwaukee, Wisconsin in 1966, and as a contrast to our newer employees, there are some people still here from the day Atlanta-Fulton County Stadium opened. There is a great deal of loyalty amongst our workers. When we played the last game in the old stadium we honoured the staff who had worked there from the beginning. Including our game

staff close to thirty people had been there in excess of thirty years. That's a lot of baseball games.

Although Kasten's commitment to long-term development both on and off the field was a major sea-change for the organization, this policy could not come to fruition unless the staff were organized around an overarching vision and, more importantly, a method of achieving it. By 1989, as the benefits of investing in the minor league system started to become apparent, Kasten undertook an extensive search for a new general manager, an inspirational player who could take the Braves to the highest level in baseball.

Kasten first turned to John Schuerholz, who was then GM of the Kansas City Royals. Under Schuerholz's stewardship the Royals had already won one World Series, and more importantly, in the process had garnered the reputation of being the 'IBM of baseball'. Schuerholz had been with the Royals for twenty-three years, so Kasten's approach was initially to ask Schuerholz if he knew of any good GM prospects. Inevitably, they found themselves discussing Kasten's dilemma at a baseball game in New York. Schuerholz now admits that at the very moment when Kasten broached the issue of the GM position with the Braves, unbeknown to Kasten, he was hooked:

I have to be honest with you. At the moment when he said that, the light bulb went on. I said to myself 'this is pretty startling', and I began to build some interest in the position myself, but I also recommended some other people, then contemplated my internal feeling that this was of interest to me. Then I talked to my wife about it, and decided to pursue it. The Royals gave me permission to talk with the Braves. We talked, and ultimately they offered me the job. Then the time came for the big decision – needless to say it was difficult. I vacillated between accepting and rejecting the Braves position. Finally our owner in Kansas City, Mr Ewing Kauffman, said, 'If you are interested enough even to entertain going, you need to go and satisfy yourself and to take this opportunity.' So once I got past that decision emotionally, I was ready to dive headlong into the challenge. Mr Kauffman gave me that little push and I was on my way.

When Kasten finally realized that after several months of probing and discussing, he might be able to snare Schuerholz, he moved quickly.

> I brought him in twice under the cover of darkness, so no one knew he was here. I didn't let him go over to the stadium because it was shabby and, obviously not the Olympic stadium. That would have turned him off, so he didn't even see his office until he was already hired. We met here at CNN, which is very nice. He told me afterwards, that was a very smart move. The fit between us was very good.

The organization needed a general manager who would complement Kasten's blue-sky visions and consummate deal-making. John Schuerholz brought with him what he describes as, 'an unrelenting, uncompromising, total commitment to being a first-class organization'.

It is not easy to imagine John Schuerholz finding himself lost. Walking briskly towards his office through the maze-like corridors, elevators and walkways of the brand-new spring-training stadium at the Disney complex in Orlando, Florida, his stride is uncompromising and purposeful. A very clear-thinking, clean-cut figure, there can be no mistake that Schuerholz relishes a challenge. He maintains the trappings of a renaissance man, writing poetry and identifying with the endeavours of others. His favourite baseball player is George Brett, the Kansas City Royals offensive star with a lifetime batting average of .305, 3,154 career hits, thirteen All-Star appearances, and batting titles across three decades. Yet the qualities that Schuerholz cherishes in George Brett are more to do with attitude than numbers. 'No one loved the game more than George. His infectious enthusiasm was legendary. No matter what the circumstances, when George came to play, he was going to have fun, work hard and give it his all.' Likewise, Schuerholz exudes selfless commitment and honesty.

Unsurprisingly, the Braves organization that he inherited did not fit his image of what and how it should be. This was compounded by the wider perception that the Braves were not well respected within the baseball community. Schuerholz's observations were brutal and direct:

It was an organization that, in the eyes of the industry, was simply floundering administratively – it didn't seem to have direction. There was no clear goal. The development plan for the team, driven by Stan and Bobby Cox, was working, but administratively it was as though there was no continuity, and no clear plan for how the organization was going to function. The organization was in dire straits in terms of operations, management, direction and administration. The biggest stumbling block was apathy. There really wasn't a sufficient energy level, either individually or collectively, with the administrative staff. They were beaten down. Apathy had taken a stranglehold and people didn't think they *needed* to care, because no matter how much they did, it wouldn't change anything.

One man's inspiration started off a transformation in the Braves organization. Schuerholz felt that many people who were department heads had not been given the opportunity to express their own individuality or function effectively, so initially he involved himself in many organizational functions beyond baseball. These included public relations, marketing, promotions and even ticketing operations. The key point of this involvement was to enable him to communicate more effectively with people who were responsible for these areas. Schuerholz wanted them to understand what the administrative direction and goals of the organization were going to be. The aim was to establish a clarity of focus which technical experts could work towards:

We did that through communication with the various department heads and through group meetings. We talked about how we were going to redefine this organization, how we were going to establish new and higher goals. Next, we talked about what the goals were, and about how we would reach them. Then, more than anything else, we empowered the staff who were already here, who had previously been viewed as non-productive and not very talented, to make this plan work. Through communication with them and considerable exchange of ideas, thoughts and emotions, we began to create a very effective organization. Mundane things such as demanding people dressing properly at work, because that is a reflection of your personal self-esteem and your job self-esteem assisted the process. I've always believed that how you present yourself is a reflection of how you care about yourself, how you care about your job, especially in an administrative and management setting.

Schuerholz intended to engage people individually, and to encourage them to talk about the importance of having pride in their work:

> I'd walk down the hall and another person would be passing me and they would drop their eyes. They couldn't look you square in the eye and feel good about themselves. We began to talk continually about feeling good about ourselves, having the power of good thoughts and positive self image, and making a commitment to doing the things that needed to be done – working harder, working more intelligently, working a bit more aggressively. Remarkably, the people who were there proved to be capable professionals. Our goal was direct. We wanted to become the premier professional baseball organization – to become a world-championship team.

Both on the field and administratively, Schuerholz's goal for the operation was to become the world champion of baseball in every facet. After he had established that specific, clearly defined goal, the entire organization became aware of it. At the very early stages, staff were provided with a road map which enabled them to envisage how the goal could be achieved, including how to work, and in some cases how to go about implementation, and finally how it would all come together. Most important of all, however, was the complete transfer of ownership, so that the master plan belonged to all the staff. This was achieved by informal means, other than the occasional large staff meeting where Schuerholz communicated his beliefs directly:

> Hopefully, they heard the passion in my voice and saw the commitment I had to doing what needed to be done. Once we reached that point there were a lot of willing partners in this new enterprise. We lived it. We lived it by our work ethic, by our commitment, by our passion, by our professionalism. They were meaningful and people saw that. Stan gave me great sup-

port, everything I wanted to do, he allowed me to do. We made substantial changes and now we are what we are – champions in the industry.

These changes had a dramatic impact on personnel inside the Braves organization. In the first place they enabled Bobby Cox to return to his earlier role in the field as manager of the team. Second, the sharp focus on administrative excellence seemed to galvanize people throughout the whole enterprise. Jim Schultz, Director of Public Relations, who joined the Braves in 1987, describes the immediate impact that Schuerholz had on people:

> John saw no reason at all why the Braves shouldn't be the best organization in baseball. When an attitude like that came down from top management, the impact was almost instantaneous, it was incredible. He made it a point to go from office to office on a regular basis, to stick his head through the door to introduce himself, 'What are you working on, how or why are you doing things this way?' etc., and you know, that was the first time someone at that level had shown an interest in lower management or middle-level management. His commitment is to excellence. I attended a lot of speeches he made early on, and he still makes them regularly. His whole theme is, 'We are committed to provide you, the fans, with a first-class product, and a competitive world championship contending team.'

Amy Richter, Director of Advertising, expressing similar sentiments on the impact of John Schuerholz's arrival from the Kansas City Royals, notes that he picked up where Bobby Cox had left off, and, by adding some new ingredients, put a winning team on the field:

> I can't tell you what a difference that made then on the front office. Within a couple of months, once we had a real clear understanding of what his vision was, everybody was on board. John was completely dedicated to winning, and would not accept any excuses, not a single excuse from himself or anybody else, and it really had an incredible impact, I think, on everybody. It increased our confidence level significantly. You felt

safe in being able to do things, and try new things and be successful at it.

Tom Glavine, who came through the Braves farm system to be a Cy Young Award recipient and the most successful left-handed pitcher in baseball in the last ten years, also saw the difference when Schuerholz arrived:

> During the winter of 1990, when John Schuerholz came over as the general manager, we all sat down and talked, and the word commitment was used, and used a lot. We decided right then and there, that there was going to be a commitment from top to bottom to making this organization a class organization and a winning organization. That started in 1990. It was simple things at first: the way you conduct yourself as a team; the way you go about your business. The next thing you know you're winning ball games, and getting all the respect that comes along with that.

It is perhaps even more remarkable that Schuerholz started the turnaround without the benefit of any formal strategic planning. Although the Braves have a variety of marketing plans, financial plans and objectives for every season, understanding how it all actually organizes and coheres is another matter. Stabbing an index finger in the general direction of his temple, Schuerholz indicates the location of the organization's strategic activity. 'Here's the strategic plan. I'm sorry, this is where it is.' Jim Schultz echoes these sentiments:

> We have a unified theme to everything we do, but not catchphrases. We have found that catchphrases, whether they are marketing phrases or sales pitches, can backfire on you. If you try to keep them generic they are not effective. People will poke fun at them because they can apply to anything and have no real meaning. In other words, you can't make a promise in a phrase that can guarantee a World Series Championship.

The vision, values and clear focus that Kasten and Schuerholz built up, from the 1986 season onwards clearly had a cathartic impact on the culture and spirit of the organization. For Tom

Glavine, the Braves community which has subsequently emerged, is about, 'commitment, loyalty and family. A lot of guys who don't play here, look at us and say "I want to play for those guys."' The front-office staff are now located together at Turner Field, with offices that dramatically look out over the baseball diamond – very different from the sprawling and fragmented work environment at Atlanta-Fulton County Stadium. A sense of community surges through the new facility, although it deeply reflects Schuerholz's penchant for dignity, elegance, understatement and humility. Amy Richter sees the new office space as one which encourages, 'pride, decorum and professionalism, a good thing for all of us. The heartbeat of this community is nine players on the baseball field, and around that you have a broad, diverse collection of people in administration who have found some common ground, a common thread that holds us together.'

Naturally, the office walls are covered with items which celebrate the Braves. Photographs, montages, mosaics and memorabilia are around every corner, providing vivid reminders to staff and visitors of hard-earned victories. In each office are personalized commemorative cut-glass plaques that gratefully recognize the contributions of all employees. Perhaps most poignant are the championship rings that are presented not just to the players, but to all staff throughout the organization. Amy Richter:

It's not a huge event. They come around and distribute them somewhat discreetly. It is not really a very attractive ring for a woman to wear, but it symbolizes something very special and unique. When the time comes to hand out those rings you can sense the uplift in morale. Every year that we have won the pennant and the World Series we've received rings which, I think, demonstrates the organization's generosity.

Schuerholz also sets the tone for how this community celebrates its success. 'Win with grace, lose with dignity,' is his key phrase. This is not an organization that flaunts every pennant victory. Being thankful for reaching four World Series, rather than complaining about lost chances, helps maintain perspective. Nevertheless, the hunger for victory remains undiminished. Stan Kasten:

The focus is to be World Champions, no question about it, and it hurts that we didn't get it. I am disappointed that we didn't win, but I don't feel that we failed particularly. I feel we didn't get what we were good enough to get – it just didn't happen for us. There is great disappointment and frustration, but it didn't diminish, for me, the pride I have in the work that everyone did to get us there. To say that our goal was to get to the World Championship is not right. Sure, our goal is to win the World Championship and I hope to do it again. But, you can have a successful season and still not win the World Championship, otherwise twenty-nine teams out of thirty are losers every year. I don't buy that, I do not buy that.

In this way, the Braves community is constantly charged, and recharged, to drive towards contention. Wayne Long, Vice-President of Marketing and Broadcasting, says that the culture of the Braves community is continually invigorated with new challenges, each and every day, spliced with a healthy dose of fun:

When we were acquired a year or so ago by Time-Warner, they sent some HR people in to talk with the department heads, and they had their questionnaires. I think the first question was, 'Take us through one of your normal days, what does your day comprise of?' I said, 'Which one – I have been here twenty-five years and I have never had two days exactly the same. – that is the challenge for me personally. I wouldn't have been here for twenty-five years if it had been routine. It's a new challenge every day, and that's what makes it fun. Fun is an important word, because I keep repeating to my people that they have got to have fun while they are doing this.

Lisa Stricklin, Director of Human Resources, also recognizes that the Braves community is much more informal than the parent company, Time-Warner:

We've learned, because of our business, to be more flexible when it comes to human resource practices. There's never a dull moment. I can never say that I have two days that are exactly alike. We have employees with a strong sense of loyalty. There are people here who have worked for us for thirty years, primarily because they enjoy working in the game of baseball, and more specifically because they enjoy working for the Braves organization.

Stan Kasten echoes the same sentiments:

How can you not have fun? I mean, even if you've lost, you're probably having fun. You get to work in a baseball park for goodness' sake. I think you might have problems away from your work if you're not having fun. It's an inherently fun workplace.

## TURNER FIELD: SHARING THE DREAM

It is hard to conceive of Turner Field, or indeed the spring-training facility in Orlando, as being workplaces at all. The overall sense of belonging, pride and identity, rather than just moving up a few notches with the opening of Turner Field, took a quantum leap into the realm of magic making. For the first time the Braves were in their own home, and with that came a significant shift in responsibility. Possibilities for new signage, corporate sponsorships, and renewal of relationships with customers and clients, expanded hugely with the opening of the new stadium. The opportunity to share the dream with many new clients, extend the product, and amplify the brand, placed enormous pressure on the staff to deliver. The chief idea was to create a baseball theme park so that when people went to Braves games they would not just sit in the stands watching the team play on the field, but would get an opportunity to have a more intimate experience with the game and its history. In Turner Field, the Braves have established a new standard in baseball entertainment. Every stadium built subsequent to Turner Field will probably contain elements that will be directly attributable to the design and the construction of the Braves' new facility. Amy Richter explains that the opportunities presented by the converted Olympic stadium were hard to quantify, since the concept of a baseball theme park was quite new to the industry:

We have an area called 'Scouts' Alley', which is an interactive games area, mainly designed for kids. It's a combination of interactive games and mural-sized scouting reports of former and current players. Museum-type exhibits allow people to compare the various weight of bats and different kinds of mitts that players use. Fans can also learn about what the 'sweet spot' of a bat is, and what it means for a player to hit the 'sweet spot'. The anchor of Scouts' Alley is a museum that traces the history of this organization back to Boston.

So we've taken all these different elements from the game and brought them a little bit closer to the fans. We have bands. We have the 'bleacher brigade', young college-age students who run around the crowd and play with the kids and do all kinds of crazy things that just give it a little more of an upbeat festival atmosphere. There are people who argue that it's just not traditional enough for baseball, but the reality is that kids growing up today aren't tied into the traditions of the older generation of fans. Clearly we need to develop this new generation of fans.

Appealing to the fans, new and old, is precisely what Kasten wanted to achieve. He recalls, only too well, the problems at Atlanta-Fulton County Stadium.

I remember standing on the concourse in the eighties at the old stadium during the game, looking out, and the fans would come thirty minutes early, and they'd just be milling around. There was nothing to do, and as I've often said – it's not a joke, I mean it very seriously – 'Milling is bad, buying is good.' I hate milling, milling doesn't do them any good at all. Remember, milling is bad, buying is good. People will spend money if you give them something that they like, if you give them something to spend it on. If you give them a reason to come early they will come early, if you give them a reason to stay late they will stay late, and with those thoughts in mind, we went into our stadium and we developed our plaza.

The ballpark design that Kasten wanted necessitated the removal of almost half of the Olympic stadium to make way for a sweeping plaza that greets the fans before they enter the actual ground. The pillars that supported the stands to the Olympic stadium remain as an oval perimeter, providing a dramatic link to the original purpose of the facility. Fans are greeted with evocative statues of Hank Aaron, Ty Cobb (a famous Georgian who did not play for the Braves) and knuckle-baller Phil Niekro. Bob Wolfe:

> One of the things that has made this park successful is the entry way into the plaza. As people come through the turnstiles their first look at the stadium is from the plaza area. There's a video board, a retail store, concessions and a huge billboard picturing an oversized baseball. We put characters, jugglers and microphones there – full entertainment that people who come to the park can experience. That's the unique part of our ballpark. I've never seen it anywhere else, and it's one of the big reasons for our success.

Once inside the stadium fans are greeted with wide concourses where they can continue to watch the game while purchasing from concession stands. For those looking for an upmarket experience there is the 755 Club, an exclusive restaurant that honours Hank Aaron's record home-run tally. Entertainment is everywhere. Kasten clearly recognizes that the Braves are an entertainment vehicle which has to compete with every other entertainment vehicle under the sun, and that their safest bet is not to think of fans as fans, but as customers:

> You don't owe them a thing, but you're an idiot if you don't give them some reason to patronize you. I think you are safer in just thinking of it as any other business. To succeed you need to satisfy your customers. Your customer is always right – if they don't like what it is you are selling, you need to sell something else, period! They don't owe me anything, they don't have to buy their season tickets. We need to wake up every day and give them a reason to want to patronize us. It may be the game, but it may be the other things too. It may be the whole evening's experience, which is what I think, and that's why we worked as hard as we could to make this the ultimate fan-consumer's baseball park ever.

Hard-core baseball fans naturally attend games no matter what the conditions – Kasten, above and beyond this, had to make the ballpark appeal to both young and old, and more crucial still, females of all ages.

The best example that demonstrates Turner Field's positive impact on revenue streams is in the area of corporate sponsorship. Long-standing sponsors Coca-Cola were clearly anxious to push the envelope with their concept of a Sky Field. Kasten explains:

> When Coca-Cola came to us we were thinking they would have the name of the plaza, and they would write us a cheque and it would be the Coca-Cola Plaza. We gave them the plans and they said 'Do you mind if we take them and study them for a few weeks?', 'Be my guest,' I said, and they came back with a use for absolute dead space, on the roof for Christ sakes! On the roof! I said two things about the space itself – you come back and show me what you want – but two things: it can say Coke, that's fair, you're spending money; but you also have to say baseball. It had to be baseball – that's what this place is – everything had to be baseball. When they first unveiled the plans to me, I thought damn, they took me literally, it says Coke and it says baseball!

Coca-Cola had come up with a unique Sky Field that sat 23,000 square feet on top of the left-field, upper-deck stand. The chief feature is a forty-two-foot-high Cola bottle made from thousands of pieces of baseball equipment, such as gloves, bats, balls, helmets, Braves shirts. It spews out fireworks on command when the Braves hit a home run. The 'field' also includes a real pitchers' mound with a regulation ninety-foot base-path which kids run along throughout the game. A dugout replete with bench and bat racks, nine twenty-eight-foot-tall baseball cards featuring pictograms of players and, most magical of all, the promise of $1,000,000 for anyone who catches a home-run hit into the Coca-Cola Sky Field.

Turner Field has enabled the Braves to share their dream with a much wider spectrum of fans, customers, sponsors and clients than before. It is the heart of this peak performing organization. The impact has been staggering. There are now close to 30,000 season ticket holders and they, along with 20,000 other patrons for each game, do come to the park early, as Kasten intended: 'We used to swing the gate two hours before the game, no-one would be there. Well, now we swing it three hours before a game, and you know what, they are outside the gates an hour *before* we swing the gates.'

The success of Turner Field was followed by the opening of the new spring training stadium, in the Disney complex, Orlando, Florida. Strategically and symbolically placed in the heart of the entertainment world, the new facility demonstrates that, from start to finish, the Atlanta Braves are a first-class outfit. The well-appointed office complex behind the stadium façade would put to shame many a major league park, while, close to the dugout, the players enjoy unparalleled space in their new locker room. In time-honoured fashion, as the ritual of spring training gets under-way, the sharp sweet sound of bat on ball evocatively echoes around all corners of the park. Because the training stadium is, naturally, a smaller facility than Turner Field, the bleachers hug both foul lines closely, ensuring that spectators can almost touch the dream. Here, the fans can still get near to their heroes. Tom Glavine, John Smoltz and Greg Maddux, some of the greatest pitchers of the modern game, need no encouragement to spend time on top of the dugout roof, to sign autographs and chat with those who are ever eager to share the dream that is the Atlanta Braves.

## THE PERFORMANCE ZONE

The full apparatus of the Braves organization, including the minor league system, players, front-office and stadium personnel, numbers over 1,500 employees, with revenues from various sources measuring in the hundreds of millions of dollars. Formally, the organization is arranged into multiple specialities, along func-tional lines. Each department has its own game-plan, following the focus articulated by Stan Kasten and John Schuerholz. Now-adays, the notion of a first-class organization that provides top-flight entertainment and contends World Championship status each year, has long been adopted, owned, sanded, varnished and polished by all organizational participants. The mode of putting this collective vision into operation is intriguing. Even though the quality of the product needs to be reaffirmed in every game played throughout the season, the 'coming together' of all the functional or system elements does not rely on, or even use, formally organized teams.

At the individual level, employees hold themselves supremely responsible for the impact that their particular job has on the final product. Exceeding personal best is a way of life that means as much in the office as it does on the baseball diamond. In the earlier days, Schuerholz would look outside to other pre-eminent baseball franchises to get a fix on what individuals should do to try to be the best. In more recent years, however, he has shifted decisively towards internal assessment:

> Now, we use ourselves as the benchmark. The spotlight is brighter here. The heat is turned up a notch higher. Our expectations have grown higher. We have high internal expectations – the external expectations are high too, but more important to us are our internal expectations. That's where most of the pressure comes, not from the outside expectations, because you can rationalize those anyway you like. It's intimidating in one sense, but invigorating in another. It primes the engine. It makes you, as an individual, as a professional, want to be at the top of your game. Wearing this uniform, or business dress, is representative of the finest organization in baseball. You can play up to those expectations.

Larry Bowman, Director of Stadium Operations and Security, more than most, faces unrelenting pressure to deliver time and time again at the highest professional level of peak-operating condition. A mosaic of tasks, which includes ticket-taking, ushering, guest relations, security, police, first-aid co-ordination, telecommunications, maintenance and engineering, needs specific attention to the tiniest detail to get the ballpark game-ready. Bowman has to impact on several hundred employees. He faces the ultimate paradox where the unexpected is the norm. Bomb threats, special requests for prayer facilities for different religious orders and on-field runs by spectators are all standard fare. Bowman explains: 'You can have a general plan of action, but each game is unique. If we try to set something in stone, certain portions of it will become obsolete the very next day.' Managing in this environment does not lend itself to formal rules, job descriptions and routine lines of command. Bowman has a different approach to deal with constant change:

> No-one here is ever really satisfied. There's room to do more. Always. Each individual has, in large part, a desire to reach perfection. But I think my staff perform better when they are focused on *reaching* it rather than actually achieving it. And no organization ever gets there. I have the type of personnel here who are never satisfied. That is typical of this organization. Moreover, you realize that you have to be innovative in coming out with solutions.

The expectation of innovation and creativity and game-breaking ideas is another significant factor in enabling Bowman's staff to address the constant whirl of change:

> All my staff have to be innovative, simply because we are constantly confronted with situations where we might not have the resources to get something done. And we live or die by getting the job done. Whatever the circumstances, my staff need to be creative, resourceful and even visionary. These are key questions when we interview for this department: How flexible are you? Can you adapt to change? How well do you operate under stress?
>
> Here's an example of what I mean. Last year, after an on-field spectator incident, the officer that was responsible for that part of the field instituted some changes among his personnel in their deployment and positioning. He talked about what to look for, what to listen for, and how to make sure they wouldn't be caught napping again. This was good, because I got to see what this guy brings to the table. He felt personally offended by the fact that somebody got on the field while his unit was out there. And then he took steps to make sure that it wouldn't happen again. During the remainder of the regular season I noticed that the other teams saw what he did, and when they rotated onto the field, they not only wanted to do what he did, they wanted to add their own wrinkle to it.

Capturing the ideas and creative juices of the staff so that everyone in the organization is in a state of flow with each other begins with functional strength. When Bowman is searching for new staff his primary concern is to hire people who are strong in their areas of expertise. From the position of functional strength, co-operation and working in formation become the default practice. The activity is informal, unspoken and unexceptional. Larry Bowman:

> You don't want a general practitioner, you want a specialist in each area, you look for the best person for player development, and the best general manager you can find, and you build your organization around those goals. It's mandatory to have the skills to do the job, but those skills are rendered useless if you can't interact and inter-relate with the people around you. No department here is truly separate. They all interact – they have to for the ball game to happen. That is the organizational footprint.
>
> People here really buy into the organization and support it, and they want to see the organization fare well. Their concern for the organization supersedes personal agendas. To have a successful team you need to have folks that view it as a team, see their stake in it, see their interest in it and act on their interests for the overall good. That strengthens the organization because you don't have people tearing at it from within. Everyone looks at that overall goal, and if they see something in your area where they can be of help to you, then that's what they do.
>
> A good example was highlighted last year as we were working to get the ballpark open. The night before the first exhibition game, we had folks who were here all day and all night, not really because they had to, even though they did – they were here because they wanted the opening day to shine, not for themselves individually, but for the organization.

Bob Wolfe, Senior Vice-President Administration, puts the practice of flow into an organizational context. While he acknowledges that formal job descriptions can be found for most employees, he is quick to point out that 'very few of them are more than eight to ten written lines, and they're not real specific in some cases. We have a philosophy of, "this is your job description", but at any time, if something comes up, you can find yourself doing something else. We have a very good level of co-operation.' According to Wolfe, this type of work activity is also reflected in the way departments themselves avoid a purely functional mindset:

> I would rather leave it to departments to develop their own ideas. One thing that can't be emphasized often enough is the importance of communication between departments. There are very few departments within this organization that can act with complete independence from other departments. The marketing people can't get their job done without the co-operation and knowledge of the people that are running the ballpark. They go hand in hand.

Information sharing, even when there appears to be little utility in doing so, is another important dimension which encourages different groups to work together:

> In our periodic staff meetings we encourage each department to talk about what they have going on, even if it doesn't seem to relate to other departments. Different departments may be able to offer some help or assistance, and are at least aware of what's happening in the organization. Hopefully it makes them feel part of the ballclub as a whole.

Although the Braves do have a formal organizational structure chart, it has languished in someone's office drawer for quite some time. It contains numerous boxes with job titles, plenty of lines and perhaps two discernible hierarchical levels. Beyond that, its utility is unclear. Bob Wolfe, after studying it quizzically for a brief moment, apparently for the first time in ages, 'You should certainly have this, but it's not going to tell you a whole lot about the flow of business around here. Communication across departmental lines is as important as communication within a department.'

The impact of the organization, and the manner in which business gets conducted, is not lost on the players. Tom Glavine has seen the Braves during the good times and the bad. He came through the farm system and truly represents the Braves' decisive move to create the future by investing in long-term development. More than anyone else, he is in a position to observe and comment on how the organization has contributed towards the most remarkable, sustained winning performance ever witnessed in the game of baseball. This is how Tom Glavine explains the Braves' success:

Number one is a commitment from Ted Turner, who put good baseball people in charge of running this baseball organization. They have the commitment to make it a first-class organization in everything they do. This commitment has existed ever since I got here in the late eighties. The trend was towards being a team with a first-class organization from top to bottom, both at the big league level and the minor league level. What you're seeing at big league level is a direct result of hard work that was put in at the minor league level. A lot of us came through the system.

The Braves have also reaped the benefits brought in by the business side, by the owner, the team president, the general managers. They're the ones who are getting the players, signing the players, and developing the players, so they get most of the credit, but it goes beyond that. You're not just a successful organization by how you play the game on the field, or at least I don't think that's our philosophy. You also have got to have a group of guys and an organization that's committed to the community, to doing things for other people – that goes a long way towards getting people behind your team, and involved in the programme. If you've got a team full of good guys who are doing a lot of community things, that helps with that relationship an awful lot. I think the front-office people below the general manager and the owner, the public relations department and the community relations department do a great job of making sure that it all takes place. When you see that commitment from your front office, it motivates you as a player to have that same commitment.

The next thing you know, you've got tremendous confidence in what you're doing. I think it's true of anything in life. The more confidence you have in what you're doing, the better chance you have of getting the results you want. That's what happened to us.

# CONCLUSION

Ted Turner, Stan Kasten and John Schuerholz were the inspirational players who moved the Atlanta Braves off the bottom rung of major league baseball. Turner provided Kasten with the time he needed to create the future by investing in baseball players through the minor league system. In parallel, management of the club was allowed to regroup, and find a common thread that helped to define the organizational footprint. John Schuerholz was given a free hand to provide focus and direction, which managers quickly adopted and re-created to their own specifications. Bob Wolfe's mercurial and supremely balanced handling of the organization benchmarks the industry.

One inspirational player alone cannot turn an organization around, no matter how charismatic he is or how deep his pockets. The Braves are the ultimate example of how long it takes, and how hard the organization has to work, to become a peak performer. The greatest starting pitching rotation in the history of baseball, of Glavine, Smoltz and Maddux, with six Cy Young Awards between them, is a rare gift delivered by a peak performing organization.

CHAPTER • 9

# The San Francisco 49ers – Tilting the Field

*Why do the 49ers win? From the beginning, our owner has wanted to win. After we won the Super Bowl in 1981 it took off. It is amazing that through all the changes which have taken place, we have been able to sustain our winning record. As coaches and administrative people have moved on to other teams, they have taken with them the '49ers system' that is so successful. And yet that system is not written down anywhere. It's a learned process – an understanding of the operation, with buy in at a very personal level. We don't have a formal doctrine, it's all up here, in our heads.* – Murlan C. Fowell, Director of Stadium Operations

The 49ers' owner, Eddie DeBartolo Jr, who bought the franchise in 1977, faces fraud charges in the state of Louisiana and is suspended by the National Football League (NFL). Lawsuits involving the 49ers abound and the President, Carmen Policy, has taken flight to join the new NFL expansion franchise in Cleveland. Dwight Clark, Vice-President and Director of Football Operations, a footballing legend for the 49ers, and responsible for 'the catch', which is now for ever appended to his name, has likewise departed east. Steve Mariucci, the young Head Coach, walking in the substantial footsteps of predecessors Bill Walsh and George Seifert signed a new long-term contract, but this did little to stem the rumour-mill. During the first half of the 1998–9 season, standout defensive lineman Bryant Young and running back Garrison Hearst both sustained broken legs, the latter occurring at the beginning of a critical play off game for a divisional title. The San Francisco Bay area media continue to churn out pages of brutalizing commentary, pronouncing, yet again, the impending death of the franchise.

Meanwhile it's January 1999 and, for a record sixteenth time, the 49ers are in the play offs again. With a record of twelve wins and four losses in league play, the wild card brings them head to head with rivals the Green Bay Packers. In the last three seconds of the game, an improbable 'through the eye of a needle' touchdown pass, thrown by quarterback Steve Young, snatches victory, sending fans to the edge of delirium. This victory sets up a further play-off game placing the 49ers in contention for a berth in the Super Bowl and the opportunity to add to their existing five trophies – more than any other NFL franchise possesses. Despite organizational upheaval, inevitably conducted in the unrelenting glare of public scrutiny, and the draft system and salary cap, which together inexorably drive NFL franchises towards the average, the 49ers remain a peak performing organization. As well as five Super Bowls, the 49ers have amassed fourteen National Football Conference divisional titles, and since 1980, they have maintained a seventy-five per cent win record.

# THE HARD YARDS OF ORGANIZATIONAL SUCCESS

After the close victory of the weekend, Santa Clara is a good place to be on Monday. The Marie DeBartolo Centre, 4949 Centennial Boulevard, built in 1988, is the home of the 49ers. It is situated on a sparsely populated tract of land where the dramatic backdrop of the Sierra mountains creates an aura of rural tranquility. The two-story Centre is the only building nestling at the tip of a large no-exit road. Behind it, shielded by high fencing, are ten acres of land – the carefully groomed training ground. Passing through the front door, players and office workers alike exchange relaxed greetings with the security staff. Players swerve left or right to enter a maze of media, conference and briefing rooms, or the weight-lifting and locker rooms. Administrative staff go directly ahead to a sweeping flight of stairs, passing a display cabinet which boasts an improbable and decidedly magical five Super Bowl trophies, alongside many other artefacts of Conference supremacy. The top of the stairs opens out to a reception area, behind which are several eye-level shelves supporting gleaming gridiron helmets from other teams. This is NFL territory.

49er magic is on every wall, along every corridor, in every available nook and cranny. Awards, milestones, personalized plaques and literally hundreds of carefully framed and mounted photographs give us the unmistakable impression that we are mere mortals in the midst of icons. These trappings of greatness include mementoes of those world-famous inspirational players who are indelibly associated with 49ers glory: Joe Montana, Steve Young and Jerry Rice. The mere mention of these names to enthusiasts of the gridiron code is likely to elicit wistfulness and ignoble jealousies, instigated by respect for talent and ability beyond earthly comprehension.

Of this famous trio, Jerry Rice is the greatest wide receiver in NFL history. His personal statistics will, in all likelihood, never be matched again. Over a full career, the constant pressure of eluding defensive cover might weigh like a nightmare on lesser beings. However, when we interviewed Rice in the twilight of his brilliant career, his passion for the game, his legendary fitness routines and glorious capacity for fun, signalled by his infectious smile, remained undiminished. It was impossible not to be completely charmed by him. More than most, he has the right to lay claim to being a major contributor to the 49ers' winning ways, yet when asked for his assessment as to why the team had achieved so much, he chose to highlight a more strategic explanation:

> I think the San Francisco 49ers have been so successful because of the people upstairs. The organization. We have the best owner in the NFL. He's a very caring individual, and it really makes you want to go out there, and leave everything on the football field, for this guy. He takes care of his players. When I first came in, he was just like a father figure to me. I have so much respect for Mr DeBartolo, and we have such a good relationship. When we take to that football field, we always say that we're representing this guy.

Edward J. DeBartolo Jr, President and CEO of the DeBartolo Corporation, based in Ohio, purchased the 49ers in 1977. The

turnaround, from two seasons with only two wins, to championship supremacy in Super Bowl XVI, has been well documented.
Less well known is the deep personal impact which this inspirational owner had on the 49ers organization. Any conversation
with a member of the 49ers about how their twenty-year-plus
winning record has been sustained is guaranteed to start with 'Mr
D.' Over the years, DeBartolo has played an enormous part in
establishing the organizational imperatives that remain powerful
and acutely tangible to all. Steve Young:

> We have an owner who values winning more than just the
> bottom line. If only the bottom line is valued, then you don't
> have any incentive to win. He really has a desire to win football
> games, even though it might not be in the best interests of *his*
> bottom line. Having said that, he sets a tone of accountability.
> In a game like football, usually, the first thing that happens if
> you start to go downhill, is that everyone starts pointing fingers
> at who is supposedly responsible. We have an owner who is
> willing to ask, 'What did I do wrong, what do I need to do?'
> He sets the tone for the rest of the organization, so that every
> person in the building says, well if the owner says 'What did I
> do wrong?', then what did I do wrong myself? This is how
> we avoid the culture of finger pointing, which will ruin an
> organization.
>
> In 1993 we lost the championship game to the Cowboys for
> the second year in a row. It was clear that if we didn't find a
> way to beat the Cowboys, we weren't going to win the Super
> Bowl. So the owner said, 'What do I need to do to beat the
> Cowboys?' He started that whole feeling. By the time it got
> down to the players, it was like, OK, we've got everything we
> can to help us beat the Cowboys. We ended up beating them
> and won Super Bowl XXIV. That's a perfect example of
> accountability.

Alongside accountability, DeBartolo has engendered an atmosphere of care and support throughout the organization. Players
and administrators alike access a mutually supportive network
that originates from the owner's overriding concern for their
welfare. Fred Gualco, Security Co-ordinator, sees first-hand
DeBartolo's effect on the players:

If there is something wrong with them he's always involved, deeply involved, and that's important. It is just phenomenal that our owner cares personally for the players and staff. When you see that the owner is really concerned about you, it has a tremendous impact. He steps forward if there is a problem, no matter how small, and this gives everyone the feeling that the owner cares for them. It is now a large family, and everybody cares for each other. No other teams in the NFL have this to the same extent. We've been to five Super Bowls, and we've watched other teams just show up, with their players wondering about how their mother and father and brother and sister are going to get there from different locations, and about their flight reservations, but *we* do all that for our players. We make them as comfortable as possible.

These sentiments are loudly echoed by Dave Rahn, Travel Manager, who has been with the franchise for fourteen years, and who previously worked in the public relations office. Rahn has seen duty in a number of positions, and could be considered the quintessential example of a 49ers man. Unruffled by the mind-boggling complexity and intricate detail that his operations demand, he is enthusiastic about the owner's positive influence upon the 49ers community:

Mr DeBartolo has always made it a point to take care of the players in his family. He has always striven to have the utmost respect for everybody, and that includes the coaches, the staff and the players. In turn, we have tried to give the people on the field the very best. That means paying them the best, giving them the best facilities, surrounding them with the best players, and giving the people who are actually on the field the environment that is best suited for them, to enable them to concentrate on what they are here for – to play football. When we travel we always travel on a big plane, usually a DC10, where there is room for the players to spread out. Most other teams travel in a smaller plane – that is an expense that Mr D. doesn't mind incurring. We always stay at the top-of-the-line hotels, with good food. Other teams will double-up with bedrooms, whereas we give every person their own room.

Newer members of the organization, like Jim Mora, who joined the coaching staff (defensive backs) in 1997, are quick to pick up on the contrast with their previous experience. Mora's enthusiasm for this topic was evident from the sheer delight that accompanied his observations on the 49ers. Mr DeBartolo's key role in establishing the 49ers way was uppermost in his mind as he rattled off a series of personal reflections:

> The number one difference that I have noticed since I have been here is the way that people are treated in a professional sense. Everybody in this organization is made to feel that they have a part in winning football games, and yet everybody understands that the most important people in any organization are the players and the coaches. Moreover – and I think that this is really important – in the other organizations which I have been in, there hasn't been an effort by the front-office people to make the players feel as if they are special. The players have always felt, in my opinion, that they are a little more on the subservient side. Yet in this organization there is a concerted effort to make the players feel that they are special, that they are going to be taken care of so that they can concentrate on their job.
>
> For instance, I had an experience in the first training camp last year. I had a flat tyre. I asked a guy, where could I get my tyre fixed and he said, 'You don't get your tyre fixed around here, we do that, give me your keys.' This organization allows you, as a coach or a player, to focus solely on football and playing the game. They do a great job of making the players feel special.

Feeling special is not confined to the players, however. Sandy Fontana, who works closely with Bill Duffy, Chief Financial Officer (CFO) and Vice-President of Business Operations, provides insight into the texture of the organization's community. In addition to her duties for the CFO she works on benefits, health insurance, is moving towards human resources, and previously worked on travel, the portfolio now held by Dave Rahn. Fontana has been with the 49ers for fifteen years, but held her first 49er season tickets while still in high school. A self-confessed gridiron junkie, she still watches all the games from the bleachers with the rest of the fans, rather than from the more palatial surroundings that she could easily access. She describes a heady combination of magic-making and strong community affiliation:

> It is very rare in almost any organization to establish, as our owner has, the foundation for a genuine family-type atmosphere, rather than a nine-to-five routine. Mr DeBartolo always does something for the staff and the players – not just the players, but the staff as well. One year he hired a plane and we had our Super Bowl party in Hawaii – absolutely everyone went. In 1994 the whole organization went to Colorado Springs for three or four days. We had a barbecue one night, and at the Super Bowl party the rings were actually presented to the players. There was horse-back riding, golfing, hot air balloons and you could spend the entire day at the spa. It was absolutely wonderful and relaxing.
>
> At these Super Bowl retreats you really get to know everybody in the organization and their spouses or their own special guests – and it isn't like, 'That's Jerry Rice and I can't talk to him' – he is just another person. It brings more of a family and a human element into the organization. Even though we have a lot of superstars on our team they are not, 'Don't touch me, I am special.' They are down-to-earth, normal people. Down-to-earth millionaires, that is! Mr DeBartolo has made this a family. He knows everybody's name and most of their spouses too.

Murlan Fowell, Director of Stadium Operations at 3 Com Park, is another fourteen-year veteran of the organization who wastes no time in locating the origins of the 49ers' success.

> The owner of this franchise has been generous to a fault in that he has given everything to the team, the players and the employees. He's a very generous man, and I think he has built a loyalty and a camaraderie, so that you want to do the best you can for him because of what he's done for you. I don't know that there's a lot of teams that can say that. You really take pride in your job and your responsibilities, and you want to make sure you get it right. You're part of the team.

Since DeBartolo took over the franchise, the structure of the 49ers organization has remained uncomplicated. In part, the community itself acts as a substitute for hierarchical complexity, and there is no evidence of artificial mechanisms designed to achieve overall system integration. Formally, the president reports to the owner, and under the president are two vice-presidents of football operations and business. On the business side are several departments, including stadium operations, ticketing, marketing, travel, public relations and accounts. The formal organization chart is not used in any operational way. Interestingly, it is hand-drawn (given the names associated with each portfolio, it is also several years out of date) with a series of dotted lines which indicate the possibility of multiple task activities, where organizational participants, irrespective of their own functional expertise, are expected to relate to and co-operate in managing any number of ongoing scenarios. There are no teams or project leaders with official responsibility to make this happen. This $150 million operation, with up to 100 direct staff and players, and up to 2,000 part-time stadium workers, is run on simple, informal lines.

Unquestionably, the stability and continuity of the 49ers staff has enabled the 49ers to create the future. A solid cadre of coaches and administrators have been with the organization through many triumphs and, along the way, have inevitably learned how to deal with defeat – 'turning the page' as it is described here. Coaches such as Dwaine Board and Tom Rathman had played with the 49ers, and most long-serving administrators have worked in several capacities, adding to their overall fund of knowledge.

The appointment of Bill Walsh as head coach is often seen as a pivotal moment in the long-term fortunes of the franchise. His initial tenure with the 49ers lasted from 1978 until 1989, and this story is incomplete without an understanding of his contribution. Technically, Walsh is famous for the development and innovation of 'the west coast offense'. Literally a game-breaking idea of its time, as 49er coaches have been appointed to other NFL teams, so this method has been adopted by them, thus enabling direct competitors to share in the 49ers knowledge base. Mike Shanahan of the Denver Broncos and Mike Holgrem of the Seattle Seahawks both formerly coaches with the 49ers, have each tasted Super Bowl success, based on their apprenticeships in San Francisco. Indeed, Steve Mariucci, who joined as head coach in 1997, spent part of his professional career under the tutelage of Mike Holgrem with the Packers. Mariucci notes the irony of his outsider status, coming as he did from the collegiate ranks as head coach at the University of California: 'Mike Holgrem taught things the 49ers way. That's where I learned it. So they hired a guy from the outside, but I wasn't really an outsider. Hey, I was going to be a guy that was going to keep the continuity!'

Walsh's legacy is also managerial. The simple nature of the 49ers' organizational structure can be traced back to Walsh's philosophy of loyalty, and focus, to a single command structure. His managerial style had the most lasting impact on the organization. Bobb McKittrick, who Walsh describes as the finest offensive line coach the world has ever seen, explained to us how the 49er system began to take shape. McKittrick has over twenty years with the 49ers and nearly thirty years in the NFL. He has been to all the Super Bowls won by the franchise, as well as three college Rose Bowls, and now, along with the owner, is one of the few inspirational figures who can recall a losing season. With a generation of experience in pro football, McKittrick's reflections have immediate currency. A key informant in every sense of the word, McKittrick is a researcher's dream come true.

When Bill Walsh came into the organization, it had been decimated by defeat. The previous president/general manager had not been able to overcome the alienation of the people within the organization. The very first thing he did was to stress that we were going to be a first-class organization and present a good image for football. With Mr DeBartolo unable to be here every day, Coach Walsh was essentially the man in charge.

Very early on he held an important meeting with everyone except the players and coaches. He told them that their job was to assist the players and coaches in anything they needed to help the team win football games. Stressing involvement and innovation, Walsh told us that anything that we thought might help the team play a little better, to win football games, would be welcomed. Coach Walsh asked everybody for ideas, so he would get the equipment man's opinion and the trainer's opinion and the video person's opinion as well as those of the assistant coaches and general manager and other people too. You could be standing at a urinal next to him and he would ask you a question, 'What do you think about this?' He got information from everybody. Soon, the team buses ran on time.

The players had a single room instead of doubling up, they traveled on a nicer aircraft, and ate better. All the little things were hard to notice, but if you had been somewhere else you would know the difference. All this laid down the foundation for an informal atmosphere.

In this early period of the Walsh era, all other titles answered to Coach Walsh, so everybody was headed in the direction established by this informal consultative process. Crucially, the key aspect of this initiative lay in the close working relationship between 'football' and 'administration'. Understandably, no one on the administrative side calls any of the plays during a game, and each side of the business works through a season according to its own rhythm and heartbeat, yet all elements unite to maintain their focus. As the organization has expanded and taken on new operating characteristics, the simple command structure Walsh adopted, almost by default, has long-since been replaced with decentralized decision-making amid multiple sources of inspirational leadership. Nonetheless, the driving ambition of the administration to do anything imaginable to help the players focus on their game, remains powerfully intact. Walsh's reappointment to the 49ers in early 1999, as General Manager, once again emphasizes strong continuity and community within the organization.

The ability of the 49ers organization to create the future continually has also rested on its ability to hire the right people, and to slide them into critical positions without extensive upheaval. Bruce Popko, Director of Marketing until his departure in late 1998 to join the Cleveland expansion team, was himself 'watched' for two years as his career in football took him from the New York Jets to the NFL. He was actively head hunted for the position, giving him an interesting perspective on how the 49ers acquire new staff:

I don't know – it seems like the 49ers just have an uncanny knack of being able to pull out or just lose one or several pieces of the puzzle and are then always able to replace those pieces of the puzzle with a worker or coach or player just as effective as the one that departed. In a lot of other organizations, not just professional sports, there can be a total vacuum, a total void, created when certain individuals leave, but the 49ers are able to put people in there who are as effective, or even more effective, than their predecessors.

Care is also taken to ensure that the personalities on the field mesh well. When the high-profile and controversial Deion Sanders became available to the 49ers, many of the key players were canvassed to see if they thought he could 'fit' with the rest of the team. This process helped smooth Sanders' induction and acceptance by all the players. More importantly, for the one season he spent with the 49ers, Sanders proved to be a popular catalyst, and helped to inspire victory in Super Bowl XXIX.

One of the key appointments to the organization, in 1996, was that of Bill Duffy, to the position of CFO and vice-president of business operations. Even though Duffy has only been with the 49ers for a short time, he is the quintessential organization man. He understands, readily accepts and propagates the 49ers philosophy that no one is above the team. Like the famous quarterback legends Joe Montana and Steve Young, who the 49ers proudly parade as their own, Duffy is extremely adept at making swift judgements which carry the organization forward. His field of vision, like that of many hands-on managers, stretches from gritty day-to-day detail, to the highly strategic and crucial deploying of finite financial resources. Fontana confirms that, 'When Bill came in, I don't think we missed a beat, we were able to keep going, because everybody knew what needed to be done and how to help him.' Duffy's appointment was indeed a key piece of the jigsaw. So much so, that Mr DeBartolo's personal intervention is worth noting here. Bill Duffy:

One of the things that I found interesting about my interview process was that at the time I didn't know I was in the process! I had met with the president for a couple of hours and had a discussion about my philosophy and my business approach. A couple of months later he asked me to come on down for dinner on a Sunday night with Mr D., where there would be five or six people from the organization. Additionally there were many other DeBartolo family members – cousins, this and that. I kind of picked up that it was a big night for me to do well with the universe of people there. We sat down for dinner – it was a very informal big Italian dinner, 'get this, pass that', everybody is reaching and sharing, and by the time everybody has settled in, there is Mr D. right across the table from me at maybe a twenty-person-long table. I didn't think anything of it at the time, but realized later that this obviously wasn't an accident. I handled a lot of questions that night.

Ensuring continuity of purpose through careful recruitment is a way of life with the 49ers which makes it possible to lose or replace key personnel without disturbing the existing community. Such stability can also be found in stadium operations, where the tradition of working 49er games is all about family and preservation of identity. Murlan Fowell:

> Many of our 2,000 employees go back to the previous ownership. We have grandfathers, fathers and sons who between them have worked throughout the fifty years of the franchise's history. In fact, our game-day co-ordinator who organizes the ushers and gatemen, is seventy-one years old and has been here since 1946–7. We had an usher who we finally had to retire a couple of years ago because he was ninety-five years old. It was his life, he lived for the 49ers. We used to provide a chair for the guy, so he could sit down, but finally his family forced his retirement because he just wasn't capable of looking after himself. The family had to move him to his son's (his son was over seventy years old for God's sake) in Los Angeles to get him away from here so he couldn't work anymore.

Very early on in the franchise's winning sequence, the 49ers became one of the most famous sports brands, worldwide. The 'SF' logo on the side of the helmet is one of the most instantly recognizable brand images in all of pro sports. Sharing the dream is an important element of the magic that the 49ers have brought to pro football. It starts with the players and coaches. Those who go on to other teams take part of the dream with them, and get to see the magnitude of the 49ers' overall influence on the NFL. Running backs coach Tom Rathman, who believes that, 'living and dying with the 49ers start when the players walk through the front door for the first time', had the opportunity to play for another NFL team before retiring from the field. This gave him an opportunity to compare at first-hand the 49ers and his new club.

Rathman's observation is clinical: 'The difference was night and day. It wasn't even close in the way the organization was run.'

While players are most viscerally at the centre of the dream, the paying fans are only a step away from the 'the snap', and with a highly competitive entertainment industry also scrambling for scarce dollars, the 49ers must provide a reason to fill 3 Com Park each season. The stadium has a capacity of 70,000, and it has been sold out since 1981. Lynn Carrozzi, Ticket Manager, estimates that there are approximately 20,000 people on the waiting list for the existing 65,000 season tickets, which can be passed down through family. Since the stadium is currently owned by the city of San Francisco, the 49ers, who share the facility with the Giants baseball team, are severely restricted in their ability to 'customize' and market the 49ers brand according to their specific needs. Nevertheless, the existing, long-standing fan base has developed its own way of sharing the dream of the 49ers. For a 1.00p.m. Sunday game, the huge parking lot that runs all the way from the stadium down to the water's edge, starts filling up at around 7.00a.m. Those with motor-homes will arrive the night before and wait for the parking lot gates to be opened. The NFL tradition of tail-gate barbecues and parties is in full swing by mid-morning. At Christmas the carnival-like atmosphere includes bringing tons of snow down from the mountains, and Christmas trees with lights are rigged up all over the lot. Most seasoned fans will only enter the stadium forty-five minutes before the start of the game. When they enter their section of the stadium they are sharing an experience that has been passed down through each generation. They will see the same families, gate-men and ushers who have enjoyed the same rituals for years. Stadium staff go the extra mile for their customers, sometimes visiting season-ticket holders in their seats in order to address an issue or concern raised in correspondence with the ticket office. Fowell describes this technique as, 'turning negatives into positives'. Sponsors too, are very aware of this captive audience. Bruce Popko:

> The mystique of this organization and its success, year in and year out, continues to help us sell. The nice thing here is that we have been able to be more selective with the partners that we are doing business with. We don't necessarily have to jump at whatever opportunity is there. We can be a little bit more

selective and say to ourselves, let's not only align ourselves with partners that are going to help us maximize our revenue and accomplish a lot of the business, let's align ourselves with companies that we think are going down the same path that we are, philosophically. We want to partner with those at the top of their industry. That is remarkably different from a lot of the other teams in the league.

Winning the *right* way, with class, makes sharing the dream that much more potent. Popko argues that, 'This creates a much larger fan base which enables the 49ers to sustain their position, while other teams temporarily shine and then disappear from the radar screen.'

## GETTING IT DONE

The pressure on the 49ers to perform is intense and stressful. Jerry Rice personifies the way the organization reacts to their environment:

> You know, the expectations out here are so high. You start that winning tradition and the fans are very unforgiving. This team is supposed to win. It's a lot of pressure on you, but I love pressure. Life is nothing without pressure. If you could come out here every day and just run around, with no pressure on you, or go on that football field on that given Sunday, and there's no pressure, then I don't think you're going to have a good time. I love the game so much that I challenge myself during the offseason to get better. I never feel like I've really played that perfect game, and that's the extra incentive to go out there and get into the best shape of your life.

The determination to win has created a climate where the organization is able to channel individual effort successfully, according to an unremitting focus which is recognized by all. Everyone strives to be the best that they can be – to exceed their personal best. From a player's point of view this is very much *de rigueur*, even more so with the advent of the salary cap, which ensures that all the NFL teams spend roughly the same amount of money on salaries. Mariucci argues that this 'puts everyone on an even keel, making things more challenging, with a premium on superior personal performance'. Mora believes that the organization is well placed to deliver, noting that, 'You are stepping into an environment where I believe your level of performance increases because it's expected of you.' Andy Sugarman, new to the 49ers with coach Mariucci, immediately grasped the importance of exceeding personal best:

> I've noticed in my relatively short time working here, that every day you show up for work you've got to be ready to go 100 miles an hour, and it's expected that you take it another level, higher than you first thought you could. The hard part is probably getting to that level, but once you are there, it snowballs and it becomes what is expected.

Organizationally, the impact of almost two decades of winning seasons has led to a reinterpretation of what winning means. Winning better than the last win drives the organization. All portfolio holders are constantly looking to improve on their previous personal best. Whether it is travel, marketing, or stadium operations, the sense of dissatisfaction is always present. Murlan Fowell:

> In stadium operations, we don't have a direct competitor, as the guys on the field do, so I am driven to be the best in what I do. In our job, we're playing against ourselves, so we've got to be able to see how far we want to go. It's not a competition, there's not an opponent. We have a function and we want to do that the best we possibly can.

High expectations throughout the organization, aided and abetted by a culture of constant improvement in all aspects of the business, naturally lead to a proliferation of game-breaking ideas. At the same time, industry-level change is profoundly difficult when the parameters of operations appear to differ little, from year to year. Jim Mercurio, from stadium operations, explains Murlan Fowell, was determined to help the 49ers redefine industry practice:

> Let me give you an example. It's easy in this business not to make change; it's easy just to do the same old thing year after

year, but when Jim came to work here several years ago, one thing he grabbed on to was our credential and security system. He came to me with a system which we then developed over a couple of years and now it is the best, not only in the NFL, but probably in professional sports in the United States. Other people are coming to us and saying, 'Explain your system to us!' It pretty much reversed the way we did things, simplifying it and making it self-regulating. It's much more effective. Now another team would not typically have championed this initiative. We're open to new ideas.

Every single day the 49ers broker, support and develop better ways to make things happen. Efficiencies, savings and resource investments are continually calibrated to serve the focus of the organization. According to Popko this means that, 'We are always able to stay one step ahead of the curve at every point, and we do it without showing our hand to everyone else.'

Being the most successful franchise in the NFL means that all aspects of the operation are always subject to close critical scrutiny from other NFL teams as well as the media and the broader entertainment industry. This creates an added incentive to avoid negative commentary, although it is next to impossible to find evidence of organizational neglect. The defining quality of the 49er system is that of ensuring that the players can focus on the field of play, which has led to a near obsessional devotion to looking after the last detail. Every organization in this study exhibits the ability to cover detail competently, but the 49ers elevate this aspect of their work to a level of intensity that words do not adequately convey. The passion in Dave Rahn's voice was evident when he explained to us the 'details details details' of travel operations. As well as organizing bigger planes, better hotels and better food, his department looks after everything from the players, coaches and their extended families, to the logistics and layout of the hotel. In reconnaissance visits to away venues, bus and truck travel times from hotel to stadium are assiduously logged, as are the eating arrangements, right down to the condiment settings. Dave Rahn:

I will look at the specs from a hotel that we have not stayed at before and they are always extremely vague. When I ask for more information and request certain things to be done the hotels invariably come back and tell me that other NFL teams have never concerned themselves with such matters. Once we provide direction they actually appreciate the detailed outlines.

Such care for the last detail is not without psychological costs on occasion. During the 1997–8 season, as the 49ers won the divisional title and prepared for their conference championship game against the Green Bay Packers, Rahn was part of a large senior management team working on arrangements for the Super Bowl in San Diego.

I still have a filing cabinet that is full of stuff. We were in San Diego three times, mapping it all out. We had to imagine moving about 1,000 to 1,200 people. Much of this fell on my shoulders. My timetable was that we would have to be there on the Monday after winning the conference game. We didn't want the players worrying about tickets so we would have had to get them out by Monday or Tuesday at the latest. I have a whole stack of manilla envelopes with names written on them, ready for the tickets that never came.

I had my timetable and logistics in the computer, and individualized letters for everybody, ready to be printed out for another set of envelopes also to be handed out on Monday, saying, 'Here is all your Super Bowl information.' I had the whole thing orchestrated. Everything was detailed. I had every office laid out, every office diagrammed at the hotel, every phone, every computer, everything, down to the last detail. I had it all mapped out because I had to. You have to prepare for the unknown. But going right to the brink and getting knocked out . . . it was terrible.

Lynn Carrozzi, responsible for ticketing, is similarly inspired to cover all possible outcomes, for which there are no written procedures. Indeed, not for the first time, we heard the incantation, 'It's pretty much in my head and their heads.' Where a task has a direct impact on a particular customer, personal attention overrides automated systems.

If season-ticket holders change their seat location, I do that manually – one of the girls will then input what I have done manually into the computer and a third one will check it to make sure that they match. We do a lot of what seems to be double work or over work, but since detail is so important in this office, I would rather overkill than neglect something.

This level of care, for the last detail, can be found amongst all staff. Fontana believes that 'it is something that carries through the entire organization'. The same level of detailed planning that accompanies the players on away games is replicated when the 49ers take the organization on retreat. All arrangements, including ground transport, flights and accommodation are taken care of, right down to personalized gifts being placed on the bed in the hotel rooms when everyone arrives.

Such extreme concentration on getting things right means that everyone in the organization takes care of the last detail, making 'managerial control' redundant. Duffy explains:

We have no need to approach things mechanically – we don't need an IBM system of purchasing or approvals. Trust in our people, to do the detail in their own department and even in other departments too, when necessary, lets them flow creatively. With a clear focus on the corporate goal we can all do what is best for the 49ers.

The ultimate goal embraced by the 49ers is the removal of all impediments, all negative forces, to enable concentration on the game plan. Collectively, this state of flow can lead to powerful surges of self belief. Recalling his first Super Bowl ring, Jerry Rice described how it felt to know that he was about to write a page in the sports history book:

We won Super Bowl XXIII on the final drive of the game. The game had been back and forth the entire time, and now, with three minutes left, everything was on the line. When Joe ran into the huddle, even with the crowd screaming, you could hear a pin drop. The *focus* was so strong, with so much excitement, we knew we could get the job done, because we'd been in that situation before. In the huddle, we were all smiling because we knew we were going to win. Taking a ball over ninety yards, to win the Super Bowl – one mistake, and it's over. You lose.

But we were so sharp and we made the right plays, and won. Man, that's the ultimate.

Those in administration express similar sensations of superior performance, invariably commenting on moments when time seems to distort and pleasure, tension and exhaustion collide. In contrast, following a tightly disciplined training session, Steve Young described to us a distortion in 'space', and in doing so provided one of the most evocative stories encountered on the project. His job is to move the ball forward – this is the essential measure of greatness in the NFL. And Young fulfils the criteria for greatness in every way. A peerless record of playoff contentions, divisional and NFL championships, alongside a Super Bowl ring, help to define the man and his craft. There are few more powerful images in sport than that of the gridiron quarterback, who, in the face of organized opposition, inexorably drives his team down the field to secure a touchdown. Ever since the game was first played, this mesmerizing progress has been seen as symbolic. The running game represents the hard yards of life, with the promise of occasional rapid breakthrough. The passing game offers the seduction of quicker, more immediate progress, but can be an all-or-nothing gamble. On every play, these elements appear to be in balance:

> I focus on tilting the field so that we are going downhill. The sheer momentum is carrying you that way. It's funny; I've had the experience of sitting on the sidelines when the quarter finishes, and we have to switch ends – now, psychologically, we were just running downhill in one direction, and we don't want to go uphill. I really have to concentrate to make sure we are going downhill again, but in the opposite direction. Mentally, I have to retilt the field.

In metaphorical terms, the whole of the 49ers organization is dedicated to helping Young both tilt and retilt the field. This becomes most evident in the preparation and lead-up to the football game.

# GAME WEEKEND

The trust between the players and administration is supreme. This is clearly evident when the players assemble on Saturday at the San Francisco Marriott airport hotel for a Sunday afternoon home game at 3 Com Park. The players are greeted by administrative staff, who have made all the logistical arrangements for them. The atmosphere in the hotel lobby, where the 49ers have set up their own check-in system, powerfully exemplifies the community. One by one, the players muster at the 49ers' desk, staffed by the familiar face of Dave Rahn, who obviously maintains a close personal investment in the players' welfare. Their response is one of affection. Humour and good-natured banter echo around the lobby – the family is coming together. Security, though unobtrusive, is necessarily ever-present. Senior administrators like Duffy are also on hand. Duffy travels to all away games, and on this occasion is also staying at the team hotel the night before the Sunday game. He wastes no time in moving easily between players and administrators alike, softly sharing brief words of mutual recognition and support and, occasionally, more lively dialogue. There are no high fives here, or any of the overt physical demonstrations of manhood that are habitually associated with the NFL. Partners and children are a vital part of this community.

Early Saturday evening the players enter a series of team briefings in readiness for the game on Sunday. In between these meetings, which are run with clockwork precision, the players graze on inviting bowls of M&Ms, chilled sodas or healthier fare. The ambience is both relaxed and focused. At one point, future member of the Hall of Fame, Jerry Rice, attempts to co-ordinate a can of soda, a serviette and a small morsel of food. This is evidently one task too many, and 'soft' hands notwithstanding, Rice unceremoniously drops all items to the floor. Depression settles over a group of administrators who have witnessed this horrifying sight, as they hope that it is not an unwelcome omen for the upcoming game.

The final briefing is attended by all the players, assembled administrators and the odd invited guest. Coach Mariucci starts the session by showing a video montage of the previous game where the 49ers demolished the New Orleans Saints, which is set to evocative music and interspersed with humorous asides inserted from TV shows. The atmosphere is highly charged. The coach then hands out several shirts to selected players for their meritorious contribution in the victory over the Saints. Their dollar value is nominal, yet it is clear that they are prized possessions. Finally, Coach Mariucci winds up the session with a passionate, hard-driving invocation on how and why the 49ers are going to win their game on Sunday. Using finely measured oratory, he strides among his players, momentarily becoming part of the audience. A hand touches a shoulder as he slowly pivots around, incorporating the whole room into his field of vision.

> We're not going to win tomorrow because we're much better than them or because they're the rookies, or because we're at home and we're the good guys. Those aren't the reasons we're going to win this game. Don't ever kid yourself that that's how you win the football game. That stuff doesn't mean anything, doesn't mean anything. We play harder than them, we play more disciplined than them, we execute our game plan better than they execute their game plan. We take care of the ball better than they take care of the ball. That's why we're going to win the game. You've got to play to that plan.

The locker rooms at 3 Com Park are spartan and unpretentious. They have obviously seen better days. Unsurprisingly they are in sharp contrast to the 49ers' pristine, though modest, training facilities at Santa Clara, an hour's drive south on Highway 101. Nevertheless, the functional locker rooms provide a sufficient, perhaps even appropriate, setting for the team to go through the rituals of game preparation. On entering the facility there is a small ante-room off to the right where the head coach can work with players without distraction. The primary locker room area is split into two levels, making overall communication somewhat fragmented.

No matter, the 49ers have obviously long since made peace with their physical circumstances. They are at home here, preparing for their upcoming game against the Indianapolis Colts. Naturally, access to this hallowed place is restricted, but in keeping with the family orientation, a number of players' children are in evidence.

One of them is the son of Steve Mariucci, who is intent on getting a personal photograph alongside Jerry Rice. He is successful in this endeavour, but Rice takes the opportunity to bind the boy's hands and feet with masking tape. Once he is apparently securely trussed and immobilized, the rest of the locker room grinningly enjoy their adult superiority, but only briefly, as the boy upstages his hero by simply slipping off his sneakers and calmly walking away. This is evidently a team and an extended family which embellishes its strong professional work ethic with fun and empathy.

After a close-fought, thrilling 34–31 victory over the Colts, secured in the dying seconds of the game, the locker room is transformed. It is pure mayhem. The artefacts of victory in the form of binding tape, pads, helmets and endless layers of clothing are strewn around the floor, but this growing mountain fails to impede the animated movement of coaches, administrators, security guards and family. Outside in the parking lot adjacent to the stadium, thousands of fans have fired up their celebratory tailgate barbecues. Two hours after the end of the game enthusiastic fans still congregate at the players' exit gates, waiting to cheer their heroes as they and their families drive off in search of solitude. The greatest cheer is of course reserved for quarterback Steve Young. The roar of delight honours the organization's most inspirational player. The dream is shared and a community's belief in itself is upheld once more.

The morning after is soon lost to a non-stop series of the inevitable thorough game debriefs. By early lunchtime, without apparent design, administrators and players can be found eagerly lining up for salad, burgers, dogs and related trimmings. Ritually, and for longer than anyone can remember, lunch is brought in each week by a different outside caterer, to be consumed communally in one of the briefing rooms, canteen-style. The whole organization is at ease and together.

The afternoon continues with debriefings, but is also punctuated with a light workout on the training field. Steve Young lazily lobs the ball to a willing circle of receivers who rotate counter-clockwise to his anchored position. Others are stretching and politely jogging a field's width. The session is over within the hour. The previous week, Coach Mariucci gave the players Monday off for their stellar performance against the Saints. This Monday, however, marks the beginnings of a week's intensive preparations, designed to avoid the scare given to the 49ers by the Colts. Once more, they will *focus* and develop the skills and mindset that will enable them to execute, execute – to get the job done.

## 'ALL ON THE SAME PAGE'

In the face of considerable internal upheaval, together with constant turbulent external change, the 49ers have been able to establish consistency, continuity and stability in their operations. Recruitment, selection, advancement, retention and 'letting go' are the most visible techniques used to create the future. Although the franchise has grown in extraordinary and significant ways, the organizational footprint remains clearly mapped. Getting the job done is a sharp phrase which carries discipline and expectations beyond its cliché-ridden origins. Personal and organizational sacrifice are the defining contours of the footprint. Players and office staff who pursue interests, personal or otherwise, outside this tight configuration of values eventually leave the 49ers. There is no place for those who do not share the dream. Bill Walsh, apart from winning three Super Bowls, established the guiding principle that administrative functions needed to be constantly and unceasingly focused on helping the players win football games. The respect and affection afforded Mr DeBartolo provide the necessary glue which ensures that everyone is 'on the same page'. The results have been remarkable. Dave Rahn:

> Since 1981 the bar has been set so high. We have been through and won five Super Bowls, and have worked with some of the greatest players in the game. One day we will sit back and say, 'Man that was incredible, that was just an incredible run that we were part of.'

# CHAPTER 10

# Team New Zealand – The Making of Black Magic

*If it was going to be easy it wouldn't have been worth trying. We have taken on the rest of the world at the hardest game available – the America's Cup – and won. This project was a two-year 'heads down, blinkers on' campaign. It was a long-term project where only total commitment could succeed, and where a win was never guaranteed. But as long as everyone could put their hands on their hearts at the end and know that they had given everything there was to give, that was all I could ask for.* – Sir Peter Blake on the Team New Zealand 1995 America's Cup campaign

The America's Cup for international yachting is the oldest continuously contested international sporting competition in the world. Queen Victoria awarded the Cup in 1851 to John Stevens, owner of the schooner *America*, for his crushing victory against a fleet of sixteen of the best of England's racing fleet. The Cup's deed of gift specified that it should be the subject of ongoing friendly yachting competition between countries, and it has been a symbol of national pride ever since.

In the 'Auld Mug's' illustrious and often controversial 150-year history it has changed hands just three times, going to Australia in 1983, back to the USA in 1987 and to New Zealand in 1995. It has never been successfully defended except by the USA. Team New Zealand's dream is to do just that at the thirtieth defence of the America's Cup which takes place in the year 2000 in the glittering waters of the Hauraki Gulf off Auckland, New Zealand.

Six years after his initial victory Stevens handed the trophy, in fact a pitcher rather than a cup, to the New York Yacht Club for safekeeping. Since then, the names of subsequent winning yachts have all been inscribed, but the trophy itself remains nameless. It is an irony of history that countless millions of dollars have been expended in the pursuit of an unnamed cup that is actually a pitcher.

The New York Yacht Club kept winning for 132 years, the longest winning record in international sporting history, thereby cementing the myth that the Cup actually belonged to the USA. During much of this period it was bolted in place, with no thought of it ever being lost. The history of the Cup is marked by the successes and failures of some of the world's richest people – Vanderbilt, Rockefeller, Lipton, Turner, Bond, Koch, Gardini and Fay – vying to demonstrate their technical and sporting prowess in defence of national pride. Alan Sefton, who has been on board all New Zealand's America's Cup campaigns explains:

It's been an American institution. It still is, by the way. It's quite extraordinary. If you go to the East Coast of the States there are generations of American families who have grown up with the America's Cup. It's dominated their whole lives and those of some English families too. For example, when Tommy Sopwith was inducted into the America's Cup hall of fame a couple of years ago, three of his family came over from Britain. They were so emotional. And Britain has never won it in 150 years!

In 1983 wealthy Australian businessman Alan Bond went to New York, with a much publicized 'golden spanner', to unbolt the Cup, and take it home. Skipper John Bertrand came back from 3–1 to even the contest at 3 all, and then sailed through from behind in the last race to squeeze over the line first, and into the history books. Dennis Conner achieved lifelong notoriety as the first American skipper to lose the Cup, and he vowed to get it back. The winning yacht club takes possession of the trophy, and is responsible for organizing the next defence in its home waters, so in 1987 Dennis Conner set course for Australia, where he successfully atoned for his defeat and recovered his nation's honour.

After sailing straight into contention with two narrow losses in the Challenger series finals in 1987 and 1992, Team New Zealand convincingly removed 'The Auld Mug' to Auckland after a perfect

1995 campaign. They sailed away with only one loss on the water in the Challenger series (preliminary to the finals), and a 5–0 wipe-out against Dennis Conner's *Young America* in the America's Cup finals. No victory at this level of international sport has been so decisive and no welcome home could have been more magical than that which awaited the crew of *Black Magic* as they arrived in Auckland airport on a specially chartered Boeing. In Auckland, and nationwide, it was carnival time for weeks, with welcome parades and parties the length and breadth of the country.

## THE AMERICA'S CUP

The America's Cup is the fourth most-watched sporting spectacle after the Olympics, the soccer World Cup and Formula One. Tony Thomas, manager of the America's Cup 2000 Regatta events (AC2000), gave us the facts:

> The year 2000 regatta is over five months, and up to three months of that will be covered live on TV. This is up to twenty-eight days of live coverage and three hours plus per day. Last time there was a cumulative total of 600 hours of television coverage and a total reach of 382 million homes. This equates to viewers of more than 600 million.

This is a sport where campaigns can cost over US $60 million. The course to the America's Cup is long and arduous. Years of preparation (normally three to five years between competitions) are required, leading to months of trials during the Challenger elimination series for the Louis Vuitton Cup, then weeks of competition in which the current holder of the America's Cup competes against the winner of the Challenger series. So how did New Zealand, a small Pacific island nation with a population of 3.5 million (about the size of San Diego), take on the technological and financial might of wealthy syndicates from the world's richest and most technologically advanced nations, and win so perfectly? This is the story of the making of *Black Magic*.

New Zealand has the highest proportion of boat owners of any nation in the world. No New Zealander lives far from the sea or a lake, and the mild climate enables year-round, cyclone-free sailing. From as young as five, Kiwi kids start sailing blunt-bowed Optimist dinghies competitively. They graduate to eight-foot, yacht-like P Class dinghies, a class that has been raced competitively in New Zealand for more than fifty years.[1] And then, as they grow older, they go on to Starlings and Lasers. Most of New Zealand's greatest yachtsmen, such as Russell Coutts, Sir Peter Blake and Chris Dickson, grew up racing P Class. The New Zealand Yachting Federation creates the future of New Zealand yachting through an infrastructure of school, regional, national and international races for all age groups. As a result, New Zealand professional sailors have dominated world sail racing for more than a decade, from windsurfing to the Whitbread Round the World Race. Kiwis are to be found in the yachting crews of most nations. Tom Schnackenberg, Team New Zealand technical and design specialist, explains:

> One of the key factors is that the sailors become, by a process of natural selection, very self-reliant. They have to demonstrate ability at a very early age or they won't make it through the junior ranks. You can imagine the first time dad takes them down to the beach, and mum gets them organized in their Optimist and rigs the boat and unrigs, while the kids just play on the beach! But the ones who are keen find that mum and dad's enthusiasm runs out, and pretty soon they are organizing their own boat. They are bullying dad or their neighbours into fixing things, or they are working together, and then starting to do the work themselves. Then they end up as late-teenagers competing internationally. They really have to be able to manage themselves around the world. So we have got this big team of yachties who are independent, innovative and self-reliant. When the Team New Zealand guys show up in some town, they will come in from different parts of the world, either hitching a ride in a boat, being flown by someone in a private jet or just coming in conventionally on an airliner.

From this foundation in competitive sailing New Zealand has developed a world-class marine industry that attracts wealthy sailors from Asia, Europe and the USA for cruising, construction and comprehensive refits. Cutting-edge designers, skilled tradesmen, Kiwi innovation and exquisite quality can all be obtained at competitive prices. So the winds were fair for a quest for the Cup, the modern-day equivalent of New Zealander Edmund Hillary's conquest of Everest. In an age of tumultuous change and instant images the America's Cup provides a sense of history, challenge, romance and adventure.

The Kiwi quest for the cup started spectacularly in 1987, with wealthy merchant banker Michael Fay bankrolling the project, and Match Race champion Chris Dickson at the helm. The Kiwi America's Cup debut was controversial. *KZ7* was made of fibreglass. This provoked protests from other syndicates, since traditionally the 12-Metre Class had been built of aluminium, or, in the early days, of wood. The affair, which became known as 'Glassgate', was resolved in New Zealand's favour, and 'Plastic Fantastic' went on to win thirty-seven races out of thirty-eight in the Challenger selection series. In the final it was *KZ7* against Dennis Conner's *Stars and Stripes*. Alan Sefton analyses the failure:

We didn't know how to win. We didn't have the campaign experience to take the last step, and there were certain cracks appearing in organization and in the chemistry of the team right at the last, when it mattered most. There were some changes made to the boat. The boat can be configured in various ways. *KZ7*, which is the fastest light-winds twelve-metre the world has ever seen, was configured to produce even more light air speed for the series against Conner. Now, Fremantle is a strong wind area, and we struck a period of quite strong winds. In Western Australia the weather pattern is dictated by a low-pressure system in the interior which sets up the 'Fremantle Doctor' phenomenon. It sucks in the sea breeze. Now, that pattern is dominant until the first cyclone comes ashore in North Australia. The first one was sitting just off the coast. If it had come ashore it would have destroyed the 'Doctor', which was at its peak. We struck a period where it blew nineteen knots plus for six weeks, and lo and behold the night we got knocked out the cyclone came ashore. And from the next day on the America's Cup was sailed in light winds. Conner beat Australia in a set of conditions in which *KZ7* would have murdered him, which we proved later in the year in the world twelve-metre championships. Knowing we would have light air speed to burn away we should have protected ourselves by configuring more at the other end of the scale. But hindsight is a wonderful thing, and it was a fabulous campaign by anybody's standards. We just had not got every last detail right and we didn't know how to win.

Having come so close, Fay did not intend to give up the dream easily. In 1988, he changed the rules of the game with an early challenge, which is legal under the Cup's deed of gift. The Kiwi challenge came not in the twelve-metre class, but in the form of a massive monohull yacht, colloquially known as 'the big boat', which was dramatically different in its design from the traditional yachts which had featured in the America's Cup for much of its history. Fay wanted to take the contest back to the glorious J Class days of the early twentieth century, but San Diego YC defended in a catamaran[2] and won easily. The next two years were spent in the courts debating the legality of both vessels. The Kiwis won in the lower court, but lost on appeal. This sorry saga had a silver lining, since the outcome was a radical update in design which created a new International America's Cup Class yacht, spectacular in its speed. The way was clear for the America's Cup to become a massive media and marketing extravaganza. It is now no longer dependent on the very rich, but offers multinational sponsors excellent value for money, and opportunities for professional sailors to pursue both fortune and national glory.

The first of the competitions with the new design took place in 1992. The new class opened up the opportunity to develop the most sophisticated technology in all dimensions of design and construction, from meteorology to masts and mainsails, from finite element analysis and computational fluid dynamics to velocity prediction. The America's Cup campaigns attract the world's best designers and engineers, boat builders, sail makers and sailors. We even found people who had worked on America's Cup campaigns at WilliamsF1.

'Michael Fay and David Richwhite, his merchant bank partner, did everything they could to make sure the 1992 campaign was successful, and it nearly was again,' Alan Sefton affirms. The campaign lacked for nothing in funding, and had New Zealander Bruce Farr as designer. Farr was recognized as the world's best. Alan Sefton: 'The campaign was designer driven. It was knitted around the Farr office, and they wanted to make decisions ranging from the design of the boats to signing off PR releases.' In this second challenge New Zealand again reached the final of the Louis Vuitton Cup, winning with ease all the way. At 4–1 up against *Il Moro di Venezia* of Italy in the final, *NZL 20* looked unstoppable. But a legal judgement cut her challenge short.

The bowsprit that was used to help gybe spinnakers was ruled illegal by the international jury. A previous jury had approved the bowsprit earlier in the competition. One more match and it would have been all over, but the jury ruled that one match be taken away as penalty. Alan Sefton describes the consequences:

> Our focus went completely. We concentrated on contesting the allegations at a time when we should have been concentrating on boat speed. The bowsprit had certain boat handling advantages, but it probably didn't contribute anything to boat speed. This eroded the confidence of the crew. They had spent the whole time sailing with the bowsprit which had been approved for the first round-robin races, so they had become very used to the system. When the Italians got the jury to reverse the original ruling, the whole handling system had to be completely changed, and that's very difficult. It was hard in the original configuration, but they had perfected it. Peter Blake's call early in the controversy was to cut it off and accept defeat on the legal front. He intuitively knew the effect it was having on our psyche.

As the Kiwi confidence was eroded, so was their edge in boat speed. After the first races, *NZL 20* was fitted with a tandem keel. According to Sefton:

> This was a fabulous piece of engineering. It was slim keel blades at the front end and the back end, with this twenty-ton torpedo attached to both of them. The key to it was that both blades turned. That offers some very exciting prospects on the start line, but the reality was that the potential was finite. So, while we were performing close to the top of our game in the finals, *Il Moro* was still able to improve. Once the keel went on there was no going back, because of the structural changes that had to be made. I think possibly the keel was put on because it was

sexy and full of excitement, and maybe people got carried away with the potential, as opposed to the reality of it. This was part of the problem with having a designer-driven campaign.

After the jury ruling, *NZL 20* did not win another race, or lead round another mile against the experienced Paul Cayard of *Il Moro*. The campaign was at an end. *Il Moro* went on to lose in the America's Cup against Bill Koch's *America³*, and the 'Auld Mug' stayed in the USA once more.

Michael Fay and David Richwhite decided they would not try again. Peter Blake had become involved in the last part of the 1992 campaign, with the confidence of earlier success in winning the gruelling Whitbread Round the World Race after seventeen years of trying. But he became disenchanted with the politics of the America's Cup, and was uncomfortable with the competitive management style that had characterized Fay's 1992 campaign. He left early, preferring the cleanly competitive, open ocean environment of the Whitbread, where sailors pitted themselves against the elements.

Alan Sefton was convinced that New Zealand had come too far and learned too much to give up without another attempt, but he had to find new financial backing:

Michael rang up to arrange a game of golf, but really he wanted to talk. I think we played four holes in two and a half hours. You are left with this big hole in the bottom of your stomach, and you don't know what to do with yourself. It was a major hurdle to overcome. I spent the next three weeks in San Diego, watched the finals and helped wind up the campaign. Then I told Peter Blake I was coming over to England to talk, but he clearly wasn't ready, so I disappeared up to my mother's in Wales and got my head out of it for a couple of weeks. Then I went down to Elmsworth and spent a weekend with Peter, and we talked it through. He agreed that he should at least come back to New Zealand and find out what was possible. If you are looking at supporting the campaign entirely out of commercial sponsorship then that's a different kettle of fish entirely.

Sefton knew there was a lot of support in New Zealand, and he knew the value of 'the psychological support and the boost that you get from knowing the whole country is watching', but he and Peter Blake did not know whether this would translate to sponsorship. So, with Michael Fay's advice, they did the rounds of potential New Zealand sponsors. Alan Sefton:

> Yes, it could be done. But there was a very definite ceiling in everyone's mind, and we couldn't get past that ceiling. You realize that there are only so many players in New Zealand that can look at it. We couldn't afford many misses, because we would run out of candidates very quickly, but we were enthused by the reaction. Peter mortgaged his house to pay the entry fee and I paid the running expenses of the campaign. They weren't large, because we were lucky enough to have an office in the Royal New Zealand Yacht Squadron clubhouse, but by my standards they became quite large until we actually got the first sponsorship in.

World Match Race champion, Russell Coutts, soon joined these inspirational players. Alan Sefton:

> Obviously the skipper appointment was very important. I think we canvassed about fourteen different opinions from the yachting community, and the call for Russell was absolutely unanimous. It was quite unbelievable. He brings much more to the campaign than just his ability to steer a boat, and he is the best in the world at that. He is an engineer by profession, so he's got a different mindset to other sailors. The America's Cup is a design contest as much as a sailing contest, and he can bridge from one aspect to the other. By being able to talk on the level of the designers, but from a sailor's perspective, he was instrumental in how that side of the campaign was structured.

With sponsors on board – Telecom, Steinlager, TVNZ, Toyota and Lotto – the campaign got under way rapidly. Limited funds gave the campaign focus – the dream was to win the America's Cup, but the focus was 'making the boat go faster'. Peter Blake says that, 'The limited budget was a plus, because it forced us to concentrate on what would give us a quicker boat around the course.'

At this point Team New Zealand realized that a peak performing, team-based organization would be needed to succeed against intensifying international competition. Alan Sefton:

Everything very quickly became team focused and a team decision. And that really is a Blake trait. He is a natural leader, but he doesn't just act arbitrarily. If a decision needs to be made, Peter will make it, but his normal way of doing about things is to get people around him who he has complete faith in. He canvasses opinion constantly, listens and then finds the right consensus. That was also Russell's inclination from the sailing perspective, so the team just grew along these lines. Some America's Cup campaigns have been skipper driven, as with Dennis Conner or Paul Cayard, or our 1987 campaign with Chris Dickson. Then we went to the other extreme in 1992 with a designer-driven campaign. neither of these approaches worked, so there had to be a smarter way. It was agreed that this would be a campaign managed by the whole team.

This decision inevitably led to a break with designer Bruce Farr, as Tom Schnackenberg describes:

He is a really good designer, and he had been the designer for all the campaigns in the past, so he was the logical choice. But there was a desire to manage the design, to let the sailor customers be in charge of the design team, and to have it in-house so that it was a very open process. Bruce wasn't too keen on a lot of that process, because he is a very powerful designer, very good, but used to making his own decisions. He sells his designs and he works with his customers, and he lays out options for them, but he controls the work and the intellectual content. So the sailors hired the design team, and Russell charged off round the world to interview potential designers. Most of them took time to talk to us, and we just asked them how they would go about winning the America's Cup. They were quite forthcoming, because they realized that we were implicitly asking them if they were interested in working with us. We built the design team from that start.

There is a design language and a yachties language, so we had to work on communication, and the designers had to unbend to try to understand the questions they were getting, and of course the sailors had to come some way to understanding the design process. The design team would meet each morning all through the summer as the boat was being put together. There was constant interplay between sailors and designers.

Peter Blake says, 'It was important to learn by our mistakes and not to have too many repeats . . . so our collective knowledge was built into the boat.' For example, a wooden mock-up of the deck was built to enable the sailors to pinpoint perfect positioning for winches, leads and workstations.

The Team New Zealand management style was born. It was decided early on that as the sailors would have to take what was delivered around the course, they would be the customers. They made it clear that they did not want a boat from one side of the design spectrum, like *NZL 20*. They wanted a boat close to what everybody else had got, but they also wanted boat-speed edge! There is no substitute for boat speed.

Team New Zealand's vision statement for the 1995 campaign was simple and 'new age':

Our aim is to build a challenge that can win for New Zealand and that we can be proud of – to succeed in all aspects.
We want a small, informed and fully motivated team that:

• Works in an environment which encourages every member to make a meaningful contribution
• Has a high degree of personal integrity and group honesty
• Recognizes personal goals but not hidden agendas
• Continuously monitors and improves its performance
• Is fun to be in.

Alan Sefton says that 'Team New Zealand actually runs as a Team'. To achieve this, there is a raft of meetings at different levels, so that everybody is always fully informed. Alan Sefton:

For example, in 1992, if you tried to find out anything about the boat you would not have succeeded unless you had a triple A CIA classification. Even lots of people within the campaign were not allowed to go under the skirts and see the keel. We went absolutely the other way in 1995. We decided it was everybody's campaign. We always told everybody in the team exactly what we were doing . . . if we were in the test tanks in

England, they knew why we were there, what we were testing on this visit and so on.

Security around America's Cup events has to be very high, and this helps build community – it reinforces the belief in being part of something that is very special. Sefton:

> In 1995 the policy of keeping everybody informed didn't let us down. It worked very well because everybody bought into the campaign, and, in particular, they understood that the dollars were finite.

Tom Schnackenberg confirms that the sailors were central to the development process. In 1995 the two *Black Magic* boats, known by their registration numbers as *NZL32* and *38* were almost identical, so that it was possible to make small changes in one to test for an improvement in boat speed. Team New Zealand delayed the building of the first boat until the design process had been completed, so that the two boats could be built together. The Australians, French, Japanese and Americans all built their boats sequentially, so their boats leap-frogged each other whereas the Team New Zealand pair had a similar performance spectrum, and both were kept up to scratch right the way through. This matched pair, two-boat campaign was a game-breaking idea that has now been adopted by most syndicates, and is central to Team New Zealand's relentless search for speed.

> *America³* did the same thing, but the design team operated as scientists. They would change the boat but not tell the sailors what they had done, because they did not want them to have preconceived notions that might prejudice the results of the test. Whereas we did the opposite. The sailors were involved in making the decisions as to what to change. Their involvement meant that the quality of the testing was much higher, due to increased focus and concentration. I was part of the design and sailing teams, and I could see we wound up making much better decisions. The sailors were the customers, and everyone else was supplying them.

Through inclusion, Team New Zealand built community. Because people have been together for a long time, and some of the relationships go back to the formative years, there is a strong sense of family. Tom Schnackenberg:

> We squabble just like families do, and there is a sort of openness that you get in normal families, yet, just like a family, you stay tight and you work through problems, and when it comes to meeting the outside world, you depend on your family members. You defend each other against attack, and even if you agree with the criticisms, you say, 'Just a minute, you can't say that about one of us.' And we deal with the issue in the family . . .

Admission to the family takes time; personnel decisions are made very slowly and very carefully.

> We are lucky in New Zealand, because there are enough good sailors around to run several teams, so we have the luxury of choice. Enthusiasm is often the important criterion. When we are deciding on a person, one of the key factors is whether they are compatible, so that everyone is a team player. You don't want team players in the sense of 'me too' people. We have got some fiery individuals who play in our touch football games with plenty of scrapping, but again, that's like a family. The interplay of strong personalities in an open family setting builds strength. Because it's a family, we try to get a genuine consensus when hiring somebody, so that the person is accepted.

Russell Coutts says that this approach extends to all significant decisions in the sailing and design teams:

> Team is a big word. TNZ is not as it may be perceived with strong leaders directing all the operations. It is actually very much consensus–led, and ideas are aired to the group. Key decisions are made quite slowly, and discussed thoroughly. There is a high degree of individual responsibility. Team talks about lack of motivation or slackness are very rare, and when they do happen they are usually discussions where comment is two-way. We are particular about getting suitable people who fit in with this approach.

Peter Blake confirms the importance of the Team New Zealand community. According to him, success comes down to 'forward planning, a united team approach and a clearly focused goal', but to do the planning and make the correct decisions the right people are needed:

> This includes not only the sailing crew, but also the shore manager and secretary, designer, boat builders, sail makers, computer wizards, engineers, i.e. the overall team. Everyone has to buy in. There are no small jobs. Everyone is important. The weather boat up the course is as vital as the man on the bows. Every person's input is valued, and all ideas are welcome. The finer details are outlined to everyone, because if you haven't got trust you haven't got anything. Success comes from a combination of all the factors, so the less meaningful jobs must not be overlooked. We keep the team small by the standard of other syndicates, and we pay them as well as we can. We don't pamper people too much, and we don't force them to live in each other's pockets or impose curfews, as happened in the 1992 campaign. Everyone is given his own space and trusted not to let the team down. The chemistry has to be right, the attitudes have to be right, and people have got to be able to have fun, or they won't give everything of which they are capable.

Both expertise and a good attitude are essential, Peter Blake continues:

> We have to have people with specific types of expertise: sail makers, riggers, spar makers, boat builders, electricians, engineers, people with medical knowledge, helmsmen, sail trimmers, bowmen, mastmen, navigators, winch grinders, etc. Each person has an area of expertise for which he is totally responsible, but most people have two or three jobs, and can turn their hands to almost anything. Everyone knows from the start that if they don't perform they will let the rest of the team down. We expect them to perform right from the beginning, so we take great care about who we take on. Most of all the crew, the team, have to want to win more than anything, and be prepared to give up everything to achieve that aim. They have

to have the same goal, with no hidden agendas. To get the best out of someone it's important to make that person feel that their contribution is worthwhile. People who realize they are appreciated and that their views will be listened to will give far more of themselves. It's also important that the team like their jobs, and because they do they have an immense amount of job satisfaction.

Team New Zealand emphasizes the importance of continuity for the strength of community, but knows that new blood is always needed to sustain the dream. 'Russell and his guys know the new talented sailors and they pull them into Team NZ,' explains Sefton. Russell describes how they go about recruiting:

Obviously, sailing ability and an ability to work with the current group as a team player are important. New sailors must also take ownership of an area that will improve the speed of the yacht as a secondary function, e.g. sail development, weather programme, spar programme, boat building and deck layout, etc. They should therefore have skill or training in one of those areas. We also have an eye for creating the future, so we tend to employ and try out younger people. It is often easier for them to buy into the culture. We generally put new sailors on a six-month (or more) trial. The selection process usually comes down to a vote amongst those affected, or who will be working closely with the new candidate. We try to give new people feedback if they have some negative points but are showing overall potential.

'We do want to encourage the young guys, the twenty-year-olds who are getting really good, to feel that there are opportunities here,' confirms Tom Schnackenberg:

After this defence we will have four fast boats, four masts, lots of sails and, of course, our library of knowledge. So, next campaign we could have six boats, four sailing teams and two racing teams in new boats, with proper trials and lots of opportunity for growth. We hope to keep the Cup for the next forty years.

Tom Schnackenberg had his own reasons for choosing Team New Zealand for the 1995 campaign, having previously worked for John Bertrand's Australian syndicate:

> I felt that I could make a bigger contribution in this team, and saw that there was a need for me. John Bertrand had gathered a big team around him. I could see people there who did exactly what I did, who I respected, so it was time to move on. It was nothing to do with money, because I hadn't even asked either team what they had in mind for salary. I hadn't any notion whether I would get more or less or the same. The question for me was whether I could make a difference.

Team New Zealand expects that everybody will make a difference throughout the campaign. It is clear to everybody that they go to meetings to contribute, not just to listen. Alan Sefton reveals how this approach has led to game-breaking ideas:

> We made several very significant speed gains this way. One was in the sail area, where two or three sailors had developed a particular idea on their own. Under normal circumstances, sail design would be left to the designers and sail makers, but they raised the idea, were encouraged, and were given a bit of a budget and time. They developed a sail shape that was very significant.
>
> We got to the stage in San Diego where we could go straight from design to manufacture through computers. We could take a design for a set of wings for the keel straight to the milling machine. Now, there are endless combinations of position and pitch shape, and you could spend the rest of your life twitching around getting them right. The first set we made in stainless steel cost us nearly US$30,000, so we weren't going to be making too many! The boat builders thought about this and came up with a system using plywood and carbon fibre, and we were making wings for US$300, so that changed the ball game completely, because we could test all sorts of combinations.
>
> Tom Schnackenberg wanted to develop a twisted wind tunnel. A normal wind tunnel is a bit artificial, because it has smooth surfaces, whereas the ocean is not smooth. The wind actually does a lot of different twists and turns over the wave

pattern, and the wind at the top of the mast is quite different to the wind at the bottom. So Tom, being the boffin he is, came up with this idea. Everyone looked at him a bit sideways, but we knew that Tom comes up with game-breaking ideas, so we said, 'There is no budget, but if you can fund it, off you go.' So he went round to people like Ross Blackman in administration and me, begging and borrowing to come up with a result. Because it was for boat speed we all found some money out of our budgets, and it proved to be a great idea.

The sense of community encourages people to contribute, and to develop game-breaking ideas. It also facilitates information sharing, which assists everyone to exceed their personal best by drawing on ideas and encouragement from others.

Internal competition and politics are minimized through community, based on a key insight from the 1992 campaign. In 1992 there were three would-be skippers and two crews competing with each other. Each crew position had two crew members who were set against each other in selection trials to get picked for the final crew, thereby destroying any sense of team unity. The result was infighting and lack of focus. According to Peter Blake, 'The 1992 crew didn't know why they were out there.' Alan Sefton explains:

That was very destructive within the team. One bowman wouldn't talk to the other about procedures and better ways of doing things. Michael Fay, using market principles, thought that competition would bring out the best team, but it doesn't work that way. Last time round we named the sailing crew eighteen months out.

The intense community culture of Team New Zealand was at first strange to Tony Thomas, who was hired from a marketing background in 1997 to lead the management of America's Cup 2000:

There are no HR procedures, no strategic planning and no job descriptions. Just instant trust, to which you respond. At first I was annoyed, because everyone wanted to know what I was doing and to get involved. I interpreted this as a lack of trust, but it soon became apparent that this was the culture; everyone is interested in everything and wants to help.

Team New Zealand is organized along traditional functional lines – design, sailing, boat builders, rig, sails, sponsorship, PR and accounting – as are all our Peak Performing Organizations, and, in common with the others, there is easy movement across functional boundaries. The lines of hierarchy are flexible. Alan Sefton: 'Peter Blake is the boss, but Peter also pulls bloody strings on the boat! Because he was willing to do any job that needed to be done, people realized early on that it was a different style of campaign.' The departmental heads meet two or three times a week, or more if required. Monday meetings are held with the whole team – each department describes in a few minutes, with an overhead, what they achieved the previous week, and what they have planned for the one coming. Then, once a month, there is a full-scale team meeting where everybody is there unless they have good reason not to be. In these meetings there are more formal presentations. All the key decisions are made on a consensus basis. Tom Schnackenberg: 'If we couldn't agree on a decision, it generally meant that we didn't know enough to make the decision, so the normal course of action then was to go back and look at the question again.'

Peter Blake would give team talks to inspire the team, and to impress on everyone the importance of careful cost saving, and not leaving anything to chance. However, he rarely acted in the traditional manner of a syndicate boss when sailing. Tom Schnackenberg can only remember two occasions in the 1995 campaign:

> Peter was invited on to the boat as part of the sailing crew, but he asserted his position only twice. Once was the day when the Australians sank. He was very quick to get on the radio as we were leaving the dock, and start badgering the race committee not to run the races. Normally you would not see him anywhere near the radio. Another time was when we completely ran out of wind. He was down below with a few others to concentrate the weight on top of the keel. Eventually we ground to a halt because there was no wind. All Peter's Whitbread experience came to the fore, and he leapt on deck and started whistling, tapping the boom and doing all the little superstitious things that you do in the Whitbread race to be in the lead. It was very funny.

Blake created the focus that led to pre-eminence, but Team New Zealand is more than just Peter Blake. A crew full of inspirational players has developed the dream: Tom Schnackenberg in charge of design; Brad Butterworth the tactician; Russell Coutts; Bob Rice on meteorology; and Tim Gurr as boat builder. All together there are about seventy people in the Team New Zealand organization, including sixteen in the sailing crew. Most team members are sailors and are involved with Team New Zealand because they love sailing. According to Peter Blake, 'They are so keen they will walk over broken glass for Team New Zealand.'

Alan Sefton confirms that the organization is now so strong that it is independent of any one individual, although,

> Certain players are very important, like Russell, who is the absolute focal point of the sailing team. Russell has specific people who sail in his match race team, people like Brad Butterworth and Simon Daubney, who are like an extension of Russell. They are very talented in their own right, but they are completely sold on the Russell philosophy and the way he goes about things. The whole operation has got its own impetus running with the team philosophy. There are guys in Team NZ who the world never sees, like Laurie Davidson, Clay Oliver or Mike Drummond, yet these guys are pivotal in the programme, and in their own way as important as Russell, Brad or Peter.

Responsibility for leadership lies throughout the organization. In fact, the idea of leadership, with the implicit corollary of followership, sits uncomfortably, as Tom Schnackenberg describes:

> We've got a few followers, but not very many. Almost everyone is a part-time inspirational player. I don't see myself as a leader, but I can be a stirrer at times! Everyone is wild to get on, so they will poke at one of the other people who are maybe seen as leaders, and say you should be doing this or that. And because there is respect right across the group they have impact. It's almost like the players are running it. So the team is managing itself.

This observation was brought home to us when we realized that Peter Blake has his home in England, and that he spent several months sailing around the world on *ENZA*, winning the Jules Verne non-stop around-the-world speed record during the build-up to the 1995 campaign. Tom explains:

> Peter was the leader last time, but on the boat and among the sailors it's really more Russell. Peter described himself as 'just the catalyst', but he was much more than that. He showed a huge amount of leadership in keeping us going financially, and nobody would have got anywhere without him. The thing he did which was really good was to keep us thinking about what could go wrong. He made a big impact at the beginning, but we actually went through part of the campaign on our own while he was on *ENZA*, winning the Trophée Jules Verne, of the Association 'Tour du Monde en 80 Jours', awarded for the fastest circumnavigation of the world in under eighty days. Peter Blake and his crew completed their circumnavigation on 1 April 1994 in 74 days, 22 hours and 22 seconds. He kept in touch by e-mails from the yacht, which were pretty garbled when it was going up and down in big waves. Listen, learn, help and lead, that is Peter's style. He's in and out, but his inspiration is always there.

Peter Blake carried Fay's dream forwards, made it his own, and shared it widely. His Whitbread Round the World Race and Jules Verne Trophy wins made him an icon in New Zealand and attracted world attention (later leading to an invitation to become President of the prestigious Cousteau Society). His knife-edge exploits were widely televised, and his understated manner gave him instant media appeal in a country where people are judged by what they achieve, not what they say. As a romantic adventurer, Peter has it all.

Michael Fay's dream of wresting the America's Cup from the USA was shared by New Zealand's avid sailors, but neither the 1987 or 1992 campaigns, successful as they were, found their way into the national psyche. The publicity surrounding the campaigns was brash and corporate. From the outset Peter Blake resolved that the 1995 campaign would be based around deeds, not words. This understated approach appealed to sponsors such as Telecom, Steinlager Toyota, Lotto and TVNZ, and massive public support developed as the regatta progressed. Typical of this was the 'red socks' campaign. As *Black Magic*'s relentless voyage to victory progressed, Peter appeared in the afterguard wearing what quickly became known as lucky red socks. From a joke within the sailing team, the red socks became a national symbol of support for the sailors. Red socks were on sale everywhere, with proceeds going to assist the campaign. And so the dream was shared.

As Alan Sefton explains:

> All you have got to sell is your dream. You are asking others to invest in your dream to win the America's Cup. Some might think it's an absurd dream or a pathetic dream, but that's really all you have got to sell. But when you think that ninety-three per cent of all New Zealanders watched the last race in the last America's Cup, it's phenomenal. When you have got that kind of national interest in what you are doing and in what you are trying to achieve, then you have got something that you can go to sponsors with and get them excited about. The dream is possibly harder to sell this time than it was last time, because the world has changed. The boards are a lot more cautious, because they are increasingly responsible to the shareholders, so the sponsorship has to stack up commercially. In a campaign such as this, you are always trying to define the media exposure to demonstrate how broadly the dream is shared.

Peter's goal was to bring the Cup back to New Zealand and to create a spectacle that New Zealanders could enjoy. Tom Schnackenberg describes how, beyond defending the Cup, Peter wants to help New Zealand present itself to the world:

> He is one of the drivers for the entire marine facility here, saying international syndicates won't come unless you build decent facilities. Whereas the rest of us are more focused on getting faster boats in order to defend the Cup, Peter is very focused on trying to maximize the opportunities for New Zealand.

Russell Coutts sees the dream in the same way:

> I believe the key for NZ is to defend the Cup successfully for ten years or more. I think our success will help the economy, but it needs to be repeated to have any long-term benefit or

impact. The America's Cup in New Zealand needs to be a regular event . . . perhaps every two or three years. We don't need to get everything about the event correct this time, provided we have the chance to improve it next time. However, if mistakes are made defending we won't get the chance to correct anything next time! Therefore my primary focus is for Team NZ to win this time and to develop a broader base of skill amongst the sailors for future defences.

Sustaining a dream that has been achieved requires imagination. Alan Sefton describes the America's Cup as 'a sporting Everest; the pinnacle of the sport'. But, like all personal or organizational 'Everests', once climbed, the incentives to do it again are reduced. It is in the nature of the human spirit to seek constantly extended challenges, to sustain the dream. For Team New Zealand the dream has extended to being the first team outside the USA to defend the trophy successfully, but for individual team members the dream has to be more personal. Tom Schnackenberg revealed to us how he has retained the magic second time around:

It's difficult, because it's a longer campaign; people come and go. Last time we were together for a short time, and we had this adrenalin surge that we can win the Cup. We all had something to prove. I said this to a few of the guys, and one said, 'Well, I have got something to prove.' He was one of our dozen or so new guys. They revitalize the team.

When you start to see a dozen challenges lining up, you see what a huge task lies ahead, and that focuses people's attention. The public actually help to keep us focused by saying, 'You have got to do it.' They sense the magic behind these boats. But what really sustains the magic for me is a feeling that we can actually improve a lot from last time. I think that is the main thing that motivates people, born as individuals and as a team. They realize they can get a lot better, so people are concentrating on improving their skills as sailors and figuring out how our boats work. I think the idea of continuous improvement, even though nobody actually talks about it, provides a focus, as does the sense of being able to hang onto the Cup for a long time.

Personal challenge lies at the heart of Team New Zealand, as it does for all human endeavour. The focus on 'making the boat go faster' provides direction for the dream, and purpose for the players. The testing process has been likened by some to watching the grass grow. However, according to Tom Schnackenberg:

> Having the sailors buying in, knowing what is going on all the time, and even leading some of the ideas, means they become intensely interested in the process. The intensive testing system gets them focused, and then it's just having fun, skylarking around. If there's a sense that people are getting bored or not concentrating we just go home. There is no big hand like Peter Blake saying we have got to stay out until five o'clock. The people out there just want to stay to get the job done.
>
> Having done a few campaigns I think we will have to force ourselves to move on in the future. It's good when someone like Peter sees a new goal in the Cousteau Society, and that gives him a new focus in life. People like myself think, maybe if we can't get enthusiastic about the next defence, or the defence after that, we should bale out and let someone else do the job. Some of the older chaps could then become like coaches. We do have to renew ourselves.

The intensity of the focus on speed facilitated communication flow and peak experiences. Peter Blake:

> Communication flow between the crew was vital. Without it we weren't going to win. Tensions do build up, but talking generally cured most problems. Intuition is even more important. Mostly, we anticipate other people's needs through intuition, as we have been working together over a long period.

Russell Coutts explained to us that the sailing team does not use policy manuals or job descriptions to communicate internally:

> We have developed a crew manual, but more for recording items such as breakdowns and safety procedures and our current thinking, rather than for laying down the correct procedure. Sometimes we try to record a method just to be sure that we can define it correctly for ourselves, and that we all agree.

This flow of information through easy relationships is readily evident throughout the Team New Zealand headquarters at the Viaduct Basin in Auckland. During our several visits we were treated as guests of the family, receiving courtesy and care from everyone we met. Despite the relentless media pressure, and visits from sponsors and friends of the family we observed the same friendliness extended to all. Here is an organization that truly shares its dream.

Security there is tight but not oppressive. The premises are Spartan and open plan. The design team, weather forecasters, sail makers, engineers, electronics, boat builders and sailing team all have their separate areas, but they flow easily into one another. The site is pristine and has a feeling of understated perfection and commitment to precision. Peter Blake's office is central to the action. The Team New Zealand headquarters exudes energy, but there is a calm, relaxed rhythm of activity. No orders are given; no voices are raised; everyone knows his role.

Team New Zealand livery is proudly displayed at all vantage points, while sponsors' logos adorn the buildings and the boats. At the centre of it all stand the twin *Black Magic* boats NZL 32 and NZL 38, sleek and evocative, reminding all concerned of the central focus of the action – making the boat go faster. The silver fern, New Zealand's national symbol, is displayed along the aft topsides as a statement of national pride, alongside sponsors' logos, the symbols of those who have chosen both to share and to finance the dream to sail faster and ever more perfectly in pursuit of personal, organizational and national glory.

We are offered the opportunity to observe the twin *Black Magic* boats in testing at close quarters, from the Team New Zealand chase boat. We realize that this is where the game is won or lost, long before the race starts, so we arrive early for our day out on the water, but today members of the sailing team are shooting basketball hoops in between moving sails, since testing has been postponed at short notice. There is a problem in the rig that must be fixed. We watch identical work taking place on the twin *Black Magic* boats to remedy the problem, but it's a major defect, so they are out of action for the rest of the day. Kristen Sneyd, our guide, and manager to the sailing team, anxious that we are not disappointed, creates an irresistible alternative. We go down to the Team New Zealand dock where Peter Blake's 60-foot schooner *Archangel*, sometimes weather boat and support vessel, is readying for sea. Various tenders and chase boats also lie alongside, mostly on loan from other organizations keen to share the Team New Zealand dream. We climb aboard the *Avon* chase boat, and plane at 40 knots out towards Rangitoto Islands and the racecourse for the 1999 Road to the America's Cup regatta. The *Avon* is to be support boat for the first day of racing, and we are fortunate to witness the action at close quarters. This annual regatta features identical New Zealand America's Cup Class Yachts from the 1992 San Diego campaign in an innovative series of round-robin contests designed to maintain public and media interest in the years between America's Cup challenges.

Our skipper, Dean Barker, former New Zealand Match Race champion, world-class Finn and Laser sailor and recent Team New Zealand family member, shares insights with us about the day's racing between the America True and Italian Prada syndicates. We pass spares to the yachts, keeping pace alongside as they slice to windward at 9.5 knots. We carry sails, spares and emergency equipment; we transfer seventeenth man observers[3] between spectator vessels and the America's Cup yachts; we transfer media people between spectator craft and back to the dock; we keep spectator craft at a distance. There is no plan for this activity, but frequent conversations guide the action.

Back at the dock, Kristen is generous in emphasizing that our wish to see Team New Zealand in action on the water can be met just as soon as the *Black Magic* boats are repaired and testing resumes. And so we find ourselves back at the Team New Zealand dock a week later, where the *Black Magic* boats are being prepared for sea. The crew is focused, just going the job with quiet efficiency. Each boat has a captain, but there is no outward sign of who is in charge. Occasional social remarks are passed about the weather, or last night's activities, conversation is routine, about the day's activities: 'We need the three-two or the three-two with the three-one, let's get them out of the shed; oh, the tide's going out, so we will have to move this one round here.' It is all very businesslike. The activity is structured, as everyone has his own job or responsibility, but as soon as one area is tidied away, then those who have finished look to help the others. People know if help is needed – they don't have to be asked. Everyone lends a hand to carry the mainsail because it takes at least six people to pick it up, and it gets easier if you have seven or eight. Highly specialized teams, such as those dedicated to winches or electronics, calmly go about their work.

The Team New Zealand work boat and the *Avon* chase boat are already attaching tow ropes to *NZL 32* and *38*. The sailing team members have checked their crew assignment from the daily lists and hop on board their respective boats. Murray Jones, our captain for the day, invites us on to *NZL 38*. He explains that the *Black Magic* boats are out sailing every day, weather and repairs permitting. Some days the emphasis is on testing innovations, but today it's to be race practice.

We have already signed indemnity forms accepting the risks involved in sailing on these high-performance racing yachts. We are reminded that the previous week a Spanish America's Cup sailor was killed when a block exploded under load. We have also signed to the effect that we will abide by the Team New Zealand secrecy rules, a reminder of the extreme lengths that competitors will go to in order to discover Team New Zealand's winning formula.

As we are towed out to the racecourse crew members relax, munch carbohydrates and share good humoured banter. It was the feel of a family day out sailing, and we are treated as guests of the family. We are warned in a friendly way of potential dangers, and team members share a quiet word or a joke with us as the day races by. Once out in open water, the chase boat drops our tow and planes out 3.3 miles to windward[4] to drop the orange marker for our day's course. The start line is marked by the work boat at one end, and by another orange marker 200 metres away.

The crew take their positions in a well-rehearsed rhythm, each one in formation. There is intense focus and concentration; hardly a word is spoken; there is just the occasional comment or gesture. In no time the mainsail is attached and hauled up the mast. A crewman is whisked 32.5 metres to the masthead to look for wind and check the halyards, and is back down again almost as fast as we can watch. The jib is set with similar speed, and we accelerate rapidly to 10 knots to windward. *NZL 32* has replicated the exercise just astern of us, and we are ready to race. The ten-minute gun sees us inside the start line, vying for the windward position. Close quarters tacking at a close speed of 20 knots provides heart-pounding excitement for us, and calm fun for the crew. The only words spoken now are the countdowns to five minutes and to the start, and the occasional comment from the headsail trimmer. *NZL 38* wins the favoured windward end and we match tacks until *NZL 32* sheers off onto a split tack. *NZL 38* powers up to 11.5 knots, the mainsail is tensioned down until it is a perfect airfoil, and the running backstay[5] is tensioned to 6 tonnes. We are warned not to hold it!

Attention then turns to the battered, yellow-covered computer sitting on the afterdeck just next to us, which provides comprehensive real-time telemetry for both boats. The navigator Clay Oliver[6] explains the readings to us, and points out that, contrary to expectations, *NZL 32* is getting more wind pressure and lift[7] on the leeward side of the course. We eye the leeward skyline and suspect a south-westerly wind shift and a squall may be building. The first cross of the boats shows that *NZL 32* is five lengths ahead, having benefited from the more favourable wind, and so it remains to the windward mark. *NZL 32* ahead of us makes a perfect spinnaker set and tacks off downwind. We follow, again this complex routine is handled with scarcely a word, and we are off 'downhill', with a black squall building to leeward. The jib is prepared, ready for the anticipated wind-shaft. Rain and wind come more quickly than expected and the spinnaker has to be let go quickly to keep excessive pressure off the mast and the back-stays. The crew meets what is high drama for us with rhythmic, wordless, high-speed, confident action; the sail is gone. We are tacking to windward again after a 180-degree wind-shift. And so the afternoon goes by with good humour, good comradeship and intense, high-performance sailing on the world's fastest matched pair of America's Cup yachts. *NZL 32* maintains her five lengths' lead at the first mark to the winning line, as happens in ninety per cent of America's Cup races. The jib is dropped and stowed, and the mainsail disappears from the boom into its cover in the time it takes for us to turn around and watch the squall disappearing out to sea. We are again under tow back to the dock, as the crew holds a debrief session in the cockpit on the key lessons of the day. The telemetry will be downloaded and analysed later.

The state of flow that we witnessed in the organization and on the water takes a while for newcomers to understand. As Tom

Schnackenberg explains, time takes on a different dimension for Team New Zealand players:

> When you go out and race it's a natural adrenalin spur, win or lose. If you have won, you are feeling good. If you have lost you are feeling good in an interesting way, and you are spurred on, either way, to rush around and fix things up, and there is an urgency which keeps you going. You can run into a twelve-hour game programme very easily, as time just flashes by without you even noticing it. Then, when you have a little break between the races where you go out testing, that's like a holiday, even though you have just as long a day. It's just different, like the difference between the weekend and a week day.

'Making the boat go faster' becomes a purpose in itself. As a consequence individuals and the organization are constantly seeking to be better than they have been, to exceed personal best. Tom Schnackenberg:

> We don't think about the competition very much. We say we have got to go faster than last week, so we are out to beat ourselves. We had some weaknesses last time. We didn't lose any races, but we sure had some close calls and we were getting overtaken downwind by a couple of boats. But we just focused on improving our own boats. We have to be self-reliant and create our own competition to beat ourselves, to achieve some sort of perfection . . . it's up to us to make sure that our in-house racing is better than anything you will see on the Challenger course.

Alan Sefton confirms this enthusiasm for exceeding personal best: 'In 1987 we stopped developing during the finals. That cost us the regatta. In 1995 we made sure we kept developing all the way through.'

Tom Schnackenberg explains the process of improvement:

> For Team New Zealand, development was a process of continual adaptation, but once in a while we had a little jump, a lucky jump that hadn't been thought of before. If you keep intellectual pressure on a particular area, you skip along, and you take a

bit of a walk, and if you have all of these people knowing what is going on, somebody will come up with an idea, even by asking a question, and the next minute, puff, you have made a little jump forwards. And you work on the find, and for a while things are easy because it opens up a few possibilities. We don't really expect jumps, but as long as we keep the pressure on they just happen.

Russell Coutts says that this 'constant focus on improvement and continuous search for new ideas' is the primary ingredient of Team New Zealand success, along with good communication, especially between the sailing and design teams.

The last details are considered to be important, and organizational flow ensures that none are overlooked. The America's Cup is a game of seconds, according to Peter Blake:

One second a mile is a twenty-second gain on the course. Races have been won or lost by less than three seconds. So a one-second per mile gain is worth spending a week on to get the little bits right. Speed gains came through making minute changes to one boat during two-boat testing to measure the difference.

In the Whitbread Round the World Race, sponging out a few litres of bilge water – first having to clear away a pile of heavy and wet sails, lift the floor boards, sponge out, then put it all back when you are leaping from wave top to wave top and the yacht is leaning on its ear – just to get rid of a few unwarranted kilos of weight, was seen as just as important as steering the yacht or trimming the sails.

Before each America's Cup race we would have twenty-five people polishing the hull, having fun as they ensured that the most minute speck of weed or dirt was removed so there was nothing to impede progress.

Russell Coutts made a similar point about the testing programme:

The differences we are looking for in the research and testing programme are often small. When we test, every component must be set correctly, or it will introduce more error into the results. There is a high emphasis on checking components to eliminate as many variables as possible.

To most people, Team New Zealand's attention to the last detail would seem fanatical. To Team New Zealand players it's just the way they do business.

## CONCLUSION

To maintain interest and international competition in the build-up to the millennium regatta, Road to the America's Cup Regattas, involving several of the most competitive America's Cup syndicates, were held in New Zealand in 1997, 1998 and 1999. Team New Zealand confirmed its international pre-eminence with successive victories.

Building on Fay's dream of winning the America's Cup, Peter Blake inspired a nation: 'Coming first may not be everything, but coming second is nothing.' With the Sydney Olympics just across the water, he saw the potential for a tourism and trade bonanza of unprecedented proportions, and through charm and business acumen transformed the dream of winning the Cup to one of creating a millennium media spectacle centred on New Zealand, in the process persuading developers to transform the Auckland waterfront for ever. By living the dream Blake and Team New Zealand showed that Kiwis could be best in the world.

In 1995 *Black Magic* formula was a combination of supreme organization, sophisticated technological development and attention to the very last detail. A nation celebrated as New Zealanders who could scarcely tell bow from stern responded to their nation's obvious technological and sporting supremacy. Peter Blake's red socks became a national symbol, with even the sheep wearing them in support of the nation's heroes!

# CHAPTER 11

# PPO Theory

| | |
|---|---|
| PPO Theory | Elite[1] theory of organizing for sustained peak performance applicable to organizations that aspire to be the very best in their field. |

## INTRODUCTION

PPO principles and concepts are woven into the stories we have told – you may have noticed the consistent pattern that emerged from dramatically different dreams. Now, referring back to the PPO stories, we explain this pattern to develop a coherent, generic and enduring theory of organizing for peak performance. We define peak performance as the continuous surpassing of personal and/or organizational best.

PPO Theory explains how organizations achieve sustained peak performance. It describes the common principles and concepts that we found in our empirical research and explains their inter-relationships. There are three PPO principles: peak purpose, peak practices and peak flow[2]. Each is supported by three PPO concepts, which are brought into being by PPO actions. Peak purpose provides meaning and direction for people within organizations. Peak practices create the organizational context for people to prepare for peak performance, while peak flow explains how people work together to achieve it. An organization is based on people – people and, in particular, inspirational players, are essential to peak performance. The combination of inspirational players, PPO principles and PPO concepts makes up PPO Theory, while PPO actions explain how the theory can be implemented (discussed in Chapter 12). Together they prescribe a basis for moving towards peak performance which can be used by all organizations.

**Figure 1: PPO Theory**

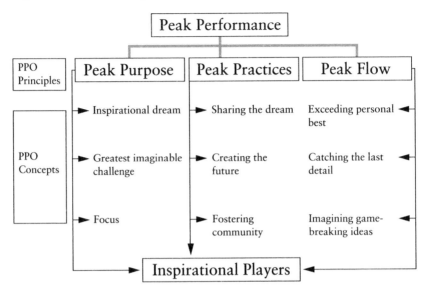

## INSPIRATIONAL PLAYERS

We use the term 'inspirational players' to denote agents within a PPO who are instrumental in actioning the PPO principles – they provide the integrating link between PPO principles and concepts. We avoid the traditional terminology of 'leadership' because of the multiplicity of theoretical perspectives about what constitutes effective leadership, and because 'leadership' necessarily implies 'followership'. There was no evidence of following in our PPO case studies; indeed, the idea is antithetical to the PPO principle of peak flow. Just as PPO principles relate to an elite subset of organization theory, so the idea of inspirational players relates to a specific subset of leadership theory that is applicable to peak performing organizations – similarities can be found in the work of Kouzes and Posner,[3] Bennis[4] and Biederman and Greenleaf.[5]

Inspirational players are central to establishing the peak purpose – the inspirational dream of greatness for the organization. Subsequent generations of inspirational players live the dream, make it happen, and inspire others to own the organizational dream in their own right, to exceed their personal best and to become peak performers. In every case they are powerful people with powerful ideas. PPOs have inspirational players positioned throughout their structure.

The dream to make the Braves the best ball club in baseball originated with Ted Turner, but the key inspirational players who made it happen, both strategically and operationally, were its President, Stan Kasten, and General Manager John Schuerholz. The dream to win the America's Cup for New Zealand originated with Michael Fay, but the inspirational players who made it happen were Peter Blake, Alan Sefton, Russell Coutts, Tom Schnackenberg and others. We found no evidence to support the idea of a charismatic leader single-handedly transforming the fortunes of the organization. Inspirational players from previous eras are honoured, and remain essential members of the PPO community. For example, the usher at the San Francisco 49ers who retired aged ninety-five was a legend in the organization and part of its inspirational dream, while inspirational soccer players from past eras are positioned throughout FC Bayern Munich.

Inspirational players are role models in that they provide a benchmark for others to emulate and exceed. They also recruit, mentor and develop people, providing for succession within the organization. The success of the Australian Women's Hockey Association owes much to past-president Meg Wilson's achievements in nurturing people in the right places throughout the management structure. Simultaneously, inspirational players are the catalysts for community. They inspire trust in themselves, in others and in the organization.

Inspirational players are actively involved, and make their own direct contributions – Patrick Head can name and explain the precise purpose of any part in the Williams factory. Inspirational players demand perfection, and their enthusiasm is infectious. They are accessible, energetic and passionate.

Some inspirational players become icons of the sport and of society as a whole. Franz Beckenbauer *is* German soccer. Michael Jordan personifies basketball; there may never be another athlete who can exceed his skill and charisma. But PPOs successfully ensure that their sports icons do not overshadow the PPO brand. The powerful Bulls brand, arguably the most evocative in all of pro-sport, was built separately from that of Michael Jordan, while Franz Beckenbauer features only lightly in the marketing of his

**Figure 2: PPO Theory –
peak purpose**

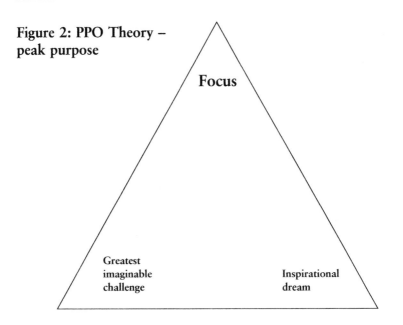

organization. They extend, rather than transcend, the inspirational dream.

## PRO PRINCIPLES

There are three PPO principles – peak purpose, peak practices and peak flow.

## Peak Purpose

The PPO principle of peak purpose comprises three PPO concepts: greatest imaginable challenge, inspirational dream and focus. These concepts are mutually reinforcing, and in combination they provide the clarity of purpose which is essential for peak performance. They are illustrated in the peak purpose triangle in Figure 2.

### GREATEST IMAGINABLE CHALLENGE

Peak performance is defined in terms of the greatest imaginable challenge – being the best that the organization can be. The greatest imaginable challenge provides purpose by defining a concrete aim.

It must be imaginable, feasible and measurable as well as important, stretching and exciting. Team New Zealand's greatest imaginable challenge is to be the first team outside North America to retain the America's Cup, while Procter & Gamble (see chapter 13) intends to double revenue within ten years. Each greatest imaginable challenge is related to the organization's unique context, circumstances and aspirations. In both sport and business it can be defined in relation to regional, national or international competition. Working towards a great challenge gives players within PPOs opportunities to achieve recognition and self-esteem by being part of the best, and by providing individual opportunities for peak performance. Once attained the greatest imaginable challenge must be reinvented to sustain success.

## INSPIRATIONAL DREAM

The challenge must inspire people to want to be a part of it, so that it becomes a shared inspirational dream. The transformation of challenge to dream is achieved through the creation of meaning, and invariably takes time. The inspirational dream makes people want to belong, since it provides a sense of recognition and collective importance. For Williams the dream derives from the joy of racing faster than everyone else, and members of the Williams community achieve global recognition for the speed of their cars on the race track. The German Soccer Federation wants to win championships but the dream that gives this meaning is 'More than 1–0': soccer working for the greater good of society.

The inspirational dream is akin to the Greek philosopher Plato's notion of Thymos,[6] 'spiritedness', or 'recognition'. People wish to be acknowledged as having worth or dignity – this enhances their self-esteem and increases their pride in themselves. This desire for recognition is extended by people to the ideas, principles or activities that they invest with value. They are prepared to make great financial and physical sacrifices for recognition, including long hours of work, physical discomfort, pain and, in extreme cases, even death. The need for Thymos lies at the heart of political and religious conflict and many wars. It urges people to enter sailing races around the stormiest waters of the world or risk death in Formula 1 racing cars. Thymos underpins the inspirational dream that lies at the heart of great endeavour and peak performing organizations.

The greatest imaginable challenge must be in harmony with the inspirational dream in order to achieve sustainable peak perform-ance, but on their own they provide no basis for action. Many people dream of doing outstanding things, but few succeed. By contrast, a PPO defines its greatest imaginable challenge and focuses systematically on achieving it. Beyond the dream and the challenge, the third essential concept of peak purpose is focus.

## FOCUS

Focus is the dream in action and the foundation of peak flow. It provides direction, and interest for participants, and is a state of mental clarity directly related to the greatest imaginable challenge. *Focus involves identifying specific actions to be undertaken, rather than targeting the end result required.* The fewer the actions in focus the better. The focus for WilliamsF1 is to push back techno-logical barriers to make the car go faster – the whole organization is aligned behind this. The focus for the San Francisco 49ers organ-ization is 'look after the team'; they do so in any and all ways possible, so that the players can focus on peak performance prep-aration.

Focus clarifies priorities. Players focus their attention and ener-gies on meaningful, challenging goals as an essential ingredient in achieving peak performance. Rolling game plans or short-term action goals provide direction and the basis for feedback. Action goals must be demanding, and are set by the individuals respon-sible for action. PPOs measure themselves continuously against these to ensure they are improving. Short-term action goals aligned to the Williams' focus might include:

1. Redesign the wheel nut to be multi-sided to increase the torque potential and reduce time for wheel changes.
2. Redesign the nose cone to reduce drag.
3. Redesign the exhaust system to increase brake horsepower.

Effective game plans will be action based, challenging, worded in the affirmative and include a time-frame. Goals derive from focus and break it into smaller units, while focus ultimately derives from the GIC.

Players must receive commensurate intrinsic or extrinsic rewards to feel valued and to increase their ability or willingness to focus on the achievement of peak performance. As Peter Blake explained, PPOs 'pay the very best they are able, and expect the very best'.

The opposite of focus is mental entropy, a state in which consciousness is jumbled with a multiplicity of anxieties, problems and uncontrolled thoughts. Most of us will experience this at times when our minds wander aimlessly, or family, health or work-related stresses and strains create such anxiety that little useful activity is possible. If, by contrast, we feel safe in our relationships, healthy, financially secure and at one with our inner selves and spirituality, this enables mental clarity, which is essential for focus and peak performance.

Table 1 sets out the relationship between the greatest imaginable challenge, the inspirational dream and focus for each of our PPO case studies.

RENEWING THE CHALLENGE

PPOs provide an organizational context in which players are able to achieve intrinsic and extrinsic rewards to the maximum of their potential through pursuit of the greatest imaginable challenge, but once achieved, the challenge is no longer a challenge. PPOs know that to sustain purpose the challenge must evolve once it has been achieved. They also understand that external forces will change the nature of the game, and that this in turn will affect peak purpose.

PPOs recognize that change can be leveraged to enhance success. Brandenburger and Nalebuff[7] explain the altering nature of competition in Co-opetition, and provide a structure for understanding and predicting the winners and losers when the game changes. In business, players must co-operate to increase the scope and value of a game but then compete intensely to extract value from it. Professional sport provides an excellent illustration of co-opetition – basketball teams co-operate in the development of the National Basketball Association to create a valuable entertainment industry, and then they compete intensely within that industry to extract value from it.

Nothing stays the same for long in any industry. Retaining

focus as the game changes is the essence of a PPO, and PPOs are frequently instrumental in changing the nature of the game.

There are four ways in which a game may change or can be changed. Each will alter the value that an organization can extract from the game, and each has the potential to move the organization off-focus. PPOs maintain focus.

1. *Changing the rules of the game.* When the America's Cup Association agreed to change the rules of the game to replace 12-Metre Class yachts with a new International America's Cup Class all design syndicates had to return to the drawing board, and prior competitiveness in 12-Metres meant little. The new America's Cup Class is bigger, faster and more exciting, creating new sponsorship opportunities and media spectacles. The equivalent rules in business are tariffs, stock exchange requirements, exchange rates, anti-trust laws, trade agreements, and environmental legislation.

2. *Changing the league.* In 1998 the New Zealand, Australian and South African Rugby Unions created the Super 12 series of provincial rugby, played within the three countries. By doing so they enhanced the popular appeal of the sport, and significantly enhanced the opportunities for sponsorship and media funding, enabling greater numbers of players to pursue a professional career. The equivalent to changing the league in business is competing in a different market, expanding from local to national to global.

3. *Changing participants changes the game.*

   • Public: enlarging or shifting the fan or customer base changes the game. The FC Bayern Munich fan club network extends globally: it even has a new fan club in China.

   • Partners: WilliamsF1 dropped their Renault engine in 1998 because Renault no longer had a strong enough commitment to development. As a consequence their 1998 and 1999 performances were off the pace. Their new association with BMW will be dramatic as BMW and Mercedes (through McLaren) race each other vicariously. The Atlanta Braves' win-win association with Coke to create a dramatic baseball theme park on top of Turner Field adds value to the Braves' entertainment experience, and induces people to drink more

Coke. Relationships, not contracts, are the basis of sustained focus.

• Players: FC Bayern Munich buys new team members who will add value on the field by winning games, and off the field through sponsorship and fan base development.

• Competitors: the addition of a new team or organization to a league will affect who extracts value. An expansion franchise in the NFL changes the game, as a new stadium is required, a city without a team gets a chance to develop municipal pride and generate revenue, more games are played, and more tickets are sold. More players are needed, but the best players will be in even scarcer supply, so their value will rise.

4. *Changing the game* itself may involve changing the dream, which cannot be undertaken lightly. One-day 'pyjama cricket' is very different from five-day Test cricket, with its attendant tradition and ceremony. 'Pyjama cricket' is fast, friendly and fun, and it opened up televised and live cricket to entirely new sections of the population, bringing in new sponsorship. The new game provides funds both for keeping the dream and traditions of Test cricket alive, and offers elite professional cricketers rewarding careers. Altering patterns of demand for entertainment meant the game had to transform itself to stay alive, but fundamental change is never successful if it destroys the dream and undermines community.

Change renews the challenge or provides a challenge for new people, and provides new opportunities or opportunities for new people. PPOs use change relentlessly to enhance individual and organizational renewal and reward and to leverage additional financial resources with which to create the future. PPOs nurture and sustain their dream in the face of external turbulence, altering the challenge to reflect or create the external environment.

## Peak Practices

Peak practices is the second PPO principle, comprising three concepts: sharing the dream, creating the future and fostering community. The peak practices provide an organizational context

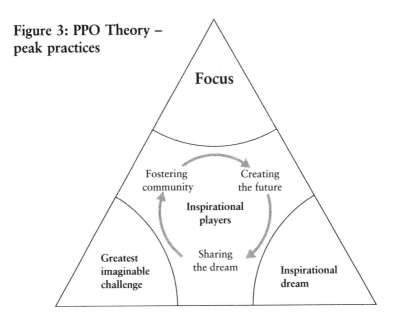

**Figure 3: PPO Theory – peak practices**

which enables players to focus on challenging goals that give meaning, purpose, direction and enjoyment to their lives. Focus is the first base for peak performance.

Peak practices are the elemental, action-based concepts of PPO Theory which describe the characteristics of PPOs and are the foundations of their success. The peak practices are closely interrelated and should be viewed in combination, as each practice plays to and draws from the others. The absence of any one practice can severely damage the ability to achieve or sustain PPO status. The relationships between peak practices and the elements of peak purpose are illustrated in Figure 3 above. Inspirational players are central both to the peak purpose and to the peak practices.

## SHARING THE DREAM

In a PPO there is an insatiable passion to win and an intense belief in being the best. Greatness is deeply entrenched in the psyche of the organization – it is built on historic performances, legends, histories and traditions, and is reinforced by the constant, collective celebration of success. There is a shared atmosphere of excitement, the mystique of belonging, and a love of the game. In each of our research organizations, players are passionate about what they do. The dream provides meaning and it sustains involvement.

PPOs share the inspirational dream widely with the 7Ps:

Principals (shareholders or owners)
Players (organization participants)
Purchasers (people who do business with the organization)
Partners (alliance partners and sponsors)
Philanthropy recipients
Public
Press

Each of these groups is made to feel valued – relationship building and dream-sharing with the 7Ps is imaginative and sustained.

The dream is made real by the compelling symbols of achievement and success that are displayed throughout the organization, and shared beyond it. These symbols emotionally connect everyone to the dream and create a belief that something amazing is going to happen – an organization in which people feel that nothing is impossible. For Williams the dream is manifested in the Formula One cars, centre stage in the atrium and the museum.

Sharing the dream widely sustains it within the organization, and extends magical experiences to others. They are enchanted with the special nature of their relationships with PPOs, which generates new business horizons. There is a tangible aura of association.

Philanthropy featured in all the case study organizations. They invest in the community and society in which they live, thereby extending their dreams to others and sustaining their meaning. The Charitabulls take the Bulls Basketball dream into the Chicago community through work with schools, hospitals and youth centres, through player appearances and through care for community causes. They belong.

By sharing the dream widely PPOs inspire confidence and belief in their own greatness, and sustain and enlarge the horizon of business possibilities. Clients buy more than a game, more than a product. They experience association with an inspirational dream. The dream both sustains and is sustained by peak performance

## Table 1

| Organization | Greatest imaginable challenge | Inspirational dream | Focus |
|---|---|---|---|
| FC Bayern Munich | To be the world's greatest soccer club | More than 1–0 | Recruit and develop the very best players |
| WilliamsF1 | To win all Formula 1 championshiops | The joy of speed | Push back technological barriers to make the car go faster |
| Australian Netball | World Champions for ever and Australia's number 1 participant sport | Netball achievements for life | Develop the Netball Australia brand as an athletic, exciting, and entertaining sport |
| Australian Cricket Board | To win every international game | To inspire the Australian nation by maintaining their winning tradition | Develop potential elite players |
| New Zealand Rugby Football Union | To win the World Cup and all international matches | Inspire the New Zealand nation with their rugby achievements | Build a portfolio of world-beating brands |
| Women's Hockey Australia | To win gold medals | To capture the imagination of the next generation | Develop potential elite players |
| Chicago Bulls | To be in contention for NBA championships | Making magic | Build a global sports entertainment brand |
| Atlanta Braves | To be the most successful baseball team | To live the American dream through sustained baseball supremacy | Be first class in everything they do |
| San Francisco 49ers | To win the Super Bowl | The quintessential football family | Look after the team |
| Team New Zealand | To retain the America's Cup for ever | Sailing and technological supremacy for New Zealand | Increase the speed and manoeuvrability of the boat |
| Procter & Gamble | Double global revenues in ten years | To make every day better in every way we can for people around the world | Creating unique, high quality brands |

and winning. Through celebration of achievements, PPOs make magic for all involved.

## CREATING THE FUTURE

To develop the dream, PPOs create the future through people, infrastructure and financial systems – they live and die on their organization infrastructure, which must nurture relationships between each of the 7Ps. Without exception our case study organizations have carefully constructed physical and financial infrastructures which enable them to create the future. Federal structures, alliances and information networks all served this purpose; the precise form and the degree of formality seemed of little consequence as it is the personal relationships rather than the formal organizational structure which make the difference. Hence the importance of the continuity of key players. The future of PPOs is grounded in tradition. They have all built excellent processes for scouting, selecting, attracting and progressing the best elite players, both on the field and in the organization.

PPOs make an enormous commitment to mentoring and development. Pam Tye of the Australian Women's Hockey Association explained that mentoring and development lay at the heart of their success. The high numbers of women leaving the game due to family commitments, mean that development must be proactive and enduring. No talent or potential can be overlooked.

There is a clear preference across all the PPOs for promoting internally and growing people within the organization, but this is balanced by careful recruitment to sustain the organization's energy and capacity. For example, FC Bayern Munich has inspirational players from previous eras positioned throughout the organization, but also recruits externally both within Germany and beyond to complement existing skills. Continuity is of paramount importance, but this is balanced with the acceptance that there can come a time when further growth can only occur beyond the organization. Recruitment, development and continuity create depth. Depth is the investment for the future, and enables careful succession planning. PPO seldom advertise for positions – inspirational players are selectively invited in to sustain and amplify the dream. A PPO's phenomenal record of success is built on employing the very best. For example, many inspirational players in the San Francisco 49ers have moved on to take up important roles elsewhere, but the 49ers have developed an uncanny ability to replace departed inspirational players with others of even more outstanding ability.

Each organization is financially secure, but it is not money that made them into PPOs. Financial security is achieved through peak performance, but it is not necessarily a prerequisite for PPO progress. We learned from several cases that the availability of excessive funding reduces the ability to find focus, since it shifts the perspective from 'How do we make best use of our funds to realize the dream?' to 'What do we do with the money?' The Australian Women's Hockey Association achieves greatness in part based on the intense focus that comes from using every dollar of its restricted budget to the best advantage.

## FOSTERING COMMUNITY

The rituals and relationships of community create a calm, relaxed and informal environment which facilitates the mental clarity necessary for peak performance, while the infectious sense of fun pervading PPOs strengthens the community and builds relationships. PPO members live the dream and belong to the PPO family. The family looks after its own. For example, the night before San Francisco 49ers home games, players, coaches and administrators and their families assemble and mingle at the San Francisco Marriott Hotel, exemplifying the comfortable relationships that provide the peace of mind necessary for peak performance.

The PPO community satisfies members' basic needs for security. They share joys and sorrows, successes and failures; and together they overcome adversity, celebrate achievements and enjoy financial rewards. Everyone benefits from success, as bonuses are based on the success of the organization as a whole. PPO players are paid well, but their deep rewards are intrinsic – being part of the best. Relationships are built on mutual trust, respect, pride, tradition, loyalty and a sense of belonging. In sport this pride in belonging is made visually apparent through 'pulling on the jersey', the symbolic representation of the best. The championship rings given to all community members in our North American PPOs symbolize this elite involvement.

The longevity in relationships within PPOs leads to 'sacrificial plays' – sacrificing personal glory for the benefit of other team members, or the organization. In addition, while some participants move on to other challenges, they never really leave. In 1999 Bill Walsh returned as general manager of the San Francisco 49ers, eleven years after departing the coach's bench as the most successful coach of his era.

Community provides the mental calm and confidence which dispels entropy, enables focus, and encourages the exceeding of personal best. Community members are not just empowered, involved or included – they are the PPO. Motivation is not an issue.

## Peak Flow

Peak flow is the third, and primary, PPO principle. It embraces, but extends beyond, the PPO concepts of exceeding personal best, imagining game-breaking ideas and catching the last detail. Peak flow and peak performance are often used interchangeably in sports psychology, but we distinguish between them. Peak flow is the experience, while peak performance is the achievement. Peak flow describes the calm and effortless flow of mind and body in perfect synchronization and harmony with their surroundings in the achievement of goal-directed, complex, actions and techniques.[8] It can be experienced in any challenging activity for which you are well prepared, whether rock climbing, ocean sailing or work. People experiencing peak flow achieve extraordinary awareness, confidence and power. They are totally focused and totally absorbed. They expect to succeed, and feel intense pleasure when experiencing this state. Peak flow can be a mystical or spiritual experience. We have observed it in action throughout our organizations, both on and off the court or field of play, but most obviously in netball. The intuitive free flow of ball and players in an unchoreographed, ballet-like ball game, and the netball concept of the 'flow-on', prompted our investigation of the psychological concept of flow.

The concept of flow has been developed and popularized by Mihaly Csikszentmihalyi[9] over more than two decades of research. He explains that 'the most basic requirement (to achieve flow) is to provide a clear set of challenges', leading to 'discovery, exploration, and problem solving'.[10] The individual must perceive the challenges to be demanding yet attainable. To achieve flow the activity must be engaged in out of choice, be intrinsically rewarding and provide clear and immediate feedback, and necessitate the active use of skills, which may be physical, cerebral or both.

Flow is best understood on a continuum varying in intensity, with peak flow at one end and low level flow at the other. Many young adults experience flow when playing computer games which stretch and develop their skills of fine motor movement and rapid thought, yet these games may have only low-level intrinsic meaning for them beyond pleasure of the moment. By contrast, other youngsters may be engrossed in developing their artistic skills, with tangible end results that can be shared by others. Flow experiences also vary according to the individual and across cultures – activities capable of providing flow experiences to one person may be intensely boring to another. Clarity of focus enables PPOs to develop an environment in which peak flow can occur.

Many of us will have momentarily experienced peak flow during our working or social lives. It can occur when we have tackled a task that we feel exceptionally well prepared for, and undertaken it beyond our best expectations. We feel at one with surroundings, friends, team mates, colleagues and ourselves. We feel unbeatable, and have an extraordinary joy in life. To sustain peak flow goals that extend our skills and abilities must be continually developed and redeveloped.

Players achieve calm through community and obtain control over consciousness through focus to achieve a state of intense awareness and readiness for peak flow. The peak practices facilitate peak flow, which leads to peak performance. Csikszentmihalyi developed his theory of flow in relation to the psychology of individual performance and experience, and we have chosen to extend the theory to the domain of organizations. We observed that teams and organizations can share flow experiences in circumstances when common goals are pursued, and the team feels well prepared and mutually constitutive. In PPOs the collective thoughts and actions of individual participants combine to achieve sustainable organizational peak performance. Peak *organizational* flow describes the apparently effortless achievement of demanding organizational tasks in harmony, to the intense satisfaction of participants. Peak flow develops between PPO members as they learn how each other thinks and acts and can anticipate each other's needs intuitively. They interact in ways that enable the organization to be greater than the sum of its players. Information flows easily before it is needed, and forms the play. Flexibility, sacrificial plays and making space for others are the accepted norms, while players are committed to their own and others' intellectual and technical development. The existence of organizational flow minimizes the utility of formal organization charts, policy manuals or job descriptions, and these artefacts of managerial control are replaced by relationships.

Flow eliminates the need for management-inspired cross-functional teams. Instead we found traditional teams of functional specialists, each expert in their own domain. The easy flow of information and assistance between members integrates activity across the PPO, focused on the dream in action.

We observed this organizational flow state many times within our case study organizations. In the Williams pit-lane garage at the 1998 Canadian Grand Prix the preparations for the race were marked by harmony, rhythm, focus and the calm, ordered completion of multiple and complex tasks by a team in flow. Intuitive understanding, a nod, or a brief gesture was all the communication needed.

A PPO workplace flows. Rituals and routines create a calm environment in which action and complete awareness can merge, leading to intense pleasure. Peak practices provide the organizational context in which flow can occur. Peak performance is imagined not managed.

## EXCEEDING PERSONAL BEST

Individuals exceed their personal best by striving for the greatest imaginable challenge and finding focus. The emphasis is on beating one's own best performance and the actions necessary to achieve that, rather than on results and beating the competition. PPO players exceed personal best through hard work, commitment and discipline. They have a deep commitment to improving their own knowledge, skills and personal performance, and are never satisfied. Creativity, risk taking, flair and intuition are regarded as vital to 'finding the edge' – failure is acknowledged openly and learnt from. Employees hold themselves supremely accountable for the impact that their particular job has on the final product, and take responsibility for themselves and the organization. There is a commitment to deeds rather than words. The passion for improvement is relentless and never ending – PPOs continually set more challenging, focused and previous-best-benchmarks, and beat them. In a PPO individuals' focus on exceeding personal best in their areas of professional expertise results in the activities becoming an end in themselves. Pride in accomplishment and a commitment to improving on prior performance have intrinsic value for participants.

Because focus is aligned to the greatest imaginable challenge, when individuals exceed personal best flow will lead to exceeding *organizational* best. In the Atlanta Braves organization, exceeding organizational best is a way of life that means as much in the office as it does on the baseball diamond. In the early days of his tenure, General Manager, John Schuerholz would look outside to other pre-eminent baseball franchises to get a fix on what individuals should do to try and be the best. When the Braves became a winning team, that focus shifted decisively towards internal assessment. 'The spotlight is brighter here. The heat is turned up a notch more. Your expectations grow higher. We have high internal expectations, the external expectations are high too, but more important to us are our internal expectations.'

Responsibility for personal performance extends to responsibility for others. Exceeding personal best extends to exceeding organizational best, which effectively renders performance management obsolete. Command and control, and traditional leadership are redundant features in PPOs.

## IMAGINING GAME-BREAKING IDEAS

PPOs bring about radical changes to the rules, the league, the players and the game itself to enhance their ability to live the dream and renew the greatest imaginable challenge. In addition, game-breaking ideas change the way the organization's game is played to create winning opportunities. Intellectual pressure is constantly applied to all aspects of the organization's activities, and there is continuous, experimentation, derived from exceeding personal best. Focus provides direction.

New ideas flow naturally and there is an enthusiasm for risk taking because innovation gains recognition and credit. PPO people are not penalized for failure – the emphasis is upon putting things right, not allocating blame when things go wrong. Innovation often goes through considerable periods of failure before success is arrived at, and ideas which do not work are regarded as opportunities for further learning, while a powerful institutional memory prevents the repetition of earlier mistakes. Innovation and game-breaking ideas flourish in this atmosphere because there is no fear of failure. Progress is achieved through experimentation, and, as a consequence, nothing is regarded as impossible – there is always a better way. Everyone contributes, and people with ideas are able to make them happen, regardless of whether or not the issue in question falls within their area of responsibility. To assist in this process, information is freely shared within the organization, but carefully protected from outsiders, while frequent informal communication crosses functions and structures. Mental space is created for individual and group creativity, and the calm environment and easy relationships fostered by community encourage clarity. As a consequence there is a cross-fertilization of ideas which enables new ways of seeing. Imagination drives innovation, fuelled by the inspirational dream.

Infinitesimal gains and revolutionary change can both win the game for PPOs. The world of Formula One is a dramatic combination of high technology and seemingly minute incremental gains – the industry is littered with constructors who have tried to find game-breaking ideas to get to the chequered flag first. Williams, the dominant force in Formula One over the last two decades, relies heavily on new ideas. Chief Executive Frank Williams ensures that 'Ideas come forward all the time. As engineers in a highly competitive environment, we have to respond to the continuous staircase of change.'

Community provides the context in which game-breaking ideas proliferate, while focus provides direction. Responsibility for exceeding personal best ensures that ideas come forward from everyone, all the time, and organizational flow means that these ideas are harmonized. Game-breaking ideas sustain peak performance.

## CATCHING THE LAST DETAIL

Catching the last detail can win the game and is the essence of PPOs – a single point or 1/500th of a second can make the winning difference. Contracts can be won or lost on small details, and customer satisfaction can be undermined by seemingly trivial product defects or negative service experiences. PPO people are committed to paying attention to each and every last detail. They exhibit personal discipline in the use of their professional judgement, because they care for the organization and its people. Individual responsibilities rather than organizational rules guide action. Each organizational process, no matter how small, is vital as it could make the difference between winning and losing.

Information flows freely throughout PPOs, enabling players to anticipate tasks rather than wait for instructions. People are aware of the tasks of others, and because all actions are aligned through focus, they help others when their own tasks are complete or when others are seen to need assistance. As a consequence, problems are fixed rather than talked about and anticipated rather than reacted to.

In the sports industry the last detail matters for players and customers alike. The Atlanta Braves need to ensure that their product is competitive alongside many other entertainment attractions, including, of course, other professional sports. Failure to catch the last detail may cause the customer to turn away for ever. On the baseball diamond, in the quintessential game of inches, failing to catch the last detail will cost the game! Catching the last detail is a state of mind which ensures that peak performance is achieved through the perfect attention to all aspects of the game.

The relationship between focus and peak flow is illustrated in Figure 4. Inspirational players are central to peak flow, just as they are to the peak purpose and peak practices.

## THE PEAK PROFILE

Our investigation of elite sports organizations revealed three PPO principles and nine PPO concepts, three for each principle; Inspirational players start the play and are instrumental in bringing

**Figure 4: PPO Theory –
peak flow**

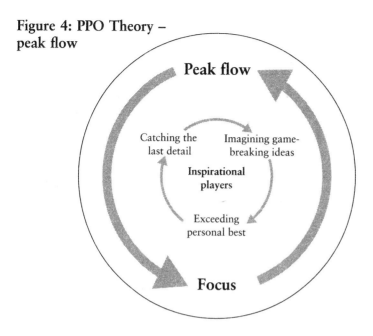

into being and implementing the principles and concepts; the inspirational dream provides meaning; the greatest imaginable challenge provides purpose; focus provides direction; goals focus action (see Chapter 12); peak practices enable focus and facilitate peak flow, and peak flow sustains peak performance. PPOs provide financial and social rewards for participants, together with the opportunity for having fun and achieving recognition and self-esteem.

A model of PPO Theory, showing the relationships between these elements is provided in our peak profile in Figure 5. The peak profile integrates peak purpose, peak practices and peak flow.

In summary, PPO Theory progresses as follows:

- Inspirational players imagine inspirational dreams.
- Focus provides direction and purpose which facilitate the achievement of peak flow.
- Sharing the dream creates an aura of association.
- The future is created by careful recruitment and development and long term commitment to infrastructure.
- Fostering community creates trusting relationships and a calm environment which enables focus.

## Figure 5: PPO Theory – peak profile

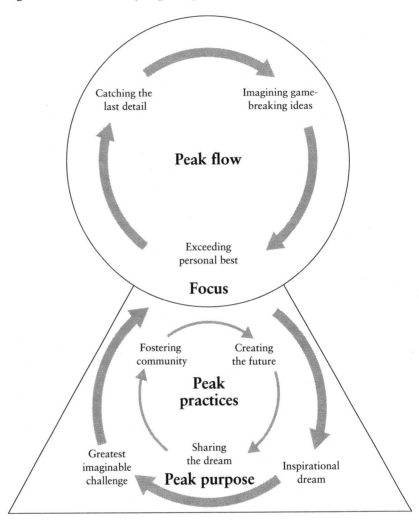

- The harmony of thought and action achieved through peak flow enables, and is enabled by, exceeding personal best, imagining game-breaking ideas and catching the last detail.
- PPOs in peak flow continuously surpass organizational best in the endless pursuit of the greatest imaginable challenge. This is peak performance.

In chapter 12 we explain PPO progression in more detail.

# PPO Progression

## INTRODUCTION

Organizations which adopt PPO Theory will be capable of developing sustainable peak performance. It offers a long-term development plan for organizations seeking to achieve and sustain their maximum potential. It can also provide a benchmark against which organizational achievements can be assessed. In this chapter we explain how organizations can use our theory to create sustainable peak performance, and provide a step-by-step process for evaluating an organization's preparedness for PPO progression.

Progression towards peak performance begins with inspirational players who are the conduits to the greatest imaginable challenge. The preparatory practices have to be carefully constructed, usually over several years. How they are implemented and which ones are emphasized will vary from organization to organization. We are not suggesting 'one best way'. There are an infinite variety of PPO progressions, depending on the resources available and the inspirational players, but all the principles and concepts of PPO Theory must be developed to achieve sustained peak performance.

PPO progression is evolutionary, but PPO regression can be rapid and dramatic. The loss of inspirational players, the destruction of the dream, the undermining of the infrastructure or the destabilization of any of the peak practices can lead to PPO regression. Peak practices need to be nurtured constantly for an organization to remain in contention. Potential PPO progression is illustrated in Figure 6 (see p. 265). Organizations can assess their current progress on the PPO development cycle.

## Figure 6: Peak performance progression

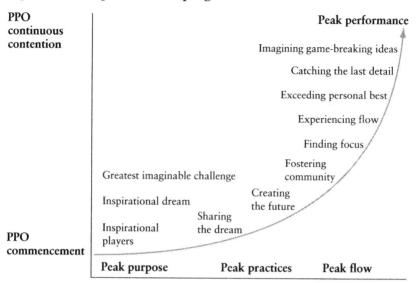

GETTING STARTED

PPO Theory is generic and transferable, but the implementation of each principle and concept is unique to each organization, and the starting lines will be different. PPO Theory can be used to enable new organizations to establish organizational practices which will assist them in progressing towards peak performance. Any existing organization will already have in place formal or informal organizational policies and procedures which will need to be assessed against PPO Theory. The PPO principles (peak purpose, peak practices and peak flow) are supported by PPO concepts and are brought into being by PPO actions. The checklists in the following pages will assist you in this regard – PPO actions are arranged beneath PPO concepts in the order of their effective achievement.

PPO progression should be developed in the sequence of the three PPO principles, peak purpose, peak practices and peak flow.

## Peak Purpose

Peak purpose depicts the relationship between the greatest imaginable challenge, the inspirational dream and focus. These PPO concepts define meaning and direction and provide the foundation for peak performance. Peak purpose starts the play and needs to be developed before significant progress can be made towards Peak practices.

## Peak Practices

Peak practices ensure the organization is in position for peak performance. Sharing the dream, creating the future and fostering community must be put in place systematically and nurtured constantly. In combination they enable peak flow. The sequence of development of the three peak practices is not important, and they are mutually reinforcing.

## Peak Flow

Peak flow is a shared state of mind. It can only be fully achieved when peak purpose and peak practices are established, and must be nurtured concurrently. Once PPO players have experienced peak flow they can be expected to do all in their power to sustain it. Peak performance is the consequence of thought and action in harmony due to peak flow.

## A PPO GAME PLAN

Checklists follow to assist you in developing a game plan for progression to peak performance. The checklists follow the sequence of the PPO progression in Figure 6. Each checklist includes a series of PPO actions necessary for the achievement of the relevant PPO concept. For examples of how these actions may be undertaken, we refer you to the PPO stories.

## Inspirational Players

Inspirational players will be instrumental in inspiring an organization to achieve peak performance. They will start the play. But they need not be the people who have formal managerial authority or who are in recognized positions of leadership. Several inspirational players will be positioned throughout the organizations. They should:

- Be powerful people with powerful ideas
- Be role models and icons
- Be actively involved with the 7P's.
- Be accessible, energetic and passionate
- Inspire belief in the organization's greatness
- Inspire others to exceed their personal best continuously
- Coach others to become peak performers, not followers
- Carry the inspirational dream
- Drive the future

Once PPO progression is under way PPOs will:

- Position many inspirational players around the organization
- Develop inspirational players internally
- Carefully recruit the very best externally
- Plan succession, but stay flexible
- Maintain the legendary status of former inspirational players

Inspirational players will be inspirational through creating purpose, fostering excellent organizational practices and inspiring flow.

## Peak Purpose

### THE GREATEST IMAGINABLE CHALLENGE

This should be:

- Feasible but stretching
- Exciting
- Measurable
- Specific to the league and level in which the organization plays
- Related to the inspirational dream
- The basis for focus
- Re-imagined once achieved

## INSPIRATIONAL DREAM

The inspirational dream should:

- Have intrinsic value beyond winning
- Provide a sense of recognition and meaning
- Be widely shared
- Derive from deep conversations with the 7Ps
- Emerge from the histories and traditions of the organization
- Not be measurable
- Not be a forecast or a vision of the future
- Relate to the greatest imaginable challenge

## FOCUS

This should be:

- Crystal clear
- Aligned with the greatest imaginable challenge
- Related to the actions required to achieve the greatest imaginable challenge, not to the desired results
- The basis for aligning everyday tasks
- The basis for determining priorities
- The basis for assessing performance
- Broken down into realistic, short-term goals which provide for regular feedback
- Actioned through rolling game plans
- Re-energized through changes to the rules of the game, the league and players

# Peak Practices

## SHARING THE DREAM

Sharing the dream with principals, players, purchasers, partners, philanthropy recipients, the public and the Press [the 7Ps] is a key role of inspirational players, and ultimately of all organizational participants, who together should:

- Foster an intense desire to be the best and an insatiable passion to win

- Create a physical environment where everyone feels that nothing is impossible
- Display compelling symbols of success
- Reinforce greatness by maintaining histories and traditions
- Build on historic success
- Celebrate new success
- Emotionally connect everyone to the organization
- Build powerful brands
- Share tangible symbols of association
- Ensure accessibility for, and nurture relationships with, the 7Ps

## CREATING THE FUTURE

Inspirational players must play a key role in this. PPOs should:

- Recruit only the best
- Invest in functional depth throughout the organization
- Promote from within and nurture people
- Balance 'up and out' with continuity in the organization
- Build long term financial stability
- Align the organization's infrastructure to stakeholders [the 7Ps]

## FOSTERING COMMUNITY

This builds on sharing the dream, creating the future and inspirational players. Fostering community creates a calm ordered environment, which is a necessary condition for reaching peak flow. In order to foster community PPOs should:

- Develop mutual trust, respect, pride, tradition and loyalty
- Minimize formal rules
- Encourage a relaxed, informal work environment
- Ensure that everyone benefits from success
- Share information
- Celebrate sacrificial plays
- Enable and celebrate initiative
- Learn from failure
- Encourage humour to flourish
- Celebrate long-lived relationships

## Peak Flow

In order to achieve peak flow all the peak practices must be in place and a crystal-clear focus must exist. In particular, fostering community minimizes the potential for organizational entropy, as peak flow is an organizational state of mind. To create and sustain peak flow PPOs should:

- Create meaning for organizational participants
- Ensure that organizational players are able to undertake ever more challenging tasks, for which they are fully prepared
- Focus on actions not outcomes
- Imagine peak performance, not manage for it
- Ensure real-time feedback on achievements
- Create a calm environment
- Ensure information is accessible and readily shared, enabling people to anticipate each other's plays
- Facilitate the development of mutual trust and respect

PPOs will achieve peak performance through peak flow, which involves exceeding personal best, imagining game-breaking ideas and catching the last detail. These concepts are all mutually reinforcing. Peak flow embraces but extends beyond the PPO concepts.

### EXCEEDING PERSONAL BEST

Exceeding personal best is an individual commitment which is expected of everyone within a PPO. It is based on focus, and is an essential element of peak flow and peak performance. To exceed personal best PPO players should:

- Set higher and higher personal goals, and beat them
- Take personal responsibility for self and organization
- Master their area of responsibility
- Research and experiment to discover more
- Try new ways of performing their daily responsibilities
- Educate others about their own area
- Learn about the responsibilities of others in order to interact with them better

- Take action to maintain excellent health, minimize stress, and assist others to do the same

## IMAGINING GAME-BREAKING IDEAS

Exceeding personal best will inexorably lead to imagining game-breaking ideas, which must be created if peak performance is to be achieved. In order to imagine game-breaking ideas PPOs:

- Minimize entropy by fostering community
- Value experimentation
- Pursue incremental gains in all areas
- Encourage risk taking
- Encourage ideas to come from everyone
- Apply intellectual pressure to all aspects of the organization
- Hold frequent informal meetings
- Create time and mental space for imagination

## CATCHING THE LAST DETAIL

PPOs know that the game can be won or lost by catching the last detail. As a consequence PPOs:

- Attempt to be perfect
- Value each and every task, no matter how small
- Ensure that personal responsibility, not organizational rules, guide action
- Fix problems rather than talk about them
- Create an expectation that people will assist each other
- Expect tasks to be anticipated
- Review all aspects of their activities for potential problems

# CAN ANY ORGANIZATION BE A PPO?

The answer to this question is an unequivocal yes. Because each organization chooses its own greatest imaginable challenge and inspirational dream, it chooses the league in which it wishes to play. PPO Theory can assist any organization to be a peak performer for its greater imaginable challenge, in the context it chooses – to be the best it can be.

## PPO DIAGNOSIS

For established organizations intent on PPO progression we recommend completion of an initial PPO diagnostic profile:

1. Assess your organization in relation to each of the above checklists.
2. Identify areas where further work is required.
3. Determine a game plan to enhance these areas.

The PPO actions should be listed below each PPO concept in the order of their effective achievement by the organization. A line should be drawn at the point where the organization is not taking the necessary actions to achieve PPO progression. Actions below the line require further work. How each of the identified actions should be undertaken will be contingent on the existing organizational relationships and practices. The game plan will be developed through deep conversations among all participants and by applying intellectual pressure to aspects of organizational practice that are seen to be deficient. PPO Theory is more a state of organizational mind than a series of actions or activities. If the organization believes it can be a peak performer it is well on the way to becoming one – the process of collective thinking about how to become a PPO will be instrumental in achieving sustainable success.

## TAKING TIME OUT

An organizational health warning – PPO Theory is not a quick fix. To become a PPO takes time. From the start of the Atlanta Braves' PPO development almost ten years passed until their first winning season and World Series appearance. Michael Jordan joined the Chicago Bulls in 1984; their first NBA Championship did not come until 1991. Procter & Gamble has taken 160 years to become arguably the most sustained peak performing organization in the business world! We believe that your organization can become a PPO in your league in a much shorter time than that, but not overnight.

We recommend taking time out as an organization to reflect on current practice and to develop a game plan for becoming a PPO, while focusing on the actions necessary to achieve this. The time out should involve everyone, as PPO Theory cannot be imposed from above – it has to be embraced from within. But inspirational players start the play.

## SUSTAINING PEAK PERFORMANCE

Achieving peak performance is easier than sustaining it. Achievement of peak performance requires high levels of organizational fitness and skills development, and these must be maintained, but the key factor which enables sustainable winning lies in the requisite mental state. This can be achieved through the sustained application of all the concepts of PPO Theory to the organization. Yet it is not quite as simple as this.

The psychology of flow experience tells us that challenges once met are no longer challenges. The greatest imaginable challenge, once achieved is no longer an energizing driver. To sustain peak performance the three concepts of peak purpose – greatest imaginable challenge, inspirational dream and focus – must remain in a strong relationship, while the challenge itself must be enriched or renewed periodically.

Focus provides direction and interest, and it ensures that organizational players 'know why they are out there'. The challenge provides purpose, and the dream provides meaning, but flow is achieved only through activity. Unless the focus of the organization, which directs action, is intrinsically rewarding and challenging there is no prospect of peak performance. Focus needs to be developed over time to ensure that it remains clear, and aligned to the inspirational dream and to the greatest imaginable challenge.

# CONCLUSION

The elements of PPO Theory have been described in a linear progression – this should be seen as a literary convenience rather than an indication of how the project of PPO progression should be approached. You should start with the peak purpose, but beyond that you should emphasize the areas where your organization's actions fall below the line in your PPO diagnostic profile. While concentrating on areas of weakness, you should also develop all the principles and concepts of PPO Theory simultaneously, since each affects the others.

For a PPO progression project to be successful, it must be embraced by everyone within the organization and extended to the 7Ps. We believe that the PPO stories and theory are accessible at all levels within potential PPOs and as such we see our book as an important vehicle for 'making it happen'. We have also developed a series of videos that take viewers on a unique tour behind the scenes of high profile international sports organizations to show how these organizations make it happen. Through these images you will be able to envisage peak performance, thereby facilitating the PPO progression of your own organization.

What is the purpose of your organization? Now translate that into the greatest imaginable challenge; feasible but stretching and exciting. Why does it matter? How does the purpose provide meaning to organizational participants? Can it fulfil the need for recognition; does it sustain Thymos? What is your inspirational dream? PPO Theory can help you to make it happen!

# CHAPTER 13

# Procter & Gamble – the Consummate Corporate Peak Performer

In our work with both large and small organizations we have concluded that the most effective way of understanding an organization is to use the PPO methodology of investigation, described in chapter 1. Comparing PPO Theory with the principles of organizing found within such companies as Procter & Gamble (P&G) and Saatchi & Saatchi Plc proved invaluable in testing the robustness of our theory. In the following pages we explain how PPO Theory helps to explain the success story of Procter & Gamble. By doing so we demonstrate the relevance of PPO Theory to business organizations, in the context of one of the world's most highly regarded companies.

## THE PROCTER & GAMBLE STORY

After renewing our friendship with the San Francisco 49ers with a brief visit to their Santa Clara training facility we flew east to the sub-zero climate of Cincinnati in winter. The two marbled towers of the worldwide headquarters of P&G attest to the status of this peak performing consumer goods corporation. P&G has a presence in 140 countries, more than 110,000 employees and annual revenue in excess of US$37 billion. With a global advertising spend in excess of US$3 billion, P&G has the world's most sophisticated brand-management programme, and with more than 30,000 products and 20,000 applications for patents every year, it is one of the world's most innovative companies. P&G has been winning in the market place for more than 160 years – a passion for winning is one of its core values. 1998 marked the forty-third consecutive year of increased dividend payments. Winner of countless awards for global excellence, including *Fortune* magazine's most admired company award, P&G is the archetypal corporate peak performer. As such, it is the perfect organization against which to test the ability to apply PPO Theory beyond its origins in sports organizations. We researched our ideas through analysis of P&G documentation and publications and conversations with senior P&G people. The purpose of our visit to Cincinnati was to discuss PPO Theory with John Pepper[1], Chairman and CEO of P&G Worldwide, and Mark Schar, then in charge of the P&G Organization 2005 global change project, together with members of the top management team.

In the following paragraphs we compare P&G organizational practice to PPO Theory. Quotations are from P&G documentation. The narrative follows the sequence of PPO Theory described in chapter 11.

The P&G inspirational dream is 'to make every day better in every way we can for people around the world'. To achieve this, P&G learns all it can about its customers, their wants and their potential needs. It continuously creates great ideas to meet these needs and to make life that little bit better. The greatest imaginable challenge is based on a 'passion for winning' – it is to double the business in ten years. P&G 'is determined to be the best at doing what matters most . . . has a compelling desire to win in the market place'. It wants to have the best brands in each of its product lines: laundry and cleaning, paper products, beauty care, health care, and food and beverages. A tangible measure of this is the aim to double global revenues within ten years. The crystal-clear focus is on building brands that are unique, high quality and innovative. This focus enables P&G to live the inspirational dream.

P&G scores one hundred per cent on the PPO concepts of inspirational dream, greatest imaginable challenge and focus. P&G does not speak of vision statements. The vision of traditional strategic thinking conveys a spiritual metaphor, or perhaps some idea of what the future may look like. By contrast, the concept of inspirational dream reveals how the future can be created, which in turn creates meaning for participants.

The P&G approach to leadership is similar to the PPO practice of inspirational players: 'We are all leaders in our areas of responsibility, with a deep commitment to deliver leadership results.' There is an emphasis on being a good coach and on helping others learn. Mistakes are treated as opportunities for learning, rather than causes of blame. P&G managers are actively involved with people and products; they make things happen by gaining the support of others. By making sacrificial plays, they enable others to win, and thereby build support and trust. Leadership is based on relationships, not upon rules. P&G acknowledge the requirement to develop more inspirational players who have entrepreneurial ability and the intuition to dream 'big ideas' and to make them happen. As part of its Organization 2005 overview:[2]

> P&G is making a number of changes to reward systems, training and other drivers of corporate culture to produce greater stretch, innovation and speed. It aims to create a culture that rewards going for breakthrough goals; supports taking risks; stimulates robust innovation; encourages courageous leadership; values speed; fosters fast, streamlined decision-making; and capitalizes on diversity.

P&G shares the dream widely:

> We will provide products of superior quality and value that improve the lives of the world's customers. As a result, consumers will reward us with leadership sales and profit growth, allowing our people, our shareholders and the communities in which we live and work, to prosper.

The company trusts its consumers totally. They are the judges of its success – consumers define the nature of value and determine what is wanted, and how it is to be packaged and presented. Needs are discovered through systematic research, and the company keeps listening long after the sale is made. Performance and functionality determine the quality of a product, which must deliver what it promises. Beyond this, P&G wants consumers to develop an emotional relationship with its branded products, so they become the products of first choice. To achieve this, although its market place is global, it is very sensitive to local market conditions and culture.

P&G builds partnerships and long-term relationships, and looks to combine its strengths with those of its partners across all aspects of the business:

> We collaborate with our suppliers. We enhance our technology expertise by leveraging the knowledge and creativity of the business partners who provide the raw materials for our products. In many cases, for example, our suppliers play a crucial role in the development of new ingredients that are often the foundation of major product innovations.
>
> We work hand-in-hand with customers. Our customer business development teams provide customers with all the expertise we have available. We bring teams of more than 17,000 experts in finance, logistics, marketing, product development, human resources and information systems to more than 10,000 wholesale customers worldwide.
>
> We live with others to make life better. P&G works with hundreds of professional associations, educational institutions and governments that share our interest in improving health and quality of life for people around the world. We support global health education programs, for example, through organizations like the World Dental Federation. We work with government agencies such as the Philippine Department of Health to promote public hygiene. And we help advance medicine through relationships such as the Partnership for Women's Health at Columbia University.

Sharing the dream extends well beyond those with whom P&G conducts business. The benefits that P&G provides to its people are among the best in the world. The company was a pioneer in the development of employee benefits that make employees owners of the business through stock options and shareholdings, enabling them to share the tangible financial benefits of the P&G dream. Part of the P&G legend is that P&G people from the shop floor have become very wealthy through their participation in the company. P&G's commitment to its people extends to all aspects of employee relations including 'diversity, job creation and security, wages and benefits, a safe and healthy work environment, and the training and education necessary to the development of challenging and rewarding careers'. Throughout its existence P&G has enjoyed an enviable record of successful industrial relations across the world.

P&G is closely involved with the communities in which its employees live and work, in the same way as our PPO case study organizations:

> Each year, P&G and The Procter & Gamble Fund contribute more than [US] $50 million worldwide to improve the quality of life in the communities where we live and work. We lend a hand to those in need. We pitch in when disaster strikes. We support the arts. We invest our resources – and ourselves, through tens of thousands of volunteer hours – in our neighbourhoods around the world.
>
> Education, from pre-school to graduate school, receives priority attention from P&G. In China we are helping to build schools in rural areas through Project Hope. In India, we are helping young girls receive an education through CARE's Primary Education Project. And throughout the world, we provide scholarships and other education assistance to the children of P&G employees, and to other deserving young people.

The commitment to corporate philanthropy derives from P&G's core values and is articulated in P&G's statement of purpose: '. . . allowing our people, our shareholders and the communities in which we live and work to prosper'. The evidence of this was all around us as we spent time exploring the P&G city of Cincinnati. Stakeholders, retired employees and past employers with whom we spoke, to gain a less formal sense of P&G's organization, all said the same. Here is a highly respected company that is deeply involved in its community and lives its dream.

Sharing the dream also involves celebrating P&G's legacy of achievements, which dates back 160 years. Full-time archivist Ed Rider maintains memorabilia including 12,000 product samples, 200,000 photographs, 4,000 films and videos and 400,000 advertisements. The collection dates back to the early days of P&G's history with products such as a case of 1865 candles discovered in an abandoned mine. Each product has its own history, for example, the famous Tide detergent represents over fifty years of technological innovation in the domain of laundry products.

The P&G dream goes well beyond the products themselves.

The company is committed to providing extensive consumer information and education about each of its products and product domains, provided through a comprehensive web site, consumer services and retail sales outlets.

P&G creates the future by attracting and recruiting 'the finest people in the world'. A P&G internship is regarded as better than a formal qualification by the many organizations which seek to recruit P&G-trained personnel. The organization 'is built from within by promoting and rewarding people [based on] performance'. Senior managers are appointed from within the organization: all of the twenty-five top managers have been with P&G for at least twenty years, and most have been brand managers at some stage during their careers.

This policy of promoting from within, means that P&G people are appointed for the long term. Only the very best are recruited – to achieve this P&G has strong relationships with universities, and testing of applicants for jobs is rigorous and lengthy. Employees are then given the very best training and development opportunities to become as good as they can possibly be. Promotion is based on peak performance, both in terms of results, and the ability to act as a coach and role model for others. Succession is considered continuously to ensure that there is a pool of people available for the future, and succession planning is flexible, not pre-determined.

P&G does everything for the long term, and as sustained profitability is built on the strength of brands, the company lives on the strength of its marketing. Long-term relationships are built with advertising agencies. Training is central to the psyche of the organization, and is primarily in-house, with senior managers conveying on their experiences and the organization's tradition, market wisdom and inspirational dream to the new generation of brand managers. Training practices, concepts and methods are global, yet modified to meet local needs. P&G is the world-recognized leader in consumer goods marketing, so it continuously benchmarks against *itself* to exceed previous best.

The sense of P&G community is universal. P&G people feel passionate about their company, and it is deeply committed to them. They accept personal responsibility 'to meet the business needs, improve systems and help others improve their effectiveness', consistent with the PPO action of exceeding personal best. The PPO community principles of:

- Trust, integrity, honesty and straightforwardness
- Respect for colleagues, customers and consumers
- Confidence in each other's capabilities and intentions
- Keeping commitments that are made and having confidence that others will keep their commitments

are lived within P&G. These provide the mental calm and confidence essential for peak performance.

Strong cultural characteristics lead to a global sense of community, despite language and ethnic differences. Global Business Units (GBUs) have responsibility for business strategy, planning and profit, brand innovation, design and new business development. GBU employees are located throughout the world, not just at HQ. Market Development Organizations (MDOs) develop market strategy and customer and external relations. They collaborate with GBUs on brand plans for local markets. Global Business Services (GBS) provide key business services such as accounting, payroll, order management, product development logistics and systems operations on a global basis. Corporate Functions (CF) develop cutting edge functional knowledge in customer business development, finance, human resources, information technology, legal, marketing, product supply, public affairs and research and development. They transfer best practices, lead corporate services (for example, financial reporting and shareholder communication) and develop leadership potential.

Every year the heads of the various local units meet in an annual convention to share stories of success and failure, so fostering community. Those who feel comfortable in the community often stay for their whole working lives, while those who leave seldom forget their roots, and carry P&G's values, principles and practices to their new organizations, where they are held in high regard.

One of the challenges in the P&G community is how to develop diversity in the context of the policy of promotion and development from within. PPO Theory emphasizes long-term development from within, but supplements this with carefully chosen selection from outside the organization to diversify the gene pool and introduce alternative perspectives which create constructive tension. Diversity is important to Procter & Gamble because 'differences often bring fresh perspective and important insights into how we do business – a rich source of competitive advantage'.

The company sees business opportunities as increasingly related to diverse consumers throughout the entire world. Diversity provides a 'broader, richer, more fertile environment for creative thinking and innovation'. To achieve diversity P&G seeks to attract and develop talent for future leadership from the 'full range of the world's rich cultural base'. To complement this recruitment strategy P&G also embraces close alliances with advertising and ideas organizations such as Saatchi & Saatchi, and with academic and research communities through such means as:

- University Exploratory Research Grants (for primary research in areas of interest to P&G)
- The annual Research and Technical Career in Industry Conference (to share ideas about how science researchers can find rewarding careers in industry)
- Doctoral Candidate Internships (to provide doctoral students with the opportunity for short periods working in the company to achieve practical industry-based research experience)

Brands provide focus for P&G as a whole. P&G lives the dream of making every day better for consumers around the world through its innovative brands. Brands are created, nurtured, and protected at all costs. Nothing must compromise the brand or how the customer thinks about the brand in the long term, even if this means short-term sacrifice. For example, even when volatile coffee and raw materials prices increase, P&G will not compromise its Folgers coffee brand by switching to low-quality ingredients. If, for competitive reasons, they are unable to recover cost increases through prices, they will accept the profit hit rather than take actions that might compromise the long-term positioning of the brand.

Additional benefits or technologies are added to a brand only if they are consistent with, and relevant to, the brand's overall competitive position. In the first twenty-one years after its launch in 1949 Tide had twenty-two significant product improvements and the innovation drive is ongoing throughout the Tide 'family' of products. It now has US$2 billion sales annually; 11.6 billion washing machine loads are washed with Tide each year in the United States alone. All these product improvements were focused on cleaning, whitening or on heightening the consumer's perception that Tide provides unsurpassed cleaning and is a brand you can always count on. P&G would not invest in any upgrade that did not deliver when measured against these principles – nothing must contradict the brand's essential market positioning. Ivory stands for purity. When it moved from hard soap to flakes, those flakes had to be pure white, as this brand can only be applied to products that are white, clean and pure. Fairy in the UK stands for mildness. You cannot put Fairy on any product unless it provides superior mildness, since this is the essence of the brand. Brands must not be extended in any way that contradicts the brand's essential market positioning.

P&G is a house of brands, not a branded house. Although its brands are household names throughout the world, the P&G name itself is less well known outside corporate circles. This is deliberate; customers choose to buy brands, not the company. Building the brand is the task of the brand manager, upon whose creative and marketing ingenuity the brand will depend. Brands managers are the front-row players of the organization – they have to win.

P&G accepts that 'mutual interdependency is a way of life'. P&G people 'respect their colleagues . . . and have confidence in each other's capabilities and intentions'. Each area has its individual focus. For brand managers it is 'build the brand'. For product supply it is 'making and shipping high-quality products in the safest, most efficient way we can'. For research scientists it is to 'create superior products that improve the lives of the world's consumers'. The routines of the P&G organization create well-being, calm and confidence. Mutual respect and confidence, focus, and community are the necessary preconditions for finding flow and peak performance.

The essence of P&G's Organization 2005 project is to enhance flow. By breaking up geographic systems and moving to GBUs by consumer product category (e.g. baby care, fabric care), P&G intends to create an organization of experts in brands. The same approach is applied to design and implementation. P&G intends to manage the development of brands globally in the design phase because it believes in the concept of a global consumer. Marketing and advertising will be done at the global level, while sales and implementation will be at the local level.

To sustain the benefits of this global approach while ensuring the input of local knowledge, communication systems are being transformed by Organization 2005 to become less formal and less hierarchical. For example, in the development process for a new brand in which one of the authors was closely involved, the evolution from concept to pilot test, test market, national roll out and global expansion was handled from day one by P&G in total partnership with an advertising agency. The agency and P&G shared all information. The agency generated the consumer data, while the company generated the performance and sales data. Results were circulated by memo to both partners within two days, and were considered as they flowed through the structures of both companies. Recipients annotated the memo by hand and recirculated it. The project group met regularly to discuss the results and to complete the communication loop by agreeing on the summary, the analysis and what was to be done. Changes took place in real time, with decisions being made on the spot. Advertising, product positioning and pricing from pilot to test markets were changed remarkably quickly. The decisions were taken intuitively, without much formality, in the rhythm of a twelve-month cycle from pilot test to national expansion. Massive amounts of information and the reflections of a wide variety of people throughout the network of communication informed the decision-making process.

One of the ways in which P&G is experimenting with peak flow is through the 'hot-house' concept, in partnership with one of its advertising agencies.[3] In a hot-house you bring together up to a dozen people who have advertising skills, passion and imagination, and put them in a room with three people who have knowledge and experience of a particular problem. A hot-house was used on a new shampoo product where the test market positioning, advertising and pricing were not completely aligned. The hot-house team included project experts and international creative staff from the agency who had not been involved with the project previously. The hot-house team went into the test market, looked at the consumers and the trade in the field, and threw away all the written research. They hot-housed two new positionings which were then taken back into the P&G system.

By combining knowledge and expertise with passion, flair and imagination the team as a whole becomes more passionate and knowledgeable, and truly new ideas can emerge. The hot-house team understands the clearly focused task – in the case above, to reposition the brand – and they don't leave the hot-house until the project is accomplished. It might take three, five, seven days or more. They achieve peak flow, which enables them to remain 'in the zone' until the work is completed.

Creative solutions involve flow of communication across geography, functions and structures. Multi-layered, convergent conversations will take place around the organization in a situation where:

- Information flows easily and informally
- There is a shared knowledge base
- There is an intense focus on the brand
- Everyone shares the dream and is passionate about the business

This fosters and is fostered by community. Organization 2005 seeks to move P&G towards a state of community peak flow.

P&G thrives on exceeding personal best, and is, 'determined to be the best at doing what matters most. There is a healthy dissatisfaction with the status quo. There is a compelling desire to improve and win in the market place.' P&G's passion to win is affirmed by real-time feedback on brand positioning and product performance, and products are continuously improved. The focus is not on the brands of competitors, although eyes and ears are constantly extended in this direction, but it is on constantly exceeding personal best in all imaginable ways to enhance brand performance. It is about continuously exceeding goals in pursuit of the greatest imaginable challenge. The passion to win is intense, and a way of life. It is the same passion that we observed in our sports case study organizations. The concept of exceeding personal best also extends to internal brand competition – P&G prefers to introduce new brands to compete against its existing brands rather than allow space for competitor brands from other companies.

P&G strives to catch the last detail. The people at P&G plants are focused on one clear objective, 'making and shipping high-quality products in the safest, most efficient way we can, the men and women of product supply truly help make every day better for consumers around the world.' P&G products must be perfect. Infinite care is taken at all stages of product research and design, market research, manufacture, packaging and supply to ensure high-quality, fault-free products. P&G knows that competitive advantage depends on consistent quality and value, delivered globally. Errors cannot be tolerated.

Perhaps the best illustration of intense attention to the last detail is the cornerstone of P&G communication, the recommendation memo. This is the primary means of decision-making communication. It has a prescribed format that entrenches, and is entrenched by, the organization's sense of community – It *is* the way P&G conducts its internal business. The P&G memo relates action to the organization's purpose and focus, and is all powerful. Every memo is written the same way: this memo recommends that we do X; the cost is Y, the signoffs are Z; the background to the recommendation; key bases for the recommendation; some discussion; then the next steps. All of it has to be on one page, plus supporting exhibits! The P&G memo is formal and requires clear, analytical thinking, supported by detailed quantitative analysis, and exposes illogical thinking or the absence of supporting evidence. Because all P&G memos follow the same logical format they provide a sense of security in decision making and efficiency in processing. The standardized, careful and simple presentation on paper of creative ideas enables speedy decisions. Nothing happens unless the ideas are on paper. The best memos are the simplest, where the idea stands out, supported by logical rationale and undebatable evidence. They are an essential ingredient of P&G communication.

Everyone starts at the same level within P&G, that of brand assistant. You do that for a year or so, then after appropriate sales training you become an assistant brand manager, then within a further three years you become brand manager or marketing manager. A key aspect of early training is how to write a P&G memo. Early in his career one of the authors had to write a P&G memo in connection with Ariel. His manager made him rewrite the memo seventeen times until it was word perfect and on one page! Every P&G person will remember their worst (or best!) number, whether thirteen, fourteen, fifteen, sixteen, seventeen or even more. Every phrase, every line is reworked until it is perfect. If there are spelling mistakes the memo is sent back, because these errors are seen as examples of sloppy work. Failure to catch the last detail is seen as reflecting lack of care, lack of thought or lack of love for the proposal. The product and related advertising are constructed in the same meticulous way – P&G people tend not to make errors. This stems from the focus on the last detail in every layer of management. Employees learn how to write the world's most concise business memorandum, and written communication provides the discipline, and weight necessary for good decision making.

From its origins in formality and structure, use of the P&G memo has shifted to reflect the increasing informality of information flows. We were told:

> Everybody kind of scribbles on the memo, and then it's face-to-face meetings or phones or video conferences, on a weekly basis, that are not scheduled or planned. Intuitive relationships develop through longevity. You will find that people have moved through the company together for twenty-five years or more on different brands and different assignments. Their relationships have been forged and bonded through working on business problems. For example, Wolfgang Berndt is the head of P&G Europe and Cliff Francis is the worldwide creative director for P&G at Saatchi & Saatchi. When they were both younger Wolfgang had a problem with positioning the Oil of Olay brand to make it into a global brand. Cliff, who was his agency partner, solved that problem with him, and in meetings with these two people in their elevated positions you can spend ten minutes listening to them tell their war story of how they solved this Oil of Olay problem together!

P&G is dedicated to game-breaking ideas. Tide was the world's first heavy-duty synthetic detergent; Pampers created the global disposable diaper business; Olean was the world's first fat-free cooking oil. P&G combines new insights about consumer wants and needs with deep technological understanding. This has led to the development of more than 200 technologies that can only be found in P&G products. Ideas, research and development drive the P&G dream. P&G holds 80,000 patents, and files 20,000 patent applications every year. It produces 30,000 products. 7,000 scientists work at P&G's seventeen research centres around the world. $1.2 billion is spent annually on research and development, and there is a drive to add value continuously to existing brands. For example, P&G wanted brands such as Tide to do more than get clothes clean. They wanted to keep clothes looking like new, so Carezyme was created; while new ideas like Olean create whole new product categories.

One P&G project to create game-breaking ideas is the futures group. Their only job is to find new business categories. Creative people are left to themselves to work on this 'best job in the world', and incredible concepts emerge which may eventually become billion-dollars businesses. However, P&G also recognizes that minor performance advantages or improvements can be game breaking, since they can lead to winning brands. Winning by one point is still winning. P&G does not like to play in any product league unless it has a winning formula. Leading the product league yields economies of scale in production, marketing and advertising. It is also the only place to be which is consistent with the organization's psyche and its greatest imaginable challenge.

To create game-breaking ideas P&G attempts to know all that it is possible to know about the wants and needs of consumers, and to understand lifestyle trends, behaviours and attitudes so that it can create new products, such as Pampers or Olean, to make life easier in ways that the consumer has not even imagined. Market research is always combined with careful and systematic observation of lifestyle trends.

Fabric care has always been part of P&G's core business, with Tide as its best-known brand in the US. While the product itself has been constantly improved, so its advertising has altered to reflect the changing nature of American lifestyles. For example, their renowned 1998–9 'Family Ties' TV advertising campaign portrayed the diversity of the modern American family, rather than the mum, dad and two children stereotype. There were families adopting ethnic babies, families with their parents coming to live with them, families with large age gaps between their children, and families with mothers having babies later in life. Tide captured consumers' hearts by reflecting these new trends.

Knowledge and ideas are built into the products, and intellectual pressure is applied to all aspects of the product to reveal how it could make life easier. P&G attempts to understand consumer lifestyles fully, and combines this with its game-breaking technology capability to create products that keep on winning.

Game-breaking ideas do not always proceed in a linear fashion. Failures or mistakes can lead to game-breaking ideas if the cause of failure is investigated and the problem reflected upon from different perspectives, and without failures progress will be limited, because the edge is insufficiently tested. P&G learns globally – 'Scientists in Asia, Latin America, Europe and North America share ideas and successes to create superior products the world over' – and searches the world for game-breaking ideas.

Although P&G is widely recognized as the consummate house of brands, P&G Chairman John Pepper sees the company as first and foremost being about technology, research and innovation. There is a tendency to rely upon technological enhancements to product performance, while recognizing that it may take time before the benefits are perceived by consumers. According to the P&G experience technology that genuinely makes life a little better will usually lead to sustainable, winning brands. This means that P&G is committed to leading the industry in research expenditure and innovation practice, with a careful process of patent protection. Patented game breaking ideas help to create the future.

## CONCLUSION

Meaning is created through the inspirational dream of making superior quality, good-value products which improve the lives of the world's consumers. P&G creates purpose through the greatest imaginable challenges of doubling revenue in ten years, while focus on brand development provides direction.

P&G's approach to leadership nurtures inspirational players – the Organisation 2005 project seeks to deploy more inspirational players throughout the organization. The corporation is exemplary in sharing the dream across the 7Ps (P&G principals, purchasers, players, partners, philanthropy recipients, the public and the Press). The future is created through relentless recruitment and development of the very best people. The sense of P&G community is all encompassing, and it provides the security, confidence and calm for necessary focused peak performance. A relentless drive towards innovation and game-breaking ideas, exceeding personal best and catching the last detail provides the winning formula.

# The PPO Story

## INTRODUCTION

We now tell our own story and explain how we conducted our research. We spent two years travelling to sports organizations around the world, prompted by a deep dissatisfaction with old-world management ideas and a belief that there had to be a better way. Because we were forced to reject long-cherished academic concepts of what leads to highly effective organizations, the intellectual journey took us much further than the miles we covered. Our former ideas simply did not plot with what we heard and observed.

We have used conventional organization theory throughout our professional and academic lives, and have observed with great interest the new theories of management super stars such as Peters and Waterman,[1] Senge,[2] and Collins and Porras.[3] Yet we have been troubled both by the frequent appearance of opposite ideas of effective organizing and their tendency to appear and disappear without trace. The ephemeral nature of many of these ideas led us to examine their origins, and to discover new terrain. We were particularly interested in the sustainability of outstanding performance.

One discovery was that metaphor has been at the origin of the majority of significant developments in organization theory. A longitudinal study by the authors of articles in the *Harvard Business Review* over the last thirty-five years revealed that metaphor is prevalent throughout the language of business. More than twenty-five per cent of articles relied upon the deep use of metaphor to convey their central meaning. In particular, concepts or characteristics from the military, the human body, organisms, journeys, the brain and sports were metaphorically attributed to organizations.

# THE METAPHOR OF PEAK PERFORMANCE

Metaphor is defined in the *Oxford Dictionary* as an 'application of name or descriptive term to an object to which it is not literally applicable.'[4] Metaphor can enable the rapid and memorable transfer of characteristics or concepts from a source domain (such as sport) to a target domain (such as organizations).

'Deep' metaphors define 'centrally important features'[5] of the idea or object being examined. In *The Fifth Discipline* Peter Senge's 'Learning Organisation',[6] which used the metaphor of the organization as a brain, explained organizational relationships at a 'deep' structural level. Alternatively, 'shallow' metaphors are used superficially to illustrate an idea or enrich a description. For example, in *The Age of Unreason* Charles Hardy uses the metaphor of the boiled frog to illustrate how people can be oblivious to change going on around them. He claims that if a frog is dropped into boiling water it will jump straight out, whereas if the water is heated slowly the frog will eventually be boiled alive! Inevitably, there is a continuum between the two types of metaphor, but for the purposes of this book, we are interested in the deep use of metaphor.

Deep use of metaphor is common throughout organization theory. For example, the concept of organizational culture derives from anthropology; the concept of strategy derives from the military; and the concept of organizational structure derives from architecture or building.

Primary metaphors relate to the source of the metaphor, while a secondary metaphor relates back to a primary metaphor. Sport is a primary metaphor, whereas peak performance[7] is a secondary metaphor derived from sport. In our study we discovered that, although business theories are dominated by military-based models, deep use of the sports metaphor has increased significantly in recent years. Brandenburger and Nalebuff[8] assert that both 'military' and 'sport' are commonly used metaphors in organizational writing. They use 'sport' as a primary metaphor in their *HBR* article 'The Right Game: Use Game Theory to Shape Strategy', while Tichy and Charan,[9] in their *HBR* article entitled 'The CEO as Coach', explore how Chief Executive Bossidy, of Allied Signal, uses goals to coach people to win. Given the variety of sports and the extent of their popularity, it is not surprising that a large number of both deep and shallow sports metaphors are in existence.

Sport creates riches beyond imagining for its leading participants, and involves people of all ages and backgrounds to a degree beyond the dreams of the Western religions. Sports superstars such as Michael Jordan and Franz Beckenbauer are global icons in the manner of political, military and religious leaders of times gone by. Many metaphors derived from sport are of a trivial nature, and add little to our understanding of how organizations work – these should not be confused with the aims of the PPO project. However, as sports enthusiasts we were fascinated by the passion that people develop for their chosen sport, and the total dedication of elite athletes towards peak performance. We wondered whether and how this passion and dedication could be reproduced within organizations more generally.

New ideas about organizations are often introduced with the assistance of a metaphor, and when one of our team arrived with a case full of books on peak performance in sport,[10] we realized that the peak performance metaphor offered us a new lens for analysing elite organizations. 'Re-engineering' was used as a machine metaphor by Hammer and Champy[11] to promote alternative ways of thinking about systems, and Margaret Wheatley's *Leadership and the New Science*[12] uses metaphors derived from the new sciences to create new ways of seeing organizations. Concepts of elite human performance derived from sports psychology are directly and theoretically relevant to organizations, but there is little attempt in extant literature about organization theory to explore this potential.

From these tentative beginnings, which scanned organizational theory as a whole, we narrowed our focus to concentrate on elite sport organizations. We hoped to analyze the peak of human performance to discover what lessons could be attributable to organizations in general. We aimed to develop deep and enduring theory, using elite sports organizations as a departure point for new ways of seeing.

Between us we have lived and worked on every continent and have followed our favourite sports around the globe. We soon realized that in each of our sports there were one or two organizations which had dominated their respective codes for long periods

– a quantitative analysis of their win records appears in appendix 11. We postulated that as players come and go these organizations must have established generic practices which enable them to sustain peak performance, and that these practices must be embedded in the organizations.

## TOWARDS AN ELITE THEORY OF ORGANIZING

Organization theory provided us with waypoints for our research. Richard Daft, author of the most popular textbook on Organisation Theory, defines organizations as: '(1) social entities that (2) are goal-directed, (3) are designed as deliberately structured and co-ordinated activity systems, and (4) are linked to the external environment.'[13] He explains organization theory as 'a way of thinking about organizations.'[14] He states that 'the way to see and think about organizations is based upon patterns and regularities in organizational design and behaviour.'[15] We sought these patterns in an elite subset of organizations, and presumed that while traditional generic theory would provide some guidance, the concepts were unlikely to be directly applicable, or sufficient to explain all peak performance.

Our dream was to discover ideas which would assist organizations to become exceptionally effective and meaningful places in which to work. Sports provided us with both deep primary metaphors and secondary metaphors which enabled us to develop a consistent language for the principles of PPO Theory.

The metaphorical origins of our enquiry soon led on to the empirical study of the organizational practices of an elite group of organizations. There is a long-established tradition of generating organization theory through observation of cases in a specific organizational setting. For example, Geert Hofstede developed his theories of organizational culture by studying IBM companies throughout the world,[16] while Burns and Stalker developed their influential ideas of mechanistic and organic organizations by reference to fifteen organizations in the UK electronics industry.[17]

Our work continues in this tradition, but focuses exclusively on elite organizations. The most widely promulgated work in this genre in recent years has been that by Peters and Waterman[18] and Collins and Porras.[19] In their book *In Search of Excellence*, Peters and Waterman conducted anecdotal enquiry in an array of unrelated clients, which were defined as excellent by attribution rather than by reference to objective criteria. In *Built to Last*,[20] Collins and Porras identified the distinguishing characteristics of eighteen 'visionary' companies which have maintained high performance, and compared these with the practices of a group of good but not outstanding performers. The organizations were selected by explicit criteria (premier institutions in their industry, widely admired by their peers, have made an indelible impact on the world, have experienced multiple generations of chief executives, and were founded prior to 1950). The resulting group has outperformed the stock market by over fifteen times since 1926. However, they used secondary data to analyse these companies rather than in-depth empirical investigation, and the result lacks the richness of first-hand enquiry, which leads to difficulty in implementation.

By contrast, the principles and concepts that constitute PPO Theory are based on first-hand empirical research. They are derived from what we observed and heard in the elite sports organizations that were the domain of our study.

## HOW WE CONDUCTED OUR PPO RESEARCH

Our project methodology was based on building theories from case study research, as explained by Eisenhardt.[21] Our research question was, 'How do elite organizations sustain peak performance?' This was translated more colloquially during our interviews into, 'How do you keep on winning?'

We talked to more than 300 people in sports organizations from fourteen different sports codes, in six different countries. Only ten of these stories are included within this book. Cases were excluded primarily because the record of peak performance did not, on a closer analysis, match up to our PPO criteria, and because we found that they were outliers in terms of our emergent PPO Theory. The relationship between declining team performance and the absence of, or weakness in, PPO practices strengthened our belief in the robustness of the theory.

We used multiple data collection methods, and analyzed our data as they accumulated. During the case study debrief sessions we identified words, ideas or ways of doing things that were commonly repeated or observed. We identified these as 'descriptors'. As our research proceeded we were able to aggregate these descriptors into groups which we defined as 'principles', to distinguish them from the original organization theory concepts. We related the principles to our concepts at a macro level to ensure that our theory had internal integrity and was comprehensive.

We maintained a relational database of principles and descriptors across all of the cases, and as time went by we found that a remarkable commonality developed. As we learnt more we found it necessary to return to some of the organizations after the main series of studies was completed, in order to round out our analysis. We learnt new insights from each case. Most of the principles were apparent after the first few cases, but some were subtler and took much longer to understand. One principle eluded us until we had visited all the organizations and returned to one of the very first. Naturally enough, the principles which were most difficult to define were the ones where the ideas involved were the most novel. Eisenhardt[22] explains the difficulties of searching for cross-case patterns. We concur, and note how the work proceeded with endless conversations that seemed to go round in circles, interspersed by flashes of inspiration which revealed concepts that, with hindsight, appeared obvious.

As our tentative understanding of the principles developed we were able to assign names to them. We were assisted significantly in this by our theorizing and research about the role of metaphor in the development of organization theory. Each of our principles was assigned a name which was consistent with a peak performance metaphor. This usage of metaphor is a significant departure from Eisenhardt,[23] but is a common approach in organization theory.

Peak performance provides a coherent theme and language for PPO Theory. The process of naming our principles was instrumental in our theory development because it enabled us to aggregate the description elements into coherent groupings. The descriptors were realigned many times as we struggled to understand their interrelationships.

As the principles became more robust we compared the emergent framework with the cases to determine goodness of fit, and we confirmed the empirical validity of our emergent theory with growing confidence. Not all the cases exhibited all of the principles to the same extent, but significant evidence of each one was revealed in all of the organizations included within this book. As we refined our description and definition of the principles, our qualitative data provided us with an understanding of why they are important in creating sustainable peak performance – this was crucial to determining the internal validity of the theory's development.

As we became more familiar with our data and our theory it became clear that there were qualitative differences between what we had labelled 'principles', and that more sophisticated analysis was required. We identified the three front-row PPO principles that are the basis of PPO Theory and peak performance. Each of these principles is supported by PPO concepts and each PPO concept is in turn achieved through a series of PPO actions. In addition we identified inspirational players as the agents within a PPO who are instrumental in actioning PPO principles.

We became intimately familiar with each case by writing it as a story that speaks to the essence of the organization. We agree with Dyer and Wilkins' approach to case study research, in which they call for 'an exemplar, that is, a story against which researchers can compare their experiences and gain rich theoretical insights'.[24] People within the case study organizations read all our stories, in order to ensure the accuracy of our facts and analysis. This feedback loop prompted further commentary and insights in many cases. PPO Theory cannot be properly understood without the rich insights from these stories.

We finally compared our findings to organization theory and to the theory of high-performing organizations. Early unsuccessful attempts to use organization theory to explain the performance of our selected organizations led to a decision not to compare in detail the organization theory concepts that provided our initial frame of reference with the emergent PPO Theory until the latter was substantially complete.

Given that elite organizations are a subset of all organizations, to which organization theory relates, we anticipated some commonality. The comparison enabled us to be confident that there were no areas within our data that we had overlooked and to identify areas of difference which may require the recalibration or abandonment of existing theory. By comparing our theory in this way we were able to test its robustness.

Finally, we had the privileged opportunity of meeting for half a day with the chief executive and senior management team of Procter & Gamble Inc at their Cincinnati world headquarters to present PPO Theory and discuss the Procter & Gamble organization in relation to it. This allowed us to reflect upon the applicability of PPO Theory to large business organizations. We identified Procter & Gamble for this phase of the study as it is widely recognized to be one of the world's best-managed, global organizations, with a history of excellence dating back over 160 years.

We closed the research project once we believed we had reached theoretical saturation (once further cases were adding nothing new to our theoretical insights), and when description and explanation of our theoretical framework was complete.

## CONCLUSION

When we began our research we had no idea whether we would gain access to the elite organizations that we wished to study. However, persistence paid off, and one organization led to the next. For example, the marketing vice-president of the Chicago Bulls flew to Atlanta to meet his counterpart at the Braves to see if we were worth talking to! In the end we were invited into all the organizations that we had targeted, and discovered that many of their organizational stories had never been told. The organizations valued seeing their reflections in the PPO mirror, and this assisted their relentless drive to exceed organizational best. Each of our PPOs was generous in the extreme of their time and in providing us with opportunities to watch the organizations in action. Each provided us with memorabilia of our visits which we have used to create an ongoing educational exhibition of what it takes to create and sustain elite organizations.The sports odyssey was a unique privilege for each of us. The intellectual journey will last a lifetime.

Although our research is now complete, and we have described the transformational organization practices that sustain peak performance, our inspirational dream of contributing to the creation of fun-filled, peak performing organizations lives on. We are imagining new challenges, and we are sharing our dream as widely as possible through books, videos, seminars and by acting as consultants to organizations which want to implement PPO Theory. Thank you for sharing our dream by reading this book. Please see our web site at http://www.mngt.waikato.ac.nz/ppo/ for the latest on the PPO project. To contact the authors e-mail PPO@waikato.ac.nz.

# The Teams

These win records were accurate as at 12 October 1999.

Soccer is the world's most popular sport. We were interested in studying the highly competitive European football scene. With its outstanding record in the World Cup we chose Germany as the domain for enquiry. At the time of our research in 1998 Germany was the reigning European Champion, as it has been twice before in 1972 and 1980. At the time of writing no other European nation has won more than once. *FC Bayern Munich* has dominated the German Bundesliga through its thirty-five-year history, with fourteen Fussball-Meister titles, a further seven second-placings and three third-placings. They held the Fussball-Meister title at the time of our visit and a few months later went on to win the Deutscher Fussball-Bund (DFB) cup for the ninth time. In 1999 FCB were once again crowned Fussball-Meister, winning by a fifteen-point margin, the largest in the history of the league. No other team comes remotely close to this record of continuous cup and league contention in Europe's most consistently competitive soccer nation.

Over the last 20 years up to and including the 1998 season *WilliamsF1* has won nine Formula One Constructors' Championships and seven World Drivers' Championships, outpacing more celebrated rivals such as Ferrari and McLaren, who have won eight Constructors' Championships each. The percentage win records related to Grand Prix starts as at the end of 1998 were Ferrari twenty per cent, McLaren twenty-four per cent, and Williams thirty per cent.

The *Australian Netball* team has won eight out of ten World Championships in thirty-five years, and been placed second in the remaining two. In 1998 it won the inaugural Commonwealth Games gold medal for netball. It has remained dominant over a longer period than any other national team in our study. Netball is one of the most popular participant team sports in the world with seven million players in more than forty-five countries.

Cricket, the archetypal British game, is dominated by Britain's former colony Australia. Under the auspices of the *Australian Cricket Board*, the Test team has, since 1876, maintained a forty-two per cent win record in all Test matches.* The West Indies, England and Australia have each secured three places in the finals of the seven cricket World Cups played since 1975. Although the West Indies has won twice, its last appearance in a final was in 1983, when it lost to India. England has never won. Australia has won twice, in 1987 and 1999, and was placed second to Sri Lanka in 1996.

The New Zealand *All Blacks* rugby team has a relentless win record in excess of seventy-two per cent, sustained over a period of more than 100 years. The team has been placed in the top three in each of the 1987, 1991 and 1995 rugby World Cups, winning in 1987 – a record unequalled by any other team.

Since 1988, the *Australian Women's Field Hockey* team has won two Olympic gold medals, in 1988 and 1996, the 1998 Commonwealth Games gold meal, two gold medals at the World Championships in 1994 and 1998, and gold medal for the last five Champions Trophy tournaments since 1991. The team has achieved an eighty per cent win record in over 200 international games over the last decade.

In 1998 *The Chicago Bulls* won its sixth National Basketball Association Championship in a fourteenth straight NBA Championship play-off appearance. The Bulls' championship run began in 1990, and the team secured six championship rings in the next eight years. In the strike-shortened 1999 season the Bulls dropped from first to bottom of the division after the retirement of Michael

---

* In a game with a high preponderance of draws no other nation approaches this achievement.

Jordan and Coach Jackson, and the departure of Dennis Rodman, Luc Longley and Scottie Pippen. There can be no question that the Bulls was the team of the 1990s. But can it rebuild? Will the Bulls be back? We believe they will. In a favourable omen for the creation of a new dynasty, the Bulls won first place in the 1999 lottery draft, giving the team the first pick of the new generation of players.

Since their turnaround season in 1991 when the team went from worst to first, the *Atlanta Braves* has won eight consecutive divisional titles, five National League Titles and the World Series in 1995. No other team in the history of baseball has matched this level of sustained peak performance.

Since 1980 the *San Francisco 49ers* has amassed an amazing fourteen 'Gridiron' National Football Divisional Championships, sixteen play-off appearances and sixteen consecutive winning seasons. Along the way they converted NFC Championships into five Super Bowl titles in 1981, 1984, 1988, 1989 and 1995. They have never lost a Super Bowl contest. The 49ers was the most successful NFL team of the 1980s, and the 1990s. The record of 109–35 (76.4%) in the 1990s is the highest achievement in history, surpassing the previous record of 105 wins, set by the Dallas Cowboys in the 1970s.

New Zealand, a country with a population roughly the size of San Diego, has been a dominant influence on the international yachting scene for the last decade. New Zealand reached the final of the Louis Vuitton Challengers' Cup in 1987 and 1992. In 1995 *Team New Zealand* sailed away from heavily bankrolled international competitors to seize the America's Cup by the only 5–0 grand slam in the Cup's illustrious 150-year history.

# Notes

### Introduction

1 1 billion = 100 million.
2 http://www.fia.com/.
3 http://soccertimes.com/.
4 http://www.france98.com/english/index.html.
5 http://www.nfl.com/sb33/news/981204facts.html.
6 We regard sports organizations as having no particular distinction from other types of organization. There is a long-established tradition of generating organization theory through observation of cases in particular organizational settings. For example, Geert Hofstede developed his theories of organizational culture by studying IBM companies throughout the world. Burns and Stalker (1961) developed their influential ideas of mechanistic and organic organizations by reference to fifteen organizations in the electronics industry in the United Kingdom.

### 1 FC Bayern Munich

1 From the DFB Website
2 FC Bayern Munich have always been there, some have sunk into oblivion and some have been relegated to the lower leagues.
3 Berti Vogts resigned from his position as German national team coach in September 1998. His successor and new *Teamchef* is Erich Ribbeck.
4 Data that does not fit with the general theory.

### 3 Netball Australia

1 In the remaining two World Championships they were placed second.
2 This title was claimed again in 1999 when a winning goal against New Zealand was scored in the final second of the game.

### 5 New Zealand Rugby Football Union

1 Moffett resigned at the end of 1999.
2 The Ranfurly Shield can only be won by a team that plays away from home. Thus, the holders 'put up' the Shield at every home game.

### 8 The Atlanta Braves

1 Caruso, G. *Rarest of Diamonds*, Longstreet Press: Marietta, Georgia, 1997.

### 10 Team New Zealand

1 The P Class was founded in 1943 and is named after the Ponsonby Cruising Club in Auckland, which sponsored the original design. It is said that the P Class is so difficult to sail that if you learn to sail in it you can sail anything.
2 Catamarans easily outpace monohulls of similar or larger size because of reduced wetted surface and the ability to skim over the water rather than plough through it.
3 The crew of an America's Cup yacht consists of sixteen sailors. An additional 'seventeenth man' is permitted on board under the racing rules as an observer, but must not take part in the sailing.

4 The Cup races start by going upwind 3.275 miles, then down and up for four legs of three miles each, then a final run of 3.275, for a total of six legs and 18.55 miles.

5 The backstay is actually a set of four wires, which converge on the runner block at the back of the boat: the topmast backstay, the runner (which takes most of the load), the upper checkstay, and the lower checkstay. These have varying amounts of tension, but the total is about 6 tonnes when sailing upwind.

6 Clay is a key member of the Team NZ design team, having been recruited especially for the 2000 defence. He is the author of the velocity prediction program that underpins the Team NZ design process.

7 Lift refers to a better angle of wind giving a better angle to the mark.

## 11 PPO Theory

1 Elite is a term used extensively in sport to describe the very best players in a particular sports code. We use the term elite theory to refer to the theory of organizing which is relevant to elite organizations, or organizations that are the very best in a particular sports code or industry.

2 M. Csikszentmihalyi,

*Flow: The Psychology of Optimal Experience,* New York, Harper & Row, 1990.

3 Kouzes, J. and Posner, B. *The Leadership Challenge,* San Francisco, Jossey-Bass, 1987.

4 Bennis, W. and Biederman, P. *Organizing Genius,* London, Nicholas Brealey, 1997.

5 Greenleaf, Robert K., *Servant Leadership: a Journey into the Nature of Legitimate Power and Greatness,* New York, Paulist Press, 1977.

6 In the *Republic* Plato explained there are three parts to the soul which explain much of human behaviour: desire, reason and Thymos. Desire makes people seek things beyond themselves, while reason shows how to get them.

7 Brandenburger, A. and Nalebuff B., *Co-opetition,* HarperCollins, London, 1996.

8 Derives from M. Csikszentmihalyi, ibid.

9 M. Csikszentmihalyi, ibid.; M. Csikszent-mihalyi, *Creativity: Flow and the Psychology of Discovery and Invention,* New York, HarperCollins, 1996; M. Csikszentmihalyi, *Finding Flow: The Psychology of Engagement with Everyday Life,* New York, Basic Books, 1997.

10 M. Csikszentmihalyi, *Beyond Boredom and Anxiety: The Experience*

*of Play in Work and Games,* San Francisco, Jossey-Bass, 1975.

11 Ideas about 'how to organize' are incommensurable with ideas about 'who organizes' in so far as illustration in a one-dimensional model is concerned. All organization and therefore each PPO principle and concept presume human agency. However, our theory of peak performance in organizations is empirically dependent on inspirational players, who, we suggest, are instrumental to the achievement of peak performance.

## 13 Procter & Gamble

1 Durk Jager took over as Chief Executive on 1 January 1999 with John Pepper continuing as Chairman.

2 Quotations throughout this chapter derive from P&G publications.

3 Saatchi & Saatchi originally developed this idea.

## Appendix I

1 Peters and Waterman (1982)

2 Senge (1993)

3 Collins and Porras (1994)

4 Fowler & Fowler (1964, p. 763)

5 Schön (1993, p. 149)

6 Senge (1993)

7 For example, Hodge, K., Sleivert, G. and McKenzie A. (1996); Kushel (1994)

8 Brandenburger and Nalebuff (1998)
9 Tichy and Charan (1995)
10 For example, Hodge, K., Sleivert, G. and McKenzie A. (1996); Kushel (1994)
11 Senge (1993)

12 Wheatley (1994)
13 Daft (1998, p. 11)
14 Daft (1998, p. 20)
15 Daft (1998, p. 21)
16 Hofstede (1997)
17 Burns and Stalker (1961)
18 Peters and Waterman (1982)

19 Collins and Porras
20 Collins and Porras (1994)
21 Eisenhardt (1989)
22 Eisenhardt (1989, p. 540)
23 Eisenhardt (1989)
24 Dyer and Wilkins (1991, p. 613)

# Bibliography

Bethanis, S. J., 'Language as Action: Linking Metaphors with Organization Transformation', In S. Chawla and Renesch, J. eds., *Learning Organizations: Developing Cultures for Tomorrow's Workplace*, Portland, OR, Productivity Press, 1995

Bennis, W., and Biederman, P. *Organizing Genius*, London, Nicholas Brealey, 1997

Brandenburger, A. M., and Nalebuff, B. J., *Co-opetition*, London, HarperCollins, 1998

Burns, T., and Stalker, G. M., *The Management of Innovation*, London, Tavistock, 1961

Collins, J. C., and Porras, J. I., *Built to Last: Successful Habits of Visionary Companies*, New York, HarperBusiness, 1994

Csikszentmihalyi, M. *Beyond Boredom and Anxiety: The Experience of Play in Work and Games*, San Francisco, Jossey Bass, 1975

——*Flow: The Psychology of Optimal Experience*, New York, Harper & Row, 1990

——*Creativity: Flow and the Psychology of Discovery and Invention*, New York, HarperCollins, 1996

——*Finding Flow: The Psychology of Engagement with Everyday Life*, New York, Basic Books, 1997

Daft, R. L., *Organization Theory and Design*, New York, South Western, 1998

Dyer, W. G., Jr., and Wilkins, A. L., 'Better Stories, not Better Constructs, to Generate Better Theory: A Rejoinder to Eisenhardt', *Academy of Management Review*, 16 (3), 1991

Eisenhardt, K. M., 'Building Theories from Case Study Research', *Academy of Management Review*, 14 (4), 1989

Fowler, H. W., and Fowler, F. G., *The Concise Oxford Dictionary of Current English*, Oxford, Oxford University Press, 1964

Greenleaf, Robert K., *Servant Leadership: a Journey into the Nature of Legitimate Power and Greatness*, New York, Paulist Press, 1977

Hodge, K., Sleivert, G., and McKenzie, A., eds., *Smart Training for Peak Performance: A Complete Sport Training Guide for New Zealand*

*Athletes*, Auckland, Reed Books, 1996

Hofstede, G. H., *Cultures and Organizations: Software of the Mind* (Rev. ed.), New York, McGraw-Hill, 1997

Kouzes, J., and Posner, B., *The Leadership Challenge*, San Francisco, Jossey-Bass, 1987

Kushel, G., *Reaching the Peak Performance Zone: How to Motivate Yourself and Others to Excel*, New York, Amacom, 1994

Peters, T. J., and Waterman, R. H., *In Search of Excellence: Lessons from America's Best-run Companies*, New York, Harper & Row, 1982

Schön, D., 'Generative Metaphor: A Perspective on Problem Setting in Social Policy', In A. Ortony, ed., *Metaphor and Thought*, Cambridge, Cambridge University Press, 1993

Senge, P. M., *The Fifth Discipline: The Art and Practice of the Learning Organization*, Milsons Point, Random House, 1993

Slack, T., *Understanding Sports Organizations: The Application of Organization Theory*, Champaign, Human Kinetics, 1997

Tichy, N. M., and Charan, R., 'The CEO as Coach: An Interview with Allied Signal's Lawrence A. Bossidy', *Harvard Business Review*, 73 (2), 1995

Wheatley, M. J., *Leadership and the New Science: Learning about Organization from an Orderly Universe*, San Francisco, Berrett-Koehler, 1994

# Index